THE PHONEME: ITS NATURE AND USE

THE PHONEME:

ITS NATURE AND USE

by

D A N I E L   J O N E S
M.A. (Cambridge), Dr. phil. h.c. (Zürich), Hon. LL.D. (Edinburgh)

*Professor Emeritus of Phonetics in the University of London
Corresponding Member of the German Academy of Sciences, Berlin
Honorary Member of the Royal Irish Academy*

CAMBRIDGE
W. HEFFER & SONS LTD.

First Edition - - - - - - - 1950
Second Edition - - - - - - - 1962

Printed in Great Britain at the Works of
W. HEFFER & SONS LTD., CAMBRIDGE, ENGLAND

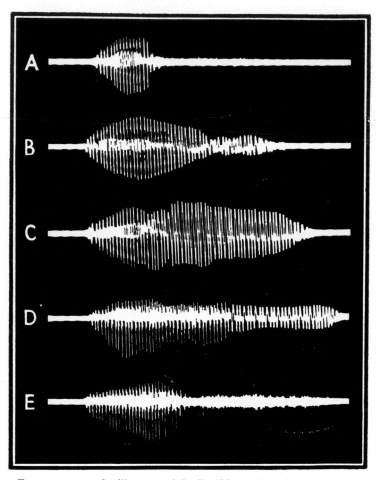

FRONTISPIECE. Oscillograms of the English words *if, is, in, Ann, ash*.
A, **if** (*if*). B, **iz** (*is*). C, **in** (*in*). D, **an** (*Ann*). E, **aʃ** (*ash*).*

---

* These oscillograms were made by the Research Department of the General Electric Company, and are reproduced here by their kind permission. The words were spoken by myself, approximately on a monotone

E♭ 𝄢 .—D.J.

PREFACE TO THE SECOND EDITION

I FIND it necessary to emphasize the fact that the theory of phonemes presented in this book is in all essentials the *original* theory as conceived in the 1870's by its discoverer JAN BAUDOUIN DE COURTENAY, but expounded mainly on "physical" (as distinguished from "psychological") lines. That theory was known in England about 1916 and has, in my opinion, never been bettered.

In its original use the term "phoneme" had reference exclusively to the *sounds* (i.e. phones or segmental elements) of speech, and I adhere to the view that separate terms such as "chroneme" and "toneme" are necessary to designate such non-segmental features of speech as are assignable to "families" in the same sort of way that phones are grouped into phonemes.

In order that readers of the second edition of this book should form a clearer conception of what is meant than can be attained by mere touchings-up of the 1950 edition, I would urge them to preface their reading by a careful perusal of my paper *The History and Meaning of the Term "Phoneme"* which was published in 1957 (by the I.P.A., Department of Phonetics, University College, London W.C.1). Not only does that paper set out at some length the development of the "original phoneme," but it also shows how, through an oversight, it has come about that many American linguisticians have unfortunately given to the term "phoneme" a signification differing greatly from that used previously in England and by the great Eastern European scholars who first gave us the theory. The paper shows too how the introduction of a single new term "signeme," to denote "any speech feature whatever (segmental or otherwise) which can be made use of for distinguishing meanings" will readily put an end to present misunderstandings.

This edition is in the main a reprint of the first edition. It has however been found necessary to make alterations in several places, and particularly where there were references to Japanese in the first edition. (See particularly §§323–331.)

References to TRUBETZKOY's *Grundzüge der Phonologie* have been supplemented by the corresponding references in CANTINEAU'S French translation of that work which appeared in 1949.

DANIEL JONES.

September, 1962.

v

PREFACE TO THE FIRST EDITION (with alterations)

CONDITIONS being what they are at the present day, the dissemination of knowledge has to be carried on to a large extent by means of books. This applies even in such a subject as phonetics, which is a science involving a particular skill that has to be imparted mainly by oral teaching. Books on scientific subjects are unsatisfactory instruments; they lag behind the advance of knowledge, but they are nevertheless liable to be taken by readers as embodying orthodoxies of one kind or another. And orthodoxies are by their nature impediments to progress in science. I would therefore express the hope that no reader of the present book will regard it in any sense as a final or unalterable exposition of the phonemic aspects of phonetics, that they will not consider the opinions expressed in it to be dogmatic pronouncements, but that they will rather look upon the work as an unfinished collection of materials which may encourage them to contribute to progress by pursuing useful lines of investigation for themselves.

It is my hope too that readers will also take due account of the limited value of writing as a means of suggesting ideas. I share L. R. PALMER's opinion that "speech is nothing more than a series of rough hints which the hearer must interpret in order to arrive at the meaning which the speaker wishes to convey."[1] Words, clever inventions though they are, form in my view a quite inadequate medium for symbolizing any but the most elementary conceptions. Most words have many meanings, shades of meaning and connotations; they therefore often have to be used loosely in order to avoid cumbrous sentences which even if set out in full would still be ambiguous. It is accordingly with intention that I have at times for convenience used loose modes of expression (such as "the sound X constitutes a single phoneme," "treating the sound X as a phoneme separate from the sound Y," "in this language the vowels are subject to wide variation") in the hope that readers will form a correct idea of what is meant.

I would ask readers further to bear in mind that certain fundamental concepts in phonetics, as in other sciences, are incapable of definition.[2] It would appear that all sciences lack firm foundations,

---

[1] L. R. PALMER, *Introduction to Modern Linguistics*, p. 82.
[2] See my article *Some Thoughts on the Phoneme* in the *Transactions of the Philological Society*, 1944

being established on unproved assumptions that certain basic units exist and that people know what they are without explanation. We assume that everyone perceives the fundamentals in the same way, and we are apt to forget that what appears to one person an obvious truth does not necessarily appear so to others. These are additional reasons why statements made in this book, as in other books of a scientific nature, must be received with reserve and treated as provisional only.

The idea of the phoneme is no new one. It was first introduced to me in 1911 by the late Professor L. ŠČERBA of Leningrad, but both the theory and the word itself date back to more than thirty years before then. According to J. R. FIRTH,[3] the term "phoneme" was invented as distinct from "phone" in 1879 by a linguistic scholar named KRUSZEWSKI, a pupil of the Polish linguistician BAUDOUIN DE COURTENAY.[4] The phoneme idea has also been (to quote FIRTH) "implicit in the work of all phoneticians and orthographists who have employed broad transcription." In particular, it is implicit in the distinction drawn by HENRY SWEET between "broad" and "narrow" transcription in his *Handbook of Phonetics* (Oxford, 1877), pp. 103–105, and in the principles of transcription formulated by PAUL PASSY for the International Phonetic Association in 1888.[5]

What I am therefore doing at present is to give as clear an account as I am able of the theory of phonemes in the form in which I have used it in practical language teaching since about 1916. I can at least certify that the theory as here set forth has done what it was intended to do for over forty years.

In view of the various opinions that have been expressed by workers in the field of phonemic research, I think it well to put on record here that my conclusions concerning the phoneme have been arrived at entirely through phonetics. Since phonetics can neither be studied nor applied without the use of phonetic transcriptions, and since adequate systems of transcription require for

---

[3] *The Word "Phoneme"* by J. R. FIRTH in *Le Maître Phonétique*, April, 1934, p. 44. See also footnote 7 to §652 of this book.

[4] The French word "phonème" appears to have been invented by L. HAVET, who employed it in 1876 to mean "speech-sound." Many other French writers on linguistic subjects have used it in the same sense.

[5] *The Phonetic Teacher*, August, 1888, p. 57.

their construction the theory of phonemes, I see no reason for regarding the theory of phonemes as other than an integral part of phonetic science.

Finally, I would remark that the phoneme theory has a certain bearing upon philosophy, and in particular upon questions relating to the "existence" or "non-existence" both of material phenomena and of ideas. For if it can be shown that phonemes are abstract things which when brought into concrete manifestation appear in different forms according to physical environment (a possibility suggested in Chapter XXIX), then they would appear to provide particularly striking examples of such types of manifestation. So since research into the nature of things in general demands enquiry into phenomena of this sort, I am in hopes that some of the facts here recorded may come to the notice of those who specialize in metaphysical problems.

D. J.

University College, London.

ACKNOWLEDGMENTS

My thanks are due to several friends who have rendered service to me in connexion with this book, and particularly to the late Professor S. BOYANUS for furnishing me with many examples from Russian and for many long and enlightening talks on the phonemic status of Russian sounds, to Professor J. R. FIRTH for a number of examples from languages of India, to Professor A. N. TUCKER who put at my disposal much information that he has collected concerning languages of Africa, to Miss E. HENDERSON for some of the examples from Japanese and for information relating to Vietnamese and Siamese, to the late Dr. G. L. LETELE for information concerning the Sotho language, to Dr. C. RABIN for some examples from Arabic and to the late Professor IDA WARD, Miss B. HONIKMAN and Professor D. B. FRY for help of various kinds. Special mention must be made of the work of my colleague Miss A. D. PARKINSON who assisted me for years with the preparation of the manuscript, and to whom I owe a debt of gratitude which it is impossible adequately to express.

D. J.

CONTENTS

xi

xii CONTENTS

LIST OF ILLUSTRATIONS

xiii

LIST OF PHONETIC SYMBOLS

The following is a list of the phonetic symbols used in this book, with short particulars of their meanings. It is to be understood that most symbols have at times values deviating from what may be considered to be their most usual values.

(1) *Consonant Letters of the Roman Alphabet.*

p, b, t, d, k, g (hard), m, n, l, f, h have their customary values.

The others are as follows:

c   breathed palatal plosive; also used when convenient to denote the affricate tʃ (Eng. *ch*).

j   voiced palatal fricative; also the corresponding semi-vowel (Eng. *y* in *yet*).

q   breathed uvular plosive.

r   stands for the various r-sounds of different languages (Eng., Fr., Ger., etc.); replaced by other symbols, ɹ, ɾ, ʀ, when necessary.

s   as in Eng. *see*.

v   as in Eng. *ever*.

w   as in Eng. *well*.

z   as in Eng. *lazy*.

(2) *Other Consonant Letters.*

ʈ, ɖ retroflex plosives.

ṭ, ṣ, etc., palatalized t, s, etc.; represented in digraphic transcription by tj, sj, etc.

ŧ   velarized t; also used for pharyngalized t.

ɟ   voiced palatal plosive; also used when convenient to denote the affricate dʒ (Eng. *j*).

ʔ   glottal stop.

ʡ   Cairene Arabic glottal stop, when corresponding to classical q.

ɱ   labio-dental nasal.

ɳ   retroflex nasal.

ɲ   palatal nasal (Fr. *gn*).

ŋ   velar nasal (Eng. *ng*).

ɲ   Japanese syllabic nasal.

ɬ   breathed l (Welsh *ll*).

ɫ   velarized (dark) l.

ɺ   a sound intermediate between d and· l.

ʎ   palatal lateral (Ital. *gl*).

ɾ   single flap tongue-tip r.

ɽ   retroflex flap.

ʀ   rolled or flapped uvular r (one variety of Parisian *r*).

ɸ, β   bi-labial fricatives.

θ, ð   dental fricatives (Eng. *th*-sounds in *thing, then*).

ɹ   fricative tongue-tip r; also the corresponding frictionless continuant, and a retroflexed variety of this; also r-coloured ə.

ʃ, ʒ   palato-alveolar fricatives (Eng. *sh*, Fr. *j*).

ʂ   velarized s; also used for pharyngalized s.

ç   breathed palatal fricative (one variety of the Ger. *ich*-sound).

ɕ, ʑ   alveolo-palatal fricatives (Polish *ś, ź*).

ɣ   voiced velar fricative.

ħ   breathed pharyngal fricative.

ʕ   voiced creaky sound made with contracted larynx and pharynx (Arabic '*ain*).

ɦ   voiced h.

ɥ   consonantal y (= y̆).

ʇ   dental click.

ʖ   lateral click.

tʃ, dʒ, ts, etc.   affricates (one mode of representation).

ph, th, etc.   aspirated plosives.

(3) *Vowel Letters.*

i   as in Fr. *si*, and sounds near to this; used also when convenient for the Eng. short *i* as in *sit*.

e   as Fr. *é*, and shades of sound near to this; also used in place of ɛ when possible, e.g. in transcribing the Eng. vowel in *set*.

ε   as Fr. *è*, and sounds near to this; sometimes used for the
       Eng. vowel in *set*.

ə   as in Parisian Fr. *là*, and sounds near to this; also used in
       the Simplified Transcription of the Eng. short vowel in
       hat and the long vowel in *half*.

ɑ   as in Parisian Fr. *las*, and sounds near to this; used for the
       Eng. long vowel in *half* in narrowèd transcription.

ɔ   as *o* in Fr. *porte*, and sounds near to this; used in narrow
       transcriptions of Eng. *saw* (long), *hot* (short), Ger. *Sonne*,
       etc.

o   as in Fr. *beau*, and sounds near to this; replaces ɔ in broad
       transcriptions of Eng. *saw, hot*, Ger. *Sonne*, etc.

u   as in Ger. *Schuh*, and sounds near to this, e.g. the vowels
       in Fr. *coup*, Eng. *too*; used also when convenient for the
       Eng. short *u* in *put, book*.

y   close lip-rounded i, as Fr. *u*, Ger. *ü*.

ø   close lip-rounded e, and sounds near to it, e.g. the Fr. vowel
       in *peu*.

œ   open lip-rounded ε, and sounds near to it, e.g. the Fr. vowel
       in *œuf*.

ɒ   open lip-rounded ɑ; used for Eng. vowel in *hot* in narrow
       transcription.

ʌ   unrounded ɔ; also used for Eng. vowel in *cup*.

ɤ   unrounded close o.

ɯ   unrounded u.

ɨ   vowel intermediate between i and ɯ.

ʉ   vowel intermediate between y and u (= a lip-rounded ɨ).

ɪ   a lowered and retracted variety of i; used in Tswana, and
       in transcribing Scottish and American pronunciation of
       sit, etc.; also in narrow transcription of Southern British
       pronunciation of such words.

ᵻ   a lowered variety of ɨ.

ᴏ   a lowered variety of u, or a very close variety of o; used in
       Tswana, and for the Igbo θ, also used in transcribing
       American pronunciation of *book*, etc., and in narrow trans-
       cription of Southern British pronunciation of such words.

ᵧ   a lowered and retracted variety of y; used for Ger. short y
    in narrow transcription.

ə   unrounded central vowel (schwa), as Eng. *a* in *along.*

ɐ   a lower variety of central vowel, as in Eng. *sofa* or in Lisbon
    Portuguese *para;* also sometimes used to denote the
    quality of long ə: in narrow transcriptions of Southern
    English.

æ   a raised a or a very open ɛ; used for Eng. short a in narrow
    transcription.

a̹, ɔ̧, r-coloured a, ɔ.

ə̧   r-coloured ə; also represented by ɹ or ɚ.

    An index letter means that the sound is that of the main
    letter modified in the direction of that indicated by the
    index. Thus hᶜ means a ç-like variety of h, and ʒᶻ
    denotes a sound intermediate between ʒ and z.

(4) *Diacritic Marks.*

~   nasalization; ɛ̃ = nasalized ɛ.

.   devoicing; n̦, l̦, ʒ̦ = unvoiced n, l, ʒ.

ᵥ   voicing; s̬ = z, t̬ = American "voiced t."

.   close variety; e̩ = a very close e, a̩ = æ.

c   open variety; ȩ = a sound between French *é* and *è.*

ɔ   lips more rounded.

c   lips more spread.

+   advanced variety; u+ or y̟ = a sound between u and ʉ.

- or ⁻ retracted variety; a- or a̠ = a sound between a and ɑ.

ᴀ   raised variety; aᴀ or a̝ = a̝ = æ.

ᴛ   lowered variety; eᴛ or e̞ = ȩ.

¨   central vowel; ü = ʉ, ë = a high variety of ə.

ʻ   slight aspiration after p, t, etc.

ʼ   glottal stop accompanying p, t, etc.; glottal contraction
    accompanying continuant sounds, Danish *stød.*

indication that a vowel is consonantal: y̆ = ɥ; also used to mean that a continuant sound is very short, as m̆ in Sinhalese m̆b, ĕ in Tswana ĕò.

. under a letter (or over it if the letter has a tail below) means that the sound is syllabic; n̩ = syllabic n.

⌢ simultaneous pronunciation of two sounds, e.g. Provençal m͡ŋ.

: length mark.

˙ half length.

ˈ at the beginning of a syllable denotes strong stress.

ˈˈ at the beginning of a syllable denotes extra strong stress.

ˌ at the beginning of a syllable denotes medium (secondary) stress.

‾ (thus ā or ‾a) high level tone.

˥ in Burmese, a level tone ending with a slight fall and pronounced with creaky voice; in Tswana a high level tone requiring that the next succeeding high tone shall be slightly lower.

_ (thus a̱ or _a) low level tone; in Vietnamese, low tone combined with a creaky voice.

´ (thus á or ´a) high rising tone, or rising tone without implication of height.

ˌ (thus a̗ or ˌa) low rising tone.

` (thus à or `a) high falling tone.

ˎ (thus a̖ or ˎa) low falling tone; in Vietnamese, low tone combined with breathy voice.

^ (thus â or ^a) rising-falling tone.

ɔ Panjabi low rising tone.

ˇ (preceding the syllable) Vietnamese rising tone combined with creaky voice.

ᴜ (preceding the syllable) Vietnamese rising tone combined with breathy voice.

CHAPTER I

SPEECH-SOUNDS

1. Speech is the uttering by the larynx, mouth, nose, etc., of various noises which people have agreed to regard as conventional symbols of certain meanings.

2. Nearly every utterance, or "speech chain," is made up of a large number of small elements no two of which are alike. That this is so can be seen by the appearance of sound-tracks or oscillograms or enlargements of the grooves of gramophone records. It is comparatively rarely that we find sections of a speech chain in which the sound has unvarying quality, intensity and pitch continued for an appreciable time, i.e. the type of sound indicated on oscillograms by a succession of waves of similar shape.

3. For linguistic purposes it is convenient to consider speech chains as divisible into sections which we call "speech-sounds" or "phones." The points of separation between successive speech-sounds are sometimes shown by abrupt changes in the patterns of sound-tracks, etc. Examples of abrupt changes are shown in the Frontispiece. More often, however, the points of separation are not clearly apparent on such tracks. It has in fact been shown that from the viewpoint of physics the "speech-sound" is non-existent, and that when one of the entities which we call speech-sounds is followed by another, the two more often than not merge into one another in a gradual manner. It has been shown that the characteristics of a "speech-sound" generally begin to appear before the preceding "speech-sound" has terminated and continue to show themselves after the succeeding "speech-sound" has begun.[1] The mechanism is such that what might be termed the characteristic part of the speech-sound is, when regarded from the standpoint of physics, generally not maintained for any appreciable time.

---

[1] See, for instance, E. W. SCRIPTURE's remarks on "overlapping of speech-sounds" in his paper on *The Nature of Speech* in the *Proceedings of the Second International Congress of Phonetic Sciences* (1936), pp. 217–219.

4. Nevertheless, the conception of the chain of speech-sounds is indispensable in all linguistic investigations. It is, moreover, justified by the means by which speech is produced. Speech is the result of certain actions performed by the articulatory mechanism. The lips, tongue, etc., take up various positions or make various movements successively, and these positions and movements can be described and classified. The conception would appear to be also justifiable on psychological grounds: when we speak, we think we utter successions of sounds most of which are held on for an appreciable time; and when we listen to speech, we think we hear similar successions of sounds. The effect is so definite to us that we have as a rule no particular difficulty in saying what the sounds in words are, or in assigning letters to them in alphabetic writing.

5. The fact that the change from one speech-sound to the next in a sequence is generally performed in a gradual manner is immaterial from the linguistic point of view. SWEET and the other pioneers of modern phonetics recognized that passing from one "sound" to another was a gradual process. In their terminology it is said that consecutive speech-sounds are linked together by transitory sounds called "glides."[2] A "glide" is the sound produced by the movement of passing in a natural manner from the position (or terminal position) of one speech-sound to the position (or initial position) of the next; it is an unavoidable sound, and has no linguistic significance. A glide may involve movements of several parts of the speech mechanism; these need not, and in fact generally do not, take place exactly simultaneously.

6. The point of separation between one speech-sound and the next in a chain may be taken to be any point in the glide which it is convenient to choose on linguistic grounds. In most cases this point does not correspond to any abrupt change in the pattern of a sound-track or oscillogram.

7. The linguistic conception of the "speech-sound" is determined by the possibility of removing a section from a chain and replacing it by a section of another chain,[3] the sections being such that the

---

[2] SWEET, *Handbook of Phonetics* (1877), §189 and elsewhere. A. J. ELLIS called them "transitional configurations" in his *Essentials of Phonetics* (1848).

[3] The glides being at the same time replaced by other appropriate glides.

exchange is capable of changing a word into another word. I do not think it is possible to give an unassailable definition of a "speech-sound," any more than it is possible to give a precise definition of a "word,"[4] but a "speech-sound" may be stated roughly to be a minimum section capable of being exchanged in the manner above indicated.

8. Thus we say that the full pronunciation of the word **az** (*as*) consists of two speech-sounds. The section we represent in writing by **a** is the minimum initial section that can be removed and replaced by a section of some other chain—say by **i** (making **iz**). Similarly, the section we represent by **z** is the minimum final section that can be removed and replaced by a section of some other chain—say, by **ʃ** (*sh*) (making **aʃ**) or by **m** (making the full pronunciation of **am**). In the last word the separation is less precise because the nasality of the consonant is anticipated in the vowel.

"Simple," "Gliding" and "Compound" Sounds

9. Speech-sounds which require for their production a static position of the speech mechanism (apart from the mechanism which propels the air and the mechanism which produces "voice") may be called "simple sounds." Speech-sounds formed by gradual movements of the lips, tongue, etc., may be called "gliding sounds." Speech-sounds which in the course of their production have an abrupt change of position of the articulating organs may be called "compound" sounds.

10. Examples of simple sounds are ordinary **m, n, l, f, z** and the "pure" vowels. Trills (e.g. rolled **r**) may also be classed among the simple sounds.

11. Simple sounds are, as a rule, represented in phonetic writing by single letters. It is occasionally justifiable to represent them by digraphs (sequences of two letters) in order to effect an economy of symbols.

---

[4] The nearest definition that can be suggested for a "word" is perhaps that given in L. R. Palmer's *Introduction to Modern Linguistics*, p. 79: "the smallest speech unit (= constantly recurring sound-pattern) capable of functioning as a complete utterance." But even this appears to need some amplification (see Jespersen, *Philosophy of Grammar*, pp. 94, 95).

12.   Examples of gliding sounds are English **w** and **j** and the diphthongs. Examples of compound sounds are the plosive consonants; for other examples, see §258 ff.   Gliding sounds and compound sounds are sometimes represented phonetically by single letters and sometimes by digraphs; for this, see §§14–19.

13.   It is to be noted that in compound sounds the amount to be designated a "speech-sound" depends upon the phonetic context. Thus the speech-sound which we represent by the letter **k** in **ˈdʒoki** (*jockey*) consists of a "stop" plus a "plosion"; nothing less can be removed and replaced by some other section to form a different word (say by **l** making **ˈdʒoli**, *jolly*).   A **k** with plosion is thus a single speech-sound in this context.   On the other hand the speech-sound which we represent by **k** in **akt** (*act*) consists of a "stop" only, in a common English pronunciation of this word; the replacement of this by, say, **n** or by the stop of **p** converts the word into other words (**ant**, **apt**).   **p** and **k** without plosion are thus "speech-sounds" in this phonetic context.

REPRESENTATION OF GLIDING SOUNDS AND COMPOUND SOUNDS

14.   In some cases a gliding sound is most conveniently represented in transcription by a single letter.   Thus the initial gliding sounds in the English words *wet* and *yard* are appropriately written with **w** and **j**.   The gliding portion of an "imperfect diphthong"[5] may also be written with a single letter.   Such a sound is that heard in one pronunciation of the French **pɑːj** (*paille*).

15.   The gliding sounds called diphthongs,[6] being sounds which begin at one vowel and immediately move in the direction of another, are best represented by digraphs of which the first letter indicates the starting point and the second the direction of movement.

16.   Compound sounds may be considered in two categories: (1) those in which a constituent part resembles a "simple" sound, and (2) those in which constituent parts have no close resemblance to "simple" sounds.   The chief examples of the first category are the affricates.   An affricate has a "stop" and a "plosion" which

---

[5] For "imperfect diphthongs," see my *Outline of English Phonetics*, eighth and subsequent editions, §227.

[6] Perfect diphthongs.

terminates with friction reminiscent of the corresponding fricative consonant; it may have an aspiration in addition to this. Affricates may be represented either by single letters or by digraphs; sometimes one method is the more convenient and sometimes the other. Thus I find it generally advisable, in the interests of symbol economy, to write the English affricate commonly written *ch* with a digraph; tʃ is chosen for this purpose since the on-glide and stop of this affricate resemble those of the English t, and the friction heard when the stop is released resembles the fricative sound ʃ.[7] Similarly, it is usual in phonetic transcriptions of German, to employ the digraph ts to represent the affricate in tseːn (*zehn*), etc. On the other hand, it is more convenient to represent the affricate sounds of such Indian languages as Hindustani and Bengali by the single letters c and ɟ (in Romanic Orthography *c* and *j*).[8] The same system is probably also advisable in transcribing Turkish, where for instance acan (the one who opens) has to be distinguished from atʃan (thirsty); the possible alternative system of writing atʃan and at-ʃan respectively is probably not sufficiently distinctive.

17. Other examples of compound sounds of the first category are the m̂b, n̂d, etc., of Sinhalese and of Bantu languages, for which see §§260 ff.; they are adequately represented by a letter representing the nasal part followed by a letter representing the plosive part. Yet others are the consonants which have double articulation and where one of the articulations terminates before the other. These can be written with digraphs, whenever the use of a single letter would be ambiguous or inconvenient. Examples are plosives pronounced with simultaneous glottal stop (p', t', etc.) and clicks pronounced simultaneously with ŋ or g. In writing the former the ' can be dropped if the other p, t, etc., occurring in the language are aspirated and therefore expressible by ph, th, etc., which appears

---

[7] In the rare cases where the phoneme t is followed by the phoneme ʃ in English, a hyphen must be inserted to make the transcription clear: e.g. ˈhat-ʃop (*hat-shop*), ˈkoːt-ʃip (*courtship*). Such instances are only found in compound words or words formed with a suffix.

[8] The Indian t and d are very dental, and it is, therefore, unsuitable to employ their symbols to denote the first part of these affricates. Moreover, when the sequence dental t + ʃ occurs, the plosion of the dental t is heard and gives to the sequence an effect entirely different from the affricate c: thus the Bengali words kutʃit (ugly) and kucit (rarely) are quite distinct. The group tc is also distinct from doubled c.

to be generally if not always the case.[9]   For the latter I recommend the notation ŋ̣, g̣ɓ, etc.[10]

18.   The second category of compound sounds comprises the ordinary (non-affricated) plosives, such as p, b, t.   These, when fully pronounced, consist of a "stop" and a "plosion" followed very often by an "aspiration."   There is as a rule no reason for writing them with more than single letters.

19.   Those plosive consonants which are made by double articulation and in which the two articulations terminate simultaneously may, however, with advantage be written with digraphs.   Thus it is justifiable and advantageous to write the velar-labial plosive of the Efik language of Nigeria with the digraph kp, for though ordinary k and p also occur in the language, p never follows k in any word.[11]

CONCRETE AND ABSTRACT SOUNDS

20.   There are "concrete" sounds and "abstract" sounds.   A concrete sound is a physical thing, a sound actually uttered on a particular occasion.   When we speak of *hearing* a sound or *making* a sound, the reference is generally to concrete sounds.   An abstract sound may be said to be that which is common to, or can be abstracted from, a number of utterances of what we call "the

---

[9] E.g. in Tswana, where for instance the p of pōla (to worry) is commonly pronounced with simultaneous glottal stop, and is distinguished from phōla (to jump off).   The Georgian language contains similar pairs of consonants. The aspirations of the aspirated p, t, etc., are, however, weaker than those of Tswana.   It is perhaps preferable in transcribing Georgian to write p, t, etc., for the aspirated consonants and p', t', etc., for the consonants accompanied by glottal stop.   See *Le Maître Phonétique*, January, 1944, p. 5. For the unusual case of Korean, see §194.

[10] C. M. DOKE has invented special letters for all these click combinations, and has used them in his *Phonetics of Zulu* and elsewhere.   D. M. BEACH has also invented special letters for the clicks pronounced simultaneously with ŋ; see his *Phonetics of the Hottentot Language*.   I venture to think that the introduction of these new letters is unnecessary, and that the notation ŋ̣, ŋɓ, etc., satisfies all requirements and is justifiable on grounds of symbol economy. When a nasal is *followed* by a click—combinations which are found in Xhosa side by side with the "single sounds" ŋ̣, ŋɓ, etc.—the letter n may be used; thus nꞆ, nɓ.

[11] See I. C. WARD, *Phonetic and Tonal Structure of Efik*, p. 7.

same sound."[12] Abstract sounds can be pictured to oneself[13]; concrete sounds are the physical manifestations of abstract sounds. When the term "sound" is used in such a book as the present one, the context shows whether a concrete or an abstract sound is meant. When one talks or writes *about* sounds, the reference is generally to "abstract sounds of the first degree."[14]

CHAPTER II

THE PHONEME

Need for the Phoneme Idea

21. It is constantly found in language study that several distinct sounds (§20) in a language have to be considered as if they were one for orthographic, grammatical and semantic purposes. Thus, although the English k's in ki:p (*keep*), ko:l (*call*) and ku:l (*cool*) are distinct sounds, it is necessary for practical linguistic purposes to treat them as if they were one and the same.

22. In fact, many of the elements of language commonly termed "sounds" or "essential sounds" are in reality small families of sounds, each family consisting of an important sound of the language together with other related sounds which, so to speak, "represent" it in particular sequences or under particular conditions of length or stress or intonation.

"Definition" of a Phoneme

23. It is to such a family that the term "phoneme" is applied in this book. The sounds included in it may be termed its "members" or "allophones."[15]

---

[12] This is no definition, since the idea of the abstract sound is implicit in the expression "the same sound." It has to be assumed that readers understand what is meant (see Preface).

[13] Though I have been told by a psychologist that not everyone can do this.

[14] See further my paper on *Concrete and Abstract Sounds* in the *Proceedings of the Third International Congress of Phonetic Sciences*. Ghent, 1938.

[15] The convenient term "allophone" was invented by the late American linguistician Benjamin Lee Whorf about 1934. Members of a phoneme have also been termed "conditioned variants." They are also said to be in "complementary distribution."

24. When a phoneme comprises more than one member, it generally happens that one of the sounds seems more important than the other(s). This may be because it is commoner than the other(s), or because it is the one used in isolation, or because it is intermediate between extreme members. Such a sound may be termed the "principal member" or "norm" of the phoneme. The other sounds in the same phoneme may be called "subsidiary members" or "subsidiary allophones."[1] Subsidiary members have also been termed "divergents" and "sub-phonemic variants."

25. Before proceeding further it is necessary to give as precise an explanation as may be feasible of what a phoneme is. I say an "explanation" rather than a "definition," because in spite of the simple appearance of the example in §21, a little consideration shows us that an "exact" definition is impossible. We cannot define what a phoneme is without making use of terms such as "language," "speech-sounds" and "words," all of which are incapable of definition like the fundamental concepts in other sciences (see Preface and §7).[2] We can restrict to some extent the meanings of these terms, but when the restrictions have been formulated, we still have to assume that the things for which the terms stand exist and that people know what they are.

26. Some have expressed the opinion that phonemes can be "defined" simply by reference to their function as units suitable for alphabetic expression. F. S. WINGFIELD, for instance, whose main interest in linguistic matters lies in the reform of English spelling, has suggested that a phoneme may be defined as "a group of speech-sounds nearly enough alike to be treated as a unit for alphabetic purposes."[3] Such a rough-and-ready definition may perhaps sometimes serve in a popular exposition; but though it underlines one of the chief uses of the phoneme theory, it will not apply in all cases, and will not, I think, be found sufficiently precise for use in those detailed linguistic investigations which

---

[1] It is, however, maintained by some that as all members of a phoneme are essential, no one member can properly be described as more important than another.

[2] See also my paper *Some Thoughts on the Phoneme* in the *Transactions of the Philological Society*, 1944, pp. 119, 120.

[3] In his *Bulletin* of reformed spelling, February, 1940, p. 5.

need the theory. In the following paragraphs, therefore, a general explanation is given of the nature of the units which we call phonemes. This will then be exemplified and amplified in the course of the book.

27. In this explanation special senses are to be attached to the terms "language" and "phonetic context," as shown in the following paragraphs.

28. A "language" is to be taken to mean the speech of one individual pronouncing in a definite and consistent style (i.e. an idiolect). It does not include sounds used in different styles of speaking. The style referred to, in the absence of indication to the contrary, is a consistent use of the forms of natural, unstudied but reasonably careful and not rapid conversation. It is the style termed by PAUL PASSY "prononciation familière ralentie." As no two people speak exactly alike, the names of languages ("English," "French," etc., or "Southern British English," "Parisian French," etc.) refer throughout the book to the speech of imaginary people using "slow conversational pronunciation" in what appears to be a typical or "average" manner. "German," in the absence of any indication to the contrary, means stage German as described in VIËTOR's *Deutsches Aussprachewörterbuch* and other works by the same author, and in the new (1957) edition of SIEBS' *Deutsche Hochsprache.*

29. The reason for restricting the term "language" in this manner is that the more general use of the term covers the speech of people who speak in ways differing considerably from each other—who use different sounds, or who use sounds in such a way that a different phonemic classification is called for.[4] See further, §658.

30. The term "phonetic context" of a sound is to be understood to mean the sounds next to it or near it in the sequence of which it is a part, together with its duration (length), stress and (if voiced) voice-pitch. "In the same phonetic context" means "when surrounded by the same sounds and subject to the same conditions as regards duration, stress and voice-pitch." For the sake of

---

[4] For instance, some Frenchmen have two a-phonemes and others only one. But they speak the same "language" as the term is commonly understood. See §§621–623, also *Some Thoughts on the Phoneme*, p. 125.

brevity it is sometimes convenient to use the term "controlling principles" to denote the phonetic contexts which condition the use of special members of phonemes.

31. With these uses of terms in mind, and regarding the phoneme as a family, we may say that a phoneme is A FAMILY OF SOUNDS IN A GIVEN LANGUAGE WHICH ARE RELATED IN CHARACTER AND ARE USED IN SUCH A WAY THAT NO ONE MEMBER EVER OCCURS IN A WORD IN THE SAME PHONETIC CONTEXT AS ANY OTHER MEMBER.

32. The restriction "related in character" is of necessity vague, since it is impossible to specify what degree of dissimilarity will prevent two sounds from belonging to a single phoneme. Many examples could be adduced to illustrate the difficulty. It does not seem possible, for instance, to prove beyond question that h and ŋ belong to separate phonemes in English (see §53). Yet they are so remote from each other that it would obviously be absurd to consider them as members of one phoneme. On the other hand, though voiceless l̥ and voiced l are acoustically very dissimilar, they clearly belong to a single phoneme in French (§73); and in German we find ourselves obliged to group into one phoneme sounds so different as eː and an ɔ-like vowel (§91).

33. The relationship between sounds in a phoneme may be acoustic or organic. For instance, in the case of t and the glottal stop (ʔ), which probably belong to one phoneme in some types of English (§§618, 620), the relationship is acoustic; to the ear they have a certain similarity in some situations in spite of the great difference in their manner of formation. On the other hand, the acoustically different sounds l̥ and l belong to the same phoneme in French by virtue of their organic relationship.

34. The restriction "in a word" is important. To extend the definition to cover word-groups or sentences would greatly complicate matters. At the best it would increase the number of phonemes in some languages[5]; it might even be found to render the elaboration of any consistent theory of phonemes impossible, since variations of sound at word junctions may take so many forms.

---

[5] For an example see §282. See also *Some Thoughts on the Phoneme*, pp. 127–132. See also my *Outline of English Phonetics*, 8th edition, 1956, Chap. XXXII, especially §1097.

35. It is to be taken as axiomatic that one sound cannot belong to two phonemes of a language. There are possibly some rare exceptions to this; they are dealt with in Chapters XIX and XX.

36. From the above explanation it will be seen that the three different k's in the English words mentioned in §21 are classed together as belonging to the same phoneme, because the variety of k used in ki:p is never used in English before o: or u:, and the k of ku:l is never used before i: or o:, and so on.

37. Sometimes a phoneme consists of only one member, or more accurately, of sounds, which are so nearly alike that they may for practical purposes be regarded as indistinguishable. We may say, for instance, that the English consonant phoneme f comprises only one member.[6] Likewise the French vowel phoneme o. H. E. PALMER suggested the term "monophone" for a phoneme comprising only one sound.

38. It must be mentioned here that in the opinion of some the phoneme may be defined in a totally different manner, namely, not as family of sounds but as a single entity—an abstract sound of the second degree[7] which appears in the first degree of abstraction as a set of abstract sounds, each of which we are able to bring into manifestation as a concrete sound. The question of regarding the phoneme in this light and in other ways is discussed in Chapter XXIX. See also my *History and Meaning of the Term "Phoneme"* (published by the I.P.A., 1957).

39. The more objective course of regarding the phoneme as a family of sounds is followed in this book because I have found it to give valuable results in practical language teaching and in connexion with the construction of systems of alphabetic writing. This manner of regarding the phoneme also presents the advantage that in certain cases of difficulty it is possible to select the phoneme to which a given sound shall belong. Some examples of this are noted in Chapters XIV and XX.

40. Neither the explanation given in §31 nor any other "definition" of a phoneme I have ever heard of is completely unassailable.

---

[6] Actually it is possible to perceive slight differences between the f's used in different phonetic contexts.

[7] *Concrete and Abstract Sounds*, p. 4.

I do not think it possible to devise an explanation which leaves no loopholes for exceptions. The above, however, gives us a workable theory which, as this book will show, is applicable in all ordinary cases as well as to many cases of an exceptional nature.

CHAPTER III

PHONETIC TRANSCRIPTION

41. Any unambiguous manner of representing pronunciation by means of writing is called a "phonetic transcription." An alphabetic system of phonetic transcription consists of letters representing sound-qualities (tambers[1]) or phonemes, together with marks or other devices[2] to indicate such of the other attributes of speech (duration, stress and voice-pitch) as may be of importance in the language to be written.

42. As the letters of a phonetic transcription may represent either speech-sounds or phonemes, so also the other marks and devices may represent duration, stress and pitch in great detail, or they may be reduced to a minimum and show only just so much as is needed to distinguish graphically the words which are distinguished in speech by these attributes.

43. A phonetic transcription in which each letter represents a phoneme is called a "phonemic" or "linguistically broad" transcription. When duration, stress and voice-pitch are denoted by the minimum of marks or devices which will serve to distinguish one word from another (in languages where these attributes are used for word distinctions), the representation of these attributes is likewise said to be "broad."

44. A phonetic transcription in which separate letters or special marks are used to distinguish two or more members of a phoneme, or in which some letters are used to represent phonemes and other letters or special marks are introduced to indicate particular members of phonemes, is called a "linguistically narrow transcription." If use is made of more marks or devices indicating duration, stress

---

[1] This convenient anglicisation of the French *timbre* was invented by ROBERT BRIDGES, the Poet Laureate.

[2] E.g. doubling a letter to indicate length.

or voice-pitch than are necessary to make visual distinction between words distinguished in speech by these attributes, the representation of them is likewise said to be "narrow."

45. Use is made of both narrow and broad transcriptions in the course of this book. Narrow transcriptions are enclosed in square brackets [ ], except where it is specifically stated or is evident from the context that the transcriptions are narrow.[3] These brackets·are to be taken to mean that the transcriptions are narrow in at least one particular; they may be narrow in several particulars. The context shows in what respects they are narrow.[4]

46. All transcriptions in this book which are not enclosed in square brackets, and which context does not show to be narrow, are broad (i.e. phonemic).

46a. A more detailed account of the theory of broad and narrow transcription will be found in Appendix A in the 8th edition (1956) of my *Outline of English Phonetics* (published by Heffer, Cambridge).

47. The phonetic alphabet used in this book is that of the *Association Phonétique Internationale*. It is assumed that readers are familiar with this alphabet. The values of the letters and the methods of using them are explained in many works, and particularly in the *Principles of the International Phonetic Association* (1949 edition) and in JONES and DAHL, *Fundamentos de Escritura Fonética*. A list of the symbols used in this book is given on pp. xiv–xviii.

CHAPTER IV

THE SEMANTIC FUNCTION OF PHONEMES

48. In §31 it was explained that no one member of a phoneme ever occurs in the same phonetic setting as any other member. In other words the different members of a phoneme are *mutually exclusive* in the phonetic contexts in which they are used. It is important to observe that this exclusion of one member of a phoneme from a position appropriate to another member of the same phoneme is inherent in the nature of a phoneme.

---

[3] E.g. in Chapters XIV, XVIII and in §§119, 323 ff., 530, 531.

[4] Square brackets are also used for another purpose, namely to enclose graphical representations of intonation. This use of square brackets cannot be confused with their use as indicating narrowness of transcription.

49. It follows from this that if two sounds of a language can occur in the same phonetic context, those sounds must belong to separate phonemes in that language. Short i and ə, for instance, belong to separate phonemes in English because they can both occur initially before the same consonant, as in the words i'luːʒn (*illusion*), ə'luːʒn (*allusion*). But in the Efik language of Nigeria, which also contains these sounds, ə is never used in the same phonetic context as i (§119); the same two sounds mutually exclude each other, and that is why they belong to the same phoneme in that language.

50. It is therefore a corollary to the explanation given in §31 that phonemes have a semantic function in languages. For since a member of a phoneme *can* occupy the same situation as the appropriate member of another phoneme, it is possible to alter a sequence by exchanging a sound for the appropriate sound of another phoneme. Such an alteration may change a word into another word. In other terms the differences between phonemes are "significant," i.e. capable of distinguishing one word from another.

51. Conversely, the difference between two members of the same phoneme cannot be "significant": it cannot be made use of for the purpose of distinguishing words. This is because, if the explanation in §31 is accepted, two members of the same phoneme never occur in the same phonetic context, and therefore a sequence cannot be changed into another possible sequence of the language by an interchange of two such sounds.

52. The fact that sounds belonging to separate phonemes are capable of distinguishing words, while sounds belonging to the same phoneme are not, is thus not part of any "definition" of a phoneme as here conceived. It follows from our explanation of its nature.

53. The sounds of separate phonemes do not *necessarily* distinguish words, but they are capable of doing so, and generally do so. It occasionally happens, however, that no pair of words can be found in which the sole difference lies in the substitution of one particular phoneme for another. Thus, as far as I know, there is no pair of English words differing by the substitution of h for ŋ. It would, however, clearly be inexpedient to assign the two sounds to a single phoneme on that ground; they are not sufficiently nearly "related in character." The same appears to apply to ŋ and ʒ in English (see §152).[1]

CHAPTER V

OTHER SIGNIFICANT ELEMENTS

54. It is the addition, subtraction or interchange of phonemes (as here conceived) which constitutes by far the commonest means of distinguishing words. There exist, however, other means of effecting word distinctions, such as differences in the duration of sounds, differences in the stress of syllables and differences of voice-pitch. It appears that there are few, if any, languages which do not make some use of at least one of these. These attributes are discussed in detail in Chapters XXI–XXV.

55. Words may also be, and very often are, distinguished by complexes of the various attributes of sounds. These complexes, which are very numerous, are discussed in detail in Chapter XXVI.

CHAPTER VI

MINIMAL DISTINCTIONS

56. When a distinction between two sequences occurring in a language is such that any lesser degree of distinction would be inadequate for clearly differentiating words in that language, the distinction is termed a "minimal" one.

57. Minimal distinctions are very commonly effected by the addition or subtraction of a phoneme. Thus minimal distinctions are shown in the following pairs of English words kwout (*quote*), ˈkwoutə (*quota*); lɔː (*law*), lɔːn (*lawn*); trei (*tray*), strei (*stray*); wet (*wet*), west (*west*).

---

[1] I would add here a word on "oppositions." The different phonemes of a language are naturally "opposed" to each other in the sense that one phoneme can, under suitable conditions, supplant another, the substitution causing a word to be changed into another word. A comprehensive theory of oppositions has been worked out by various phonologists. For this see particularly TRUBETZKOY, *Grundzüge der Phonologie*, especially pp. 59–75 (in CANTINEAU's translation, pp. 69–87).

3

58. Minimal distinctions may also be effected by the substitution of one phoneme for another. Thus, the following pairs of English words exhibit minimal distinctions: sit, sat; sit, sip; sit, fit.

59. In "chrone languages" (§381) minimal distinctions are found when a short sound is replaced by the same sound lengthened. Thus the French pair bɛt (*bette*), bɛːt (*bête*) exhibits a minimal distinction. So also does the stage pronunciation of the German words ˈtrɛne (*trenne*) and ˈtrɛːne (*Träne*), and pairs like taiko (drum), taikoː (opposition) in Japanese, are (he has) and aːre (daughters) in Kikuyu, okutuma [.. ˙ .] (to send) and okutuːma [.. ⁻ .] (to heap up) in Luganda.[1]

60. In "stress languages" (§428) minimal distinctions are found if strong stress is shifted from one syllable to another, the sounds and lengths remaining constant or approximately so. For instance, the Spanish ˈtermino (*término*, end), terˈmino (*termino*, I finish) and termiˈno (*terminó*, he finished) differ from each other by minimal distinctions.[2]

61. In "tone languages" (§470) minimal distinctions are found when two words differ in tone but not in any other respect. Thus, the Cantonese words ˎsœŋ (hurt), ˊsœŋ (photograph), ⁻sœŋ (prime minister), ˏsœŋ (pair of drawers), ˏsœŋ (ascend), ˌsœŋ (above) differ from each other by minimal distinctions. So do pairs of Tswana words such as mɷa (soot), mɷā (breath, spirit), lɪkāu (young man), lɪkau (kind of wild duck), bɒntlɛ (beauty), bɒntlɛ̄ (the outside).[3]

62. If two sequences are distinguished by simultaneous changes in two attributes, the distinction is a minimal one when the amount of change in each attribute is not of itself sufficient to differentiate words in the language in question. This case may be exemplified by such pairs of English words as ʃiːp (*sheep*), ʃip (*ship*), diːd (*deed*), did (*did*). The vowels of such words in my type of English differ

---

[1] Dots and lines enclosed in square brackets indicate the tones in tone languages. Dots show short syllables; horizontal lines show long syllables. (Oblique lines may represent short syllables as well as long ones.)

[2] The shifting of secondary stress does not appear to be adequate for differentiating one word from another. (See footnote 25 to §462.)

[3] Narrow transcriptions of these Tswana words, when said in isolation, are mɷːa̰, mɷːā, lɪkàːu̠, lɪka̰ːu̠, bɒṇːtlɛ, bɒṇːtlɛ̄. The type of Tswana referred to here and elsewhere in this book is the Rolong dialect spoken in and around Mafeking.

both in length and in quality: the vowel in ʃiːp is longer than that in ʃip, and it also has a "closer" quality.[4]

63. Other examples of minimal distinctions by a combination of quality and length are those in such English pairs as noːd (*gnawed*) and nod (*nod*), puːl (*pool*) and pul (*pull*). Minimal distinctions by a similar combination are found in German, but in that language the quality difference is notably less than in English, and the length difference correspondingly greater. Examples are ˈbiːte (*biete*), ˈbite (*bitte*), ziːç[5] (*Sieg*), ziç (*sich*).

64. Minimal distinctions are sometimes due to changes in three attributes simultaneously. In Serbo-Croat, for instance, minimal distinctions may be effected by a combination of length, stress and voice-pitch (see §§466, 547, 558–560). In Pekingese, too, we find that the difference between the first (high-level) and third (low-rising) tones is accompanied by a difference of vowel quality and of length (see §§543, 557).

65. Sequences are, of course, very often distinguished by more than a minimal difference. These wider differences may be termed "duple," "triple," etc., according to the number of minimal distinctions of which the total difference is composed. Duple distinctions are those which are the result of two minimal distinctions. These are exemplified in such English pairs as sit and sap, sit and lip, which each differ in two phonemes. Further examples are seen in the French pair bɛːt (*bête*) and bɛk (*bec*), which exhibits a difference in a phoneme and a significant length, the English pair niːd (*need*) and nod (*nod*), which exhibits a difference of quality and duration equivalent to two minimal distinctions,[6] the English ˈproutest (*protest*, n.) and prəˈtest (*protest*, v.), which differs in a phoneme and the incidence of stress, the Cantonese ˎsœŋ (hurt) and ˏseŋ (city) which differ in a phoneme and a tone.

---

[4] This does not apply to Scottish pronunciation. In Scottish English the vowels generally have about the same length (short), and the distinction between such words as *sheep* and *ship* is rendered adequate by a wider quality difference than that found in my type of Southern English.

[5] Alternative pronunciation of ziːk.

[6] niːd (*need*) and noːd (*gnawed*) are distinguished by a single phoneme, while noːd and nod are distinguished by a minimal difference consisting of a combination of quality with duration.

66. Triple distinctions are those shown in the English pairs fit and pan (three phonemes), hiːt (*heat*) and pot (two phonemes and a complex of quality and length),[7] the French pair bɛːt (*bête*) and ʃɛk (*cheque*) (two phonemes and a significant length), the English pair 'preznt (*present*, n.) and pri'zent (*present*, v.) (two phonemes and the incidence of stress), the Cantonese pair ´saːŋ (provincial) and ˏseŋ (city) (a phoneme, a length and a tone), the Kikuyu pair raːra [⁻ .] (spend the night) and rara [· ´] (be tepid) (a length and two tones), and so on.

CHAPTER VII

EXAMPLES OF PHONEMIC GROUPING

67. A few examples of the grouping of sounds into phonemes have already been given, and notably the English k-sounds (§§21, 36). In the present chapter are shown other examples of various types. They are intended to give the reader a general idea of the principles involved.

68. It will be observed that all illustrations of the phoneme require a comparison of pairs of sequences differing in two respects. In most cases one of the differences is evidently the chief means of distinguishing the sequences, and the other an incidental one accompanying or conditioned by the chief means of distinction. Thus, the English words kiːl, koːl, kuːl are distinguished mainly by their vowels. The k's are also different, but these differences are clearly subsidiary and conditioned by the vowels.

(1) VARIANTS OF SOUND CONDITIONED BY NEIGHBOURING SOUNDS IN THE SEQUENCE

(a) *Consonants*

69. In English the h-sounds in hed (*head*), haːd (*hard*), hud (*hood*) are very different sounds, but they have to be considered as belonging to a single phoneme, since their use is dependent upon the nature of the following vowel. The words are distinguished by the vowels, and the differences in the h's are evidently incidental to these.

---

[7] The number of minimal distinctions is shown by sequences like hiːt, piːt (*peat*), pit, pot, or hiːt, piːt, poːt (*port*), pot, or hiːt, hit, hot, pot.

70. The ŋ-sounds in siŋ (*sing*) and soŋ (*song*) are different sounds, as can easily be heard by isolating them; but these and other varieties of ŋ are used in accordance with the nature of the preceding vowel and must therefore all be regarded as belonging to a single phoneme. Here again it is the vowels which constitute the essential differences between the words, the variations of ŋ being incidental.

71. In Southern English, as I speak it, the l-sounds in liːf (*leaf*) and fiːl (*feel*) are different, the first being a moderately "clear" l and the second a "dark" (velarized) l. But these two l's, and other l's of intermediate types, must be looked upon as belonging to one phoneme, since their use is entirely conditioned by their situations in relation to other sounds in the sequence. (Clear l's are used whenever a vowel follows.[1] Dark l is used finally and whenever a consonant follows. Dark l does not occur before a vowel,[2] and clear l never occurs finally or followed by a consonant.)

72. The English t-phoneme is one which includes a number of members. The principal t is alveolar and slightly aspirated; it is used before vowels in strongly stressed position, as in ten (*ten*), 'teibl (*table*). Subsidiary t's are: (1) a dental t used before θ, as in eitθ (*eighth*), (2) a retracted t used in tr, as in trein (*train*), (3) an unaspirated or barely aspirated t used in weakly stressed positions, as in 'letə (*letter*), (4) a laterally exploded t used in tl, as in 'ketl (*kettle*), (5) a nasally exploded t used in tn, as in 'mʌtn (*mutton*).

73. In French, voiceless l (ļ), which is used in such words as pœpl (*peuple*), 5ːkl (*oncle*) when final, must be considered as belonging to the same phoneme as the ordinary French l. Its use is entirely dependent upon situation; for instance, in French the voiceless sound ļ can never begin a word as the ordinary l can.

74. In French different kinds of d are used in different situations. For example, the d of adʒɛktif (*adjectif*) is an alveolar sound distinct from the common French dental d, as in dut (*doute*).

75. In many languages, e.g. Italian, Hungarian, the sound ŋ is found to the exclusion of n before k and g, but not in any other

---

[1] There are degrees of "clearness," according to the nature of the vowel.

[2] Except occasionally when it is syllabic, i.e. pronounced with unusual length.

situation. In Spanish, ŋ is found to the exclusion of n before k, g and x, as in ['θiŋko]³ (*cinco*, five), [iŋ'gles] (*inglés*, English), [na'raŋxa] (*naranja*, orange), but not in any other situation. ŋ is therefore to be considered as belonging to the same phoneme as n in these languages. (Broad transcription of the above Spanish words would be 'θinko, in'gles, na'ranxa.)

76. In conversational Dutch the sound g exists, but only before voiced consonants, e.g. before d in ['zagduk] (*zakdoek*, handkerchief), where it may be said to "represent" k. g is therefore a member of the k-phoneme in that language.

77. The sounds h, ç and ɸ occur in Japanese, as in [çito] (*man*), [hana] (*nose*), [ɸuku] (*luck*). They belong, however, to one phoneme, their use depending entirely upon the nature of the following vowel. h-sounds are used before e, a and o and not before i and u; ç is used before i and not before any other vowel; ɸ is used before u and not before any other vowel. (The above words would appear in broad transcription as hito, hana, huku, and these are their forms in Kunreisiki Rōmazi orthography.)

78. In languages containing sounds of the h type varieties of "voiced h" (ɦ) are often found to occur between voiced sounds to the exclusion of breathed h-sounds, while breathed h-sounds are used in all other situations to the exclusion of voiced h-sounds. When this is so, the voiced and breathed h-sounds constitute one phoneme. This is found to be the case, for instance, in some styles of English pronunciation. Many English people, especially when speaking in a rather rapid style, use voiced h in such words as əd'hiə (*adhere*), 'bɔihud (*boyhood*), bi'haind (*behind*), though they use breathed h initially or when a voiceless consonant precedes.

79. In one form of the Kikuyu language of Kenya the sounds ɸ, β and b appear to be used in such a manner that they may be regarded as constituting a single phoneme. I refer to the speech of those natives who use ɸ initially and not elsewhere, e.g. in [ɸa:βá] [-´] (father), β medially except after m, e.g. in [ɣekãβū] [.··] (basket), and plosive b after m and not elsewhere,

---

³ Square brackets [ ] mean that the word is transcribed narrowly (§45).

e.g. in [mborī] [. ˙] (goat), [itu:mbe] [·-·] (egg).[4] These words would accordingly be written broadly as ba:bá, gekābū, mborī, itu:mbe. Similar considerations doubtless apply to the families θ, ð, d, as in [θa:ðī] [-˙] (soup), [ando] [··] (people), and x, ɣ, g in Kikuyu, but I have not had opportunities of verifying this. [θa:ðī] would be written broadly as da:dī.[5]

80. In one variety of the Igbo language of Nigeria ʃ and s belong to a single phoneme, ʃ being used to the exclusion of s before i and e, and s being used to the exclusion of ʃ before all other vowels. Examples are oʃiri [˙ . .] (he cooked), ɔʃere [˙ . .] (he said), but osɛrɛ [˙ . .] (he wrote), ɔsara [˙ . .] (he washed). In broad transcription the first two of these would be written osiri, ɔsere.

81. In the Tswana (Chwana) language of South Africa there exists a peculiar sound intermediate between d and l, which may be written narrowly with the letter ɹ.[6] It occurs before i and u but not in any other situations. There is also an ordinary l in the language which never occurs before i or u, but does occur before all the other vowels (ι, e, ɛ, a, ɔ, o, ꭥ). Thus, xꭥlīmꭥ (above), mꭥlumɔ (sound), have the d-like l, while lιlā (to weep), mꭥlιmɔ (goodness), tʃhōlɔ (hospitality) have ordinary l. It follows that ɹ must be regarded as belonging to the l-phoneme in Tswana.[7]

82. I am informed that in certain dialects of Igbo (Nigeria) a sound intermediate between l and r occurs before the vowels i, e, ꭥ, u and not in any other situations, while an ordinary single flap

---

[4] Not all native speakers of Kikuyu pronounce in this way. Many do not use ɸ at all, but use β in initial as well as in medial positions. This is the form described in L. E. ARMSTRONG's *The Phonetic and Tonal Structure of Kikuyu*. Some, influenced by English, use an English b in borrowed words such as bu:kū [-˙] (book). With them b and β are separate phonemes. (The natural unstudied pronunciation of the word for "book" by speakers unaffected by the importation of English sounds is mbu:kū [- ˙].) ‗

[5] Miss ARMSTRONG suggested a different phonemic classification, which I am disposed to think is better than that given above. She regarded the Kikuyu mb, nd and ŋg as single compound sounds constituting separate phonemes. This treatment of the sounds is clearly justifiable in this language, since when mb, etc., occur initially, the nasal element is very short and often so weak as to be almost imperceptible; it may even be absent altogether. (See ARMSTRONG, pp. 30–32.)

[6] As in the *Sechuana Reader* by D. JONES and S. T. PLAATJE.

[7] For ɹ as a phoneme separate from l see §127.

r occurs before the other vowels (ε, a, ɔ and o) and not in other situations. Thus, osiri [˙ . .] (he cooked) and ɔsere [˙ . .] (he said) have the l-like r, while osɛrɛ [˙ . .] (he wrote) and ɔsara [˙ . .] (he washed) have the ordinary flapped r. This distribution requires that the two consonants should be regarded as belonging to the same phoneme in these dialects.

83. An r-like and an l-like sound also belong to a single phoneme in Luganda. The usage in that language appears to be that the sound is l-like initially and after the vowels a, o, u, and r-like after i and e. Examples are okutoːla (to accept), emmaːli (wealth), but [okumiːra] (to swallow), [omuliro] (fire), [emmeːri] (steamer).[8]

84. In several Indian languages, e.g. Urdu, Hindi, Bengali, Telugu, Sinhalese, the retroflex consonant ɳ occurs when one of the other retroflex sounds ʈ or ɖ follows, but not elsewhere. Examples are: Urdu [ghəɳʈa] (bell), [koɳɖi] (water carrier); Sinhalese eteɳʈə (thither). ɳ must therefore be considered a member of the n-phoneme in these languages (compare §128).

85. Tamil is a language which illustrates particularly well the grouping of several quite distinct sounds into single phonemes. The grouping has been worked out by J. R. FIRTH, and details will be found in his *Short Outline of Tamil Pronunciation*.[9] One example may be quoted here.

86. Varieties of k, g, x, ç and ɣ occur in Tamil and are all members of a single phoneme. The rules governing the use of the sounds are as follows. (1) Single k occurs only initially, (2) double k occurs only intervocalically and in the group rkk, (3) g is used after ŋ but not elsewhere, (4) single x is used in most inter-vocalic positions, but (5) ç is used intervocalically when the following vowel is i, and (6) a variety of ɣ[10] is used when a or u follows in final syllables. Examples given by FIRTH are: (1) [kal] (stone), (2) [pakkam] (side), (3) [tiːrkka] (to complete), (3) [naːŋgal] (we), (4) [maxan] or [maɣan] (son), (5) [aɹuçi] (decaying), (6) [kuruɖarɣal] (blind men), [piraɣu] (after).

---

[8] See L. E. ARMSTRONG's summary of the phonetics of Luganda in WESTER-MANN and WARD's *Practical Phonetics for Students of African Languages*, p. 191.

[9] Published as an appendix to the 1934 edition of ARDEN's *Grammar of Common Tamil*.

[10] With weak friction. The sound resembles a voiced h.

87. It is noteworthy that Tamil orthography does not show any difference between all these sounds. Those who originally invented this orthography must have had a clear conception of the phoneme idea, though the theory had never been formulated. This is evidence in favour of a mentalistic view of the phoneme (Chap. XXIX).

(b) Vowels

88. In English, as I pronounce it, certain special varieties of vowel sound are used exclusively before "dark" l. For instance, the vowels in **wet** (*wet*) and **wel** (*well*) are different, the second being opener than the first. The two must, however, be regarded as belonging to a single phoneme since the opener vowel only occurs before dark l and the closer vowel is never found in that position. The opener e̯ may be thought of as "taking the place" of the common (closer) e in this particular situation.

89. Again, in my type of English, the u-sound in **ˈmjuːzik** (*music*) is not the same as that in **luːz** (*lose*); it is a "fronter" sound. The usage is that when long uː is preceded by j, the sound employed is fronter than that used in other situations. Therefore, these fronter and backer sounds must be regarded as belonging to the same phoneme in my type of Southern English.

90. An example from French is found in the sounds of the ɔ type. In Parisian French the vowel of **nɔt** (*note*), **bɔn** (*bonne*), etc., is a central variety as shown in Figure 1.[11] But when r follows as in **pɔrt** (*porte*), the variety employed is a back one. The two sounds, being used in different phonetic contexts, naturally count as belonging to the same phoneme.

91. In German there are two very different varieties of ə, a low one not far from ɔ used when r follows in the same syllable; and a high one used in other situations. Examples of words containing the low ə are [ˈbɛsər] (*besser*), [ˈzondərn] (*sondern*);

---

[11] This diagram and subsequent similar ones (Figs. 2, 3, 4, etc.) show approximate relations of vowels to a system of "Cardinal Vowels" which can be conveniently employed as a basis of comparison. For this method of indicating the nature of vowels, see my *Outline of English Phonetics*, Chap. VIII. These cardinal vowels have been recorded on a double-sided gramophone record, numbered ENG 252–3, published by the Linguaphone Institute.

examples of words containing the high ə are ['bitə] (*bitte*), [gə'laistət] (*geleistet*). As these ə's are consistently used according to the presence or absence of a following r in the same syllable, the two vowels must be classed as belonging to the same phoneme in this type of German. They probably also belong to the same phoneme as eː (see §§224, 225).[12]

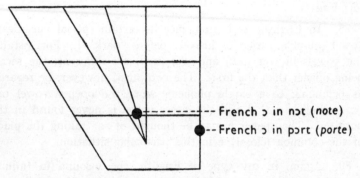

FIG. 1. Positions of the French Vowels in nɔt and pɔrt.

92. In the Danish language varieties of short a are distinguishable according as a dental (alveolar) or a velar consonant follows. A fronter variety is used, for example, in san' (*sand*, sand), 'sadə (*satte*, set), sgal (*skal*, shall), and a backer one in saŋ' (*sang*, song), tak (*tak*, thanks), slags (*slags*, sort), saɣd (*sagt*, said). A still backer variety of a is used in such a word as var'm (*varm*, hot), where a uvular r follows. These varieties of a are evidently conditioned by the following consonant and are therefore to be assigned to a single phoneme.

93. In Arabic there occur several varieties of a-sound ranging from a very front and raised a to a very back ɑ. Until quite recently it has been thought that their use is prescribed exclusively

---

[12] There are types of German in which the written r of *besser, sondern,* etc., has no consonantal value at all, but in which the *er* is pronounced as a kind of uvularized vowel resembling ɔ. This sound constitutes a phoneme separate from ə. See Part 2 of EGAN's *German Phonetic Reader,* where this special vowel is represented by the letter ɐ; *besser* is written 'bɛsɐ, *sondern* 'zɔndɐn, etc. *Nur, vier,* etc., are likewise written with ɐ (nuːɐ, fiːɐ, etc.) in transcriptions of this style of speech. See also EGAN's remarks on p. viii of his book.

by the nature of the adjacent consonants, and in consequence, if this opinion is correct, they must all be held to belong to the same phoneme. The complicated principles regulating the use of these vowel-sounds are set out in GAIRDNER'S *Phonetics of Arabic*, Chapter VII.[13]

94. The principles of phonemic grouping of vowels are particularly well illustrated in the Russian language, and it is worth while setting out the case here in some detail.

95. As is well known, the consonants of Russian fall into two sets, the "soft" consonants (viz. the palatalized consonants, together with tʃ, ʃtʃ, and the separate j) and a set of "hard" (non-palatalized or velarized sounds corresponding to the palatalized consonants, together with ʃ, ʒ and ts). Representing the palatalized consonants by digraphs formed with j,[14] the corresponding palatalized and non-palatalized sounds may be written tj, dj, sj, zj, etc., and t,

---

[13] I have recently (1945) been informed that there are some errors in GAIRDNER'S analysis of the a-sounds of Cairene Arabic, and that actually there is an ɑ-phoneme as well as an a-phoneme in that form of the language. I have had no opportunity of corroborating this. In any case it may not apply to other types of Arabic.

[14] In monographic phonetic writing the palatalized consonants would be written in international notation by the signs ṭ, ḍ, ṣ, ẓ, etc. To my mind the digraphic system is generally preferable as being simpler and more easily legible than the monographic. (Some of the monographic signs are unsatisfactory.) In digraphic representation of the soft consonants a single j can be used to show that all the consonants in a sequence of two or more are palatalized; thus, **strj** can be used to mean ṣṭ ʃ. In groups such as **vzg-lj**, where a non-palatalized consonant is followed by one or more palatalized consonants, a hyphen can be inserted after the symbol of the non-palatalized sound; in cases where this happens in accordance with one of the regular rules, the hyphen may be omitted. (These rules are set out in Chap. V of the *Manual of Russian Pronunciation* by S. C. BOYANUS, published by Lund, Humphries and Co., 1955.)

Note that, when j is used to denote palatalization, two j's must be written in such words as **pjjut** (пьют, they drink), **'bjjotji** (бьёте, you strike), **ʒi'ljjo** (жильё, dwelling place).

Incidentally, it may be observed that Russian orthography could be simplified (in the sense that an alphabet of fewer letters could be devised) by the consistent use of a letter denoting palatalization. The letter ы would then no longer be needed, nor would the letters э, ю and я. On the other hand, the sign of palatalization would occur very frequently, and would render the written forms of many words longer than they are at present. Some might consider this a drawback.

d, s, z, etc. There is no doubt at all that the corresponding palatalized and non-palatalized sounds must be considered to belong to separate phonemes, since they are as a rule quite distinct in sound from each other and the qualities of their essential parts are invariable.[15]

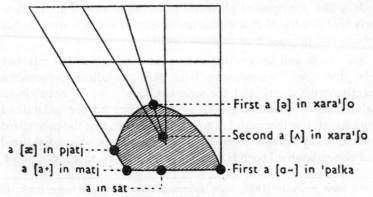

FIG. 2.   Positions of the chief Russian a-sounds.

96.   It is well known too that all the Russian vowels are subject to wide variations. These are conditioned by (1) the nature of adjoining consonants, i.e. whether they are soft or hard, and (2) the degree of stress. It is, for instance, possible to distinguish fairly easily five different shades of a in strongly stressed positions and two more in medium and weakly stressed positions. The shades occurring in strongly stressed positions may be represented narrowly by the symbols ɑ⁻ (a very back a), ɑ (a middle a), a- (a not very forward a), a (a completely forward a, near to cardinal a), a⊥ or æ (a sound between cardinal a and ɛ). (See Figure 2.) These sounds are to be heard in the following words:

'palka ['pɑ-lkə] (палка, stick),
mat [mɑt] (мат, checkmate),
mjat [mja-t](мят, crumpled),
matj [matj] (мать, mother),
mjatj [mja⊥tj] (мять, to crumple).

The principal shades occurring in medium and weakly stressed

---

[15] Though it must be noted that in some special connexions, when the sounds are so situated as to be deprived of their glides, the differences between certain hards and softs are not very clearly perceived. (See §183.)

positions are heard in xara'ʃo [xərʌ'ʃó] (хорошо, well), the first syllable of which has weak stress and the second medium stress. (See further, §§536, 539.)

97. Specially noteworthy is the case of the Russian i-phoneme, which in strongly stressed syllables comprises members ranging from a rather back ɨ to a cardinal i, and which includes in weakly stressed positions ɩ and a lowered variety of ɨ (ʇ).[16] The four most notable members of this phoneme used in strongly stressed positions may be represented narrowly by the symbols ɨ (a sound between cardinal ɨ and ɯ), ɨ̠ (a retracted variety of this), ɨ̟ (half way between this ɨ and i), i (a somewhat retracted i), i̠ (cardinal i). (See Figure 3.)   Words illustrating these sounds are:

> bil [bɨ-l] (был, was),
> bilj [bɨ+lj] (быль, a true fact),
> bjil [bjil] (бил, he beats),
> bjilj [bji̠lj] (биль, parliamentary bill).

ɩ is heard in such words as i'gra [ɩ'gra] (игра, game), 'dajtji ['dajtjɩ] (дайте, give), and ʇ (=ɨ̠) in words like 'komnati ['komnətɨ̠] (комнаты, rooms), tsi'na [tsʇ'na] (цена, price).

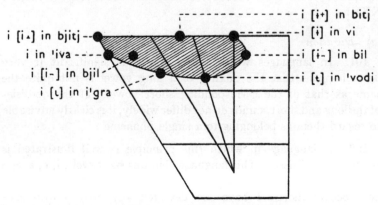

i [i̠] in bjitj ----------------------------------- i [ɨ+] in bitj
i [i̠] in bjitj -- ● ------------------------------- i [ɨ] in vi
i in 'iva ---- ● ----------------------------- i [ɨ-] in bil
i [i-] in bjil -- ------------------------------ i [ʇ] in 'vodi
i [ɩ] in i'gra

FIG. 3.   Positions of the chief Russian i-sounds.

98. The Russian e-phoneme comprises sounds ranging from a close e to a very open and somewhat retracted ɛ. It occurs

---

[16] See §§332–335. Also S. C. BOYANUS, *The* i - ɨ *Phoneme.*

exclusively in strongly stressed positions.   The following words
exemplify the use of the chief varieties:

vjesj [vjesj] (весь, all),
vjek [vjɛ⌄k] (век, century),
'etat ['ɛ⌄tət] (этот, this).

(See further, §§308, 332–336.)

99. In the case of the o and u phonemes the range of variation
is less wide, but it is noteworthy that central varieties of o and u
are used when soft consonants both precede and follow, as in

'tjotja ['tjötjə] (тётя, aunt),
'ljudji ['ljüdjʮ] (люди, people).

(2) Variations of Sound Quality Conditioned by
Duration, Stress and Voice-Pitch

100. The following are examples of different sound qualities
which are assignable to the same phoneme on the ground of their
occurrence in relation to the attributes duration, stress and voice-
pitch. They illustrate differentiations of sound sequences by
complexes of attributes, a subject dealt with more fully in Chapter
XXVI.

(a) Duration

101. In languages where vowel length is significant it very
often happens that the quality of a long vowel is not quite the
same as that of the corresponding short vowel. If the qualities
of the long and short sounds do not differ widely, it is clearly advisable
to regard them as belonging to a single phoneme.

102. A language in which this principle is well illustrated is
colloquial Sinhalese.   This language contains six vowels, i, e, ɛ, a, o
and u, to which significant length is applicable, and one, ə, which
only occurs short.   I have not detected any quality difference
between the long and short ɛ, but in the case of the other lengthen-
able vowels perceptible quality differences accompany the variations
of length.   Examples of words differentiated essentially by the
length of the vowel are si:tə (cold), sitə (mind), he:nə (beautiful),
henə (thunder), ka:lə (quarter), kalə (pots), po:rə (manure), porə
(quarrels), su:du (gambling), sudu (white).

103. The differences in the qualities of the vowels in such pairs of words are not great. Their extent may be judged from the annexed diagram (Fig. 4), in which the Sinhalese vowels have been placed in relation to cardinal vowels. The diagram shows that the differences of length are all-important; Sinhalese words, like those quoted in §102, would undoubtedly continue to be adequately distinguished if the slight differences of quality were not observed.

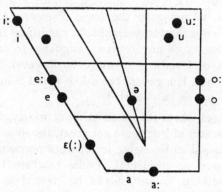

Fig. 4. Positions of the Sinhalese Vowels.

104. There are languages in which much wider differences of vowel quality accompany differences of vowel length. One of these is English, or more precisely one type of Southern English.[17] In this kind of English the closer i-sound of such words as *deed*, *sheep*, *aesthetic* and the opener sound of *did*, *ship*, *estate* (is'teit), are connected by the relation that the first is always longer than the second in similar situations: the vowel in *deed* is longer than that in *did*, the vowel in *sheep* is longer than that in *ship*, the first vowel in *aesthetic* is longer than that in *estate*, and so on. These two

---

[17] I refer here to the type of Southern English which I find it convenient to select for practical teaching purposes. Other types of English exist in which this relation is not consistently observed. There are, for instance, varieties of English in which the vowel in *bid* is in certain situations fully long like that of *bead*; with those who pronounce in this way the two sounds belong to separate phonemes (see §§130, 519, 734, also footnote 8 to §513 and footnote 1 to §592). The sounds would likewise belong to separate phonemes in the speech of any who pronounce *aesthetic* with the closer i but consistently make no difference in length between it and the first vowel of such a word as *estate*.

vowel-sounds may therefore be regarded as members of the same phoneme in this type of English. Similar considerations apply to the English long and short o and u sounds, as in *caught, cot, pool, pull*.

105. The same thing is found in German, where the long i, a, o, u, y and ø differ in quality from the corresponding short vowels.[18]

106. Further examples of a similar kind may be found in many other languages. In Dutch and in Hungarian, for instance, it seems clear that the widely differing sounds a and ɑ should be considered as belonging to the same phoneme, a being always long and ɑ always shorter under similar conditions (see §§523, 524). Sounds of these types are likewise assignable to one phoneme in various forms of English; the usage is, however, the reverse of that in Dutch and Hungarian, the ɑ-like sound being long and the a-like sound ([aˑ] or [æ]) short.[19]

107. In cases where the qualities differ widely, but the accompanying differences of length are not great, the sound-qualities may have to be classed as belonging to separate phonemes, the lengths being considered as incidental. Some teachers think that the vowels of Southern English should be treated in this way (see §§515, 516).

(b) Stress

108. The use of aspirated and unaspirated t-sounds in Southern English is connected chiefly with the degree of stress. A t with considerable aspiration is used before strongly stressed vowels as in ten (*ten*), ə'tend (*attend*); a less aspirated or unaspirated t is used before weakly stressed vowels as in 'priti (*pretty*), 'aːftə (*after*), 'letə (*letter*), as already mentioned in §72. The two varieties must evidently be regarded as members of the same phoneme.

109. In American English a "voiced t" (a kind of r-like flap) is used in many weakly stressed positions, e.g. in 'bɛʈr (*better*).

---

[18] e and ɛ belong to separate phonemes in stage German, since in that type of German 'eːre and 'ɛːre, for instance, are different words (*Ehre, Ähre*). They belong, however, to one phoneme in the speech of those who do not use a long open ɛː (i.e. those who use close eː in such words as *Ähre, spät, Nähe, ähnlich*). (See §§224–229.)

[19] Reference is made here to the types of English in which the front a ([aˑ] or [æ]) is short. There are other types in which it may be long (see footnote 8 to §513 and elsewhere).

As the use of this special sound is confined to these positions, and an ordinary t does not occur in them, it is to be regarded as belonging to the t-phoneme.

110. In French a close e is used in final positions, i.e. in syllables which receive normal strong stress, while opener varieties of e ("e moyen") are used in non-final positions, i.e. on syllables with weaker stress. They must undoubtedly be classed as belonging to a single phoneme. (See §§214 ff.)

111. In Russian a number of shades of vowel-sound are found exclusively in weakly stressed positions. They are assignable to the same phonemes as those to which strong vowels belong. (See §§332, 333, 536–539.)

(c) Intonation

112. Certain vowels of Pekingese vary with the "tone" under some conditions. For instance, when the syllable which may be written fen has the first tone (level),[20] the vowel is a rather ə-like sound, but when the syllable has the third tone (low-rising),[21] the vowel is more ʌ-like. These two vowel-sounds must be regarded as belonging to the same phoneme, for, as is shown later (§545), the tones are the essential distinguishing feature of the words, and the vowel qualities are incidental to them. (The third Pekingese tone also involves length, as mentioned in §557.)

113. I have noticed also that the Pekingese syllable which may be written broadly fou has values depending upon tone which may be shown narrowly as follows [ˉfou, ˊfǫu, ˏfɔu, ˋfɔ(ᵘ)]. In the last of these the u element is almost inaudible.

114. It would appear too that even in such a language as English, vowel-quality sometimes varies to some extent according to intonation. Professor K. Luick of Vienna made observations tending to show that the Southern English oː [ɔː] appears in a closer variety on high pitches and an opener variety on low pitches. He also came to the conclusion that ei is less diphthongal on low pitches than on high pitches.[22]

---

[20] Meaning "command" or "a tenth" (among other things).

[21] Meaning "powder" (among other things).

[22] *Germanisch-Romanische Monatsschrift*, Vol. 18, p. 364, and *Englische Studien*, Vol. 65, p. 337.

CHAPTER VIII

DIFFERENCE OF USAGE IN DIFFERENT LANGUAGES

115. It will be seen from many of the examples given in the last chapter that sounds which belong to separate phonemes in one language may belong to the same phoneme in another language.

116. Thus, we find h and ç belonging to different phonemes in German,[1] but to the same phoneme in Japanese (§77). Varieties of voiceless l (written phonetically ɬ or ɬ) occur as separate phonemes from voiced l in Welsh, Zulu and Burmese, but two such sounds belong to the same phoneme in French (§73). g and k belong to separate phonemes in most languages, but to the same phoneme in Dutch (§76). n and ŋ belong to separate phonemes in many languages, e.g. English, German, Chinese, Swahili, Tswana, but they are members of the same phoneme in Italian, Spanish, Hungarian and Hindustani (§75). θ, ð and d belong to separate phonemes in English, but may be found as members of one phoneme in one form of Kikuyu (§79).

117. Further examples are the following. The s-phoneme of Spanish, as spoken in Buenos Aires, comprises a number of sounds which occur as separate phonemes in other languages. A sound of the s-type is used before vowels, but before another consonant we find h, varieties of ç and x, m̩ and ɬ, as in

> ['pahta] (*pasta*, paste),
> ['lihʕto] (*listo*, ready),
> ['bohˣke] (*bosque*, a wood),
> ['mihmo] or in quick speech ['mim̩mo] (*mismo*, same),
> ['aɬlo] (*hazlo*, do it).

118. Varieties of a and ɑ belong to separate phonemes in some types of English (§129 and footnote 8 to §513), but similar sounds belong to a single phoneme in Russian (§96) and probably in some types of Arabic (§93).

119. In the Efik language of Nigeria there exists an i (similar to the English vowel in *eat*) and an ə (similar to the sound of *a* in *along*). In that language these sounds belong to the same

---

[1] Since they both occur initially before various vowels.

phoneme, the rule governing their use being that i is used only in open syllables and ə only in closed syllables. Examples of i are di [˙] (to come), itie [. . ˙] (a seat); examples of ə are efək [. .] (the Efik language), dəp [˙] (to hide), ɲəmme [˙ ˙] (to agree), təbbi [˙ ˙] (to dig).[2] The latter words are rightly written with *i* in the new phonetic spelling of Efik (*Efik, dip, nyimme, tibbi*). In other languages, such as English, German, Welsh, Sinhalese, i and ə sounds belong to separate phonemes.

120. s and z belong to separate phonemes in most languages in which they occur, e.g. in English, French, German, Roman Italian (see §121), Russian, Urdu, Japanese, Zulu. But in Spanish they belong to the same phoneme, since in that language z occurs to the exclusion of s before voiced consonants and not in any other situation; examples are ˈmismo, rriˈesgo (narrow transcription [ˈmizmo], [rriˈezyo]).

121. It would seem that types of Italian exist in which s and z belong to the same phoneme, the rules for the use of these sounds being that (1) s occurs initially and before breathed consonants, (2) doubled s occurs intervocalically, (3) z occurs before voiced consonants, (4) single z occurs intervocalically to the exclusion of s.

122. The common distribution of g and non-syllabic ŋ[3] in Japanese suggests that these two sounds might be held to belong to a single phoneme in that language; g occurring solely as a word initial (or in an initial-like position) and ŋ elsewhere, as exemplified by gai (harm), gakko: (school), but [kuŋi] (nail) [saŋŋai][4] (third storey [second ŋ]). It seems, however, that there are a few exceptions which cannot be explained by any rules, and which therefore render a single phoneme grouping impracticable.[5]

123. t and d belong to separate phonemes in most languages in which they occur. But it seems that in a common form of Greek they have to be assigned to the same phoneme, since in this

---

[2] All the other vowels of the language (e, a, ɔ, o, u) can occur both in open and in closed syllables. These particulars were furnished to me by Professor IDA WARD.

[3] For syllabic ŋ see §§292–295.

[4] Written in Rōmazi *kugi, sangai*.

[5] E.g. that go (five) retains the sound g when occurring as the second element of a compound, and that some recently borrowed foreign words are said with a medial g. (A summary of the chief exceptions is given in S. E. MARTIN's *Morphophonemics of Standard Colloquial Japanese*, p. 22.)

form of the language d occurs to the exclusion of t after n, but not elsewhere. Thus, in this form of Greek, ἕνδεκα[6] (eleven), δέντρο[7] (tree) are pronounced ['endeka], ['ðendro]. (Broad transcriptions of these words would be 'enteka, 'ðentro.) Similar considerations apply to the Greek p and k phonemes.[8]

124. d and ð belong to separate phonemes in English, as is shown by the existence of the words den (*den*), ðen (*then*). Other varieties of d and ð belong to separate phonemes in Danish; this is shown by such a pair as 'rɛdə (*rette*, comply), and 'rɛðə (*redde*, save). But analogous sounds belong to a single phoneme in Spanish, where a plosive d is only found after n and l[9]; the case is exemplified by such words as ['toðo] (whole), [sole'ðað] (solitude), [með'rar] (to prosper), but ['kwando] (when), [in'dulto] (pardon), [es'palda] (shoulder).

125. In most languages p and f occur as separate phonemes. A. N. TUCKER has, however, found that in certain languages of the Sudan they belong to the same phoneme, p being used exclusively before front vowels and f exclusively before back vowels. Similarly with b and v.[10]

126. Sounds of the l and r types belong to separate phonemes in European languages, but they belong to a single phoneme in some languages of Africa, as mentioned in §§82, 83.

127. It was stated in §81 that the sounds l and ɭ occur in the Tswana language and belong to the same phoneme. These two sounds also exist in the cognate language Pedi, but there they belong to separate phonemes, since the syllables li and lu occur as well as the syllables ɭi and ɭu. (See A. N. TUCKER, *Comparative Phonetics of the Suto-Chwana Group of Bantu Languages*, §146.)

---

6 Also (less commonly) spelt ἕντεκα.

7 Also (less commonly) spelt δένδρο.

8 This does not by any means apply to the pronunciation of all Greeks. Some use d, instead of the more natural nd, initially in words of modern foreign origin. They will pronounce ντους (shower-bath), a Greek rendering of the French *douche*, as dus instead of [ndus]. With speakers who do this consistently, d constitutes a phoneme separate from t. It appears, however, that the pronunciation of most Greeks is erratic (Chap. XXVIII), and that it is in consequence impossible to come to any definite conclusion as to the phonemic status of their sounds b, d and g.

9 In some styles of speech also initially.

10 TUCKER, *Eastern Sudanic Languages*, Vol. I, §780.

128. In Panjabi and Marathi the sounds n and ɳ occur in similar phonetic contexts, e.g. they may both precede any vowel. The two sounds therefore belong to separate phonemes in those languages. But in many other Indian languages the same sounds belong to a single phoneme, since in them ɳ occurs exclusively before ʈ and ɖ (§84).

129. It sometimes happens that two sounds belong to one phoneme in one dialect of a language and to two separate phonemes in another dialect of the same language. A notable case is that of English "short" vowels. It has already been pointed out in §104 that in one type of Southern English the difference of quality between the vowels in *deed* and *did* is accompanied by a difference of length. Similarly with the vowels in *cart* and *cat*, *cord* and *cod*, *food* and *good*. One may consequently assign each pair of sounds to a single phoneme, with the convention that the difference of quality accompanies the difference of length.

130. There are, however, Southern English speakers who lengthen the vowels in *bid, cat, cod, good,* while preserving the usual quality. With them these vowel-sounds constitute phonemes separate from those in *bead, cart, cord, food.* (See my *Outline of English Phonetics*, §§874–879.)

131. It would seem that types of French exist in which the front a and the back ɑ are connected by a length relation, a being always short and ɑ always long; in other words, that there exist French people who use long ɑː in such words as *page, lave, soir* as well as in *pâte, âme, croître*, etc., and who use a short front a in such words as *pas, mât, droite*, as well as in *là, patte, boîte*, etc. In such a type of French the two sounds would be assignable to a single phoneme. In a common type of Parisian French both sounds occur both long and short in similar situations; thus one meets with Parisian speakers who use short a in *là, boîte*, long aː in *page, poivre*, short ɑ in *pas, droite*, and long ɑː in *pâte, croître*. In this type of French a and ɑ necessarily constitute separate phonemes. (See also §621.)

132. In some types of German the vowels e and ε constitute separate phonemes, while in others they are to be grouped together as members of a single phoneme. (See footnote 19 to §105, also §§224–228.)

CHAPTER IX

ACOUSTIC IMPRESSIONS

133. People often get impressions that speech-sounds are other than what they are. There are two chief circumstances in which sounds are thus "mis-heard" as other sounds. The first is the common case where a person fails to estimate correctly the quality of a sound of a foreign language or of a dialect, and identifies it with a sound of his own mother tongue. When, for instance, a Frenchman hears the Southern English sound ə:, he is liable to think it the same as his French œ or the French group œr; when a German hears the Southern English short **a**, his first reaction is to identify it with the German ε, incidentally confusing the English short **e** and **a** sounds. So also, as German does not contain the sound of English **w**, Germans "hear" it as their variety of **v**. Similarly, I am informed that speakers of Spanish, having no **q** in their language, mistake the **q** of the Quechua language of Peru for the Spanish **x**, thereby confusing the two Quechua sounds **q** and **x**. Instances of this kind can be multiplied indefinitely.

134. The second case is where the various members of a phoneme are not recognized as being different from each other. It does not as a rule occur to an Englishman, for instance, that the k-sounds he uses in *keep, call* and *cool* differ in any way, nor that, in the pronunciation of many, the vowel-sound in *well* is different from that in *wet*. It does not occur to a Dane, unless his attention has been specially called to the fact, that the sound of *a* in the Danish word *sang* differs from that in *sand*. And so on.

135. Ability to make accurate estimates of sound qualities can, as is well known, be developed by phonetic training. But the linguistic investigator always has to be on his guard against the possibility of mis-hearing sounds in the two types of case above-mentioned.

136. It is possible too that a particular speech-sound may sometimes give the impression of being two different sounds in different phonetic contexts, in the same way as a given colour may appear to vary on account of the proximity of other colours. Optical illusions in regard to colour doubtless have their counterpart in aural illusions as to qualities of sound. This, however, is a subject which has not yet been investigated as far as I am aware. If it were established that any considerable aural illusions as to the quality of sounds are brought about by the proximity of other sounds, the facts would presumably have some bearing on the phoneme theory. At present, however, it would seem that such aural illusions as may exist are insufficient to invalidate any of the theory presented in this book.

137. It is the fact that people are not as a rule aware of the existence of differing members of phonemes that has led to the common confusion between speech-sounds and phonemes. The view of the phoneme propounded in Chapter II of this book is that it is a family of speech-sounds. It is only by looking at the phoneme in a different light that it can be considered in any sense as a sound. It might possibly be regarded as *a sound aimed at* by the speaker, but there is some doubt as to whether a consistent theory of phonemes can be established on this basis (see Chap. XXIX).

138. Though differences between the members of a phoneme are not readily perceived by native speakers of the language in which the phoneme occurs, yet they may be noticeable to a foreign hearer if they run counter to a usage in regard to similar sounds existing in his language. This is especially the case if the first language contains in one phoneme two sounds which belong to separate phonemes in the second language. This was brought home to me in a striking way once when a speaker of Urmian Syriac observed to me that the t's in *ten* and *letter* sounded to him quite different; it afterwards transpired that in his native tongue aspirated and unaspirated t occur as separate phonemes, so that the (to me) slight difference in the amount of aspiration between the English stressed and unstressed t was very apparent to him.[1]

139. For similar reasons English people are very conscious of the difference between the vowels in the Arabic words batt[2] (he decided) and ʃat̪[3] (shore). This difference of vowel is immaterial to an Arabic speaker; to him the only essential difference is in the consonants.

---

[1] This was in 1912. My informant was a remarkable linguist and phonetician, S. OSIPOFF, whose mother tongue was Syriac, as spoken by about 10,000 people then living in the neighbourhood of Lake Urmia. (Since then these people have had to migrate to Iraq and Syria, but they continue to speak the Syriac language.)

[2] A raised front a.

[3] A back sound of the ɑ-type.

140. The fact that speakers of one language often notice differences which are immaterial to speakers of another language has sometimes been responsible for the introduction of unnecessary complications in spelling. Thus f, ts, ch, dz, j and sh were introduced into the old (Hepburnian) Roman writing of Japanese, because that system was inspired by English people who naturally identified certain Japanese sounds with English ones; the English find it difficult to realize that these sounds belong to the h, t, t, z (or d), z (or d), and s phonemes respectively, and are, therefore, from the Japanese point of view, adequately provided for by the letters h, t, t, z (or d), z (or d) and s. (See §§323–331.)

141. *Th* was introduced into the orthography hitherto used for Kikuyu for a similar reason. The originators of this orthography were English. Being accustomed to hear d and ð as separate phonemes in English, they naturally wrote these sounds with d and *th* in accordance with English orthographical habits, wherever they heard them, not realizing that the distinction is immaterial in ordinary Kikuyu (see §79). The Kikuyu language contains the pairs b β and g ɣ used in the same way as d ð, but since β and ɣ are not English sounds there was no temptation to make similar provision for them in the orthography.[4]

142. The converse of the case referred to in the foregoing paragraphs is also very commonly met with. If two sounds are phonemically distinct in one language but not in another, speakers of the latter language are liable to confuse the sounds. Thus, English people learning Indian languages continually confuse the Indian dental t and retroflex ʈ, because sounds of this character do not occur as members of separate phonemes in English; the English learner identifies them both with "the English t."[5]

---

[4] If Kikuyu orthography had been invented by Germans, it might well have happened that b and β would have been distinguished by the letters *b* and *w*, while the distinction d ð would have been ignored. If it had been invented by Spaniards, only b, d and g would have been used to denote the plosive-fricative phonemes, since the Kikuyu use of β, ð, ɣ is similar to the Spanish; the writing would then have been the simplest possible and in accord with the needs of the language. (See §79.)

[5] "The English t" is a phoneme comprising a good many sounds. The principal member is an alveolar t intermediate between the ordinary Indian t and ʈ (but nearer in sound to ʈ). (See §72, also my *Outline of English Phonetics*, third and subsequent editions, §§ 511–513.)

143. For a similar reason English people have difficulty in distinguishing between the German sounds ʃ and ç, despite the fact that a variety of ç is used by some English speakers in such words as *huge*. They likewise find it difficult to distinguish the aspirated and unaspirated consonants of many languages, though degrees of aspiration are to be found in English. Spaniards do not distinguish the English d and ð properly, though both sounds occur in their language. The Japanese fail to distinguish between such pairs of words as *foot* and *hoot*, though their language contains both h and a variety of f.

CHAPTER X

ASCERTAINING THE PHONEMES OF A LANGUAGE

144. The fact that phonemes are the chief linguistic elements differentiating one word from another (§§50–53) generally furnishes us with the quickest and surest method of ascertaining the phonemes of languages. When an investigator desires to find out whether two sounds of a language belong to separate phonemes or not, he should try to find a pair of words distinguished solely by means of these two sounds. The discovery of such a pair of words is conclusive proof that the sounds belong to separate phonemes.

145. Thus the existence of the words bit, bet and bat in English suffices to show that the vowel-sounds in these words belong to separate phonemes; the existence of kat (*cat*), kot (*cot*) and kʌt (*cut*) show that ʌ and short o belong to phonemes distinct from these. The existence of the words ne (*nez*) and nɛ (*naît*) demonstrates that e and ɛ are separate phonemes in French. Lingual r and uvular ʀ are shown to occur as separate phonemes in Provençal, as spoken at Arles, by pairs of words like 'sɛro (evening), 'sɛʀo (saw, n.), ga'ri (to cure), ga'ʀi (oak).[1] And so on.

146. The phonemic status of a sound may also be established by discovering whether it can be added to or subtracted from a sequence. Thus the existence of the English words ad, sad, sand, stand, shows that there are s, n and t phonemes in the language.

---

[1] Examples taken from H. N. COUSTENOBLE'S *La Phonétique du Provençal Moderne*, p. 93.

147. If the observer knows that two sounds occur in a language but is unable to find a pair of words distinguished solely by an exchange of these sounds, he may still be able to prove that they belong to separate phonemes by finding two words containing the sounds in situations of sufficient similarity. The sounds belong to separate phonemes if he can show that their use is in no way dependent upon other differences that the words may contain.

148. Thus I clearly feel ə and ʌ to belong to two separate phonemes in my type of English,[2] but I am unable to find proof by a pair of words differing solely by an exchange of one of these sounds for the other. The difficulty of proof is due to the fact that ʌ rarely occurs with weak stress, while short ə is always weakly stressed. However, the fact that my speech contains such words as 'hikʌp (*hiccup*), 'hʌm̃drʌm (*humdrum*), 'katəpʌlt (*catapult*) as well as words like 'sirəp (*syrup*), kə'nʌndrəm (*conundrum*), 'difikəlt (*difficult*) demonstrates the case to my satisfaction, since it cannot be maintained that the use of ʌ and ə in these weakly stressed positions is attributable in any way to the nature of the preceding sounds in the words.[3] (For another theory concerning these sounds see §§197 ff.)

149. There is a similar case in German,[4] where there does not appear to be any pair of words differentiated solely by the use of the sounds ɛ and ə. But the existence of the word 'eːlɛnt (*elend*) beside ['feːlənt] (*fehlend*) and numerous other words ending in [-ənt] suffices to show that the two sounds belong to separate phonemes. (See further, §§224–229.)

150. It is evident too that German has two separate phonemes h and ç, though in the speech of many Germans there does not appear to be any pair of words distinguished by an interchange of these sounds. The fact that both sounds occur initially before various vowels suffices to show that there are two phonemes.[5]

---

[2] One type of Southern British.

[3] With many Southern English speakers the case is proved by the existence of a few words containing strongly stressed short ə, and notably the words pronounced by them bi'kəz and dʒəst (adverb), the latter word being distinct from the adjective dʒʌst. (This does not apply to my pronunciation. I pronounce *because* as bi'koz, and the adverb *just* like the adjective, dʒʌst.)

[4] Stage pronunciation as shown in VIËTOR'S *Deutsches Aussprachewörterbuch*.

[5] A pair is found in the speech of those who pronounce *Chorde* as 'çorde (instead of the more usual 'korde): 'çorde, 'horde (*Horde*).

151. The sounds o and ɔ of normal Parisian French probably exemplify the same point. In that type of French there does not appear to exist any pair of words distinguished solely by these sounds, but the words so:ʒ (*sauge*) and lɔ:ʒ (*loge*) suffice to demonstrate that the two vowels constitute separate phonemes.[6]

152. Sometimes when a pair of words cannot be found to demonstrate that two sounds belong to separate phonemes, proof can be given by means of a series of four words. Thus, as already mentioned in §53, I do not think there is any pair of English words differing solely by the interchange of ŋ and ʒ, and which will therefore prove these sounds to belong to separate phonemes; but, in the words of TRAGER and BLOCH,[7] "the lack of such a pair is easily supplied by the series *singer : sitter, letter : leisure* or *ring : rim, room : rouge.*"

153. One cannot have a positive proof that two sounds must belong to one phoneme. They may, however, be presumed to be assignable to one phoneme if exhaustive tests fail to reveal any case of their occurrence in similar phonetic contexts. As long as it is felt that there is a possibility of the sounds occurring in the same phonetic context, they must be presumed to belong to separate phonemes.

154. An examination of the examples in Chapter VII shows that in the great majority of cases there is no doubt at all as to what phoneme a sound belongs to. In most cases it would not occur to the average native to group the sounds otherwise than in the manner described in that chapter. He knows the grouping instinctively, and doubt only arises if different usages of other languages are brought to his notice.

155. Cases are, however, found from time to time where the phonemic grouping of sounds is by no means clear, and can only be settled after prolonged investigation. Cases even appear to exist where it is not possible to make a satisfactory grouping at all, or where the grouping has to be arbitrary. Instances are given in Chapter XIV.

---

[6] There are other types of French in which conclusive examples are numerous. In Swiss-French, for example, *peau* and *pot* are distinguished as po and pɔ.

[7] *The Syllabic Phonemes of English* in *Language*, Vol. XVII, No. 3, July, 1941, p. 229, footnote 10.

CHAPTER XI

NEED FOR ACCURATE ANALYSIS

156. It goes without saying that no phonemic classification can be made unless the sounds concerned have been analysed with great accuracy and all the conditions concerning their use have been fully established. A superficially made analysis may lead to erroneous classification.

157. As an example of this we may take the nasal consonants of modern Provençal, as spoken at Arles, particulars of which have been supplied to me by Dr. H. Coustenoble, and are set out fully in her book, La Phonétique du Provençal Moderne. That language contains the sounds m, n and ŋ. m and n occur before vowels but never at the end of isolated words; ŋ never precedes a vowel in a word, but it occurs at the ends of words; it also occurs before k and g. Examples of these sounds are 'maire (mother), nɛu (snow), tsiŋ (dog), 'blaŋko (white), veŋ'gø (come, p.p.).

158. This distribution might lead one to think at first sight that ŋ must belong to the same phoneme as n. On further examination, however, it is seen that this cannot well be the case. For we find that this language is peculiar in containing some words which when said in isolation terminate in ŋ, but which are pronounced with n when a word beginning with a vowel follows. In the case of some words this substitution is always made, in the case of others it is sometimes made and sometimes not, according to the nature of the expression. Thus: (1) suŋ (are) is always pronounced with ŋ (or before certain consonants m͡ŋ or n͡ŋ, see §160), e.g. suŋ ami (they are friends), suŋ aʀi'ba (they have arrived), suŋ eŋ tʀiŋ (they are in process (of)), but suŋ (his) is always replaced by the form sun when the following word begins with a vowel, e.g. sun us'tau (his house), sun 'uŋkle (his uncle), sun eŋ'tʀiŋ (his animation), (2) beŋ (well, very) is generally pronounced with ŋ before vowels, but it is pronounced bɛn in various common expressions, e.g. beŋ a'vaŋ (a long time before), beŋ au (very high), but bɛn ø'rus (very happy), bɛn ø'tiːle (very useful).

159. The above examples show that n and ŋ must be assigned to separate phonemes, unless it could be found possible to consider

the forms with n as prefixes forming single "words" with what follows. It does not, however, seem feasible to consider them so, since the principles, such as they are, which determine whether n or ŋ is used cannot be specified with precision. These principles are moreover syntactic or semantic, and not phonetic.[1]

160. Two other nasal consonant sounds are found in Provençal, one of which is used when p or b follows, and the other when t or d follows. To an unpractised ear they sound at first like m and n respectively, and one might easily be tempted to assign them to the m and n phonemes. By listening carefully, however, one can hear that the sounds are not ordinary m and n at all, but m and n pronounced with a simultaneous ŋ. Using the notation m͡ŋ, n͡ŋ to represent these sounds, examples can be written in narrow transcription thus: [em͡ŋpleˈgaːdo] (employée), [ˈkan͡ŋte] (I sing). The sound m͡ŋ is of course "related in character" to m, but there is nothing in the nature of a "similitude"[2] to justify assigning to the m-phoneme the sound m͡ŋ occurring before p and b. The use of a labialized ŋ before p and b is, however, a clear case of similitude involving the assignment of m͡ŋ to the ŋ-phoneme. Similarly with n͡ŋ. Provençal m͡ŋ and n͡ŋ must therefore be considered as members of the ŋ-phoneme, and should be written simply with ŋ in broad phonetic notation. The above cases thus illustrate how a superficial analysis, based on insufficient material or incorrect identification of sounds, might cause two serious errors in phonemic classification, namely, to assign ŋ to the n-phoneme and to assign m͡ŋ and n͡ŋ to the m and n phonemes.

161. The need for accurate analysis may be exemplified by two further instances of errors of classification which have been made in the past. The first concerns the Hindustani vowel sound hitherto generally written by romanizers with short a when h and another consonant follows, as in the older transcriptions pahlā (first), shahr (city), kahnā (to speak). The sound in such words is, at any rate in the pronunciation of Lahore, rather ε-like in character and resembles the Southern English vowel of bag.

---

[1] n is used when there is very close grammatical connexion between the words, or when the expressions are very common. It is probably impossible to define the required degrees of "closeness" and "commonness."

[2] See my Outline of English Phonetics, §835.

These transcriptions imply that this ε-like sound is a member of the phoneme whose principal member is the ʌ-like sound heard in the words written in older transcriptions *das* (ten), *phal* (fruit), *garm* (warm). Recent research has, however, shown that the above ε-like sound has nothing to do with the ʌ-phoneme, but is identical with or similar to the slightly diphthongal sound which the older transcribers wrote *ai*. It has also been established that there is not really a separate h following the vowel in *pahlā*, etc., but that the vowel is said with "breathy voice" which continues throughout its whole duration; the sound formerly written *ah* before a consonant is in fact an "aitchified" vowel, to use a term suggested by J. R. Firth, who was the discoverer of the correct phonemic classification of the sounds under consideration. (It is convenient to represent aitchified vowels in practical writing by digraphs[3] consisting of vowel letters followed by h.)

162. In the proposed new All-India Romanic Orthography the correct phonemic classification is followed. The ʌ-phoneme is written, very suitably, with ə, so that the old transcriptions *das*, *phal*, *garm* are replaced by *dəs, phəl, gərm*. The old *ai* is written *əy*, the old "Roman Urdu" forms *hai* (is), *baithnā* (to sit), etc., being replaced by *həy, bəyṭhna*, etc. And words formerly written with *ah* + consonant are in the proposed new orthography properly written with *əyh*, in accordance with the correct phonemic classification of the vowel, thus *pəyhla, ʃəyhr, kəyhna*.

163. Similar considerations apply to the Hindustani sound written *əwh* in All-India Romanic, e.g. in *bəwht* (much). In the older romanic transcriptions this word was written *bahut*, a form indicating a misconception of the phonemic make-up of the word. The vowel really is the aitchified form of the slightly diphthongal sound əꞷ heard, for instance, in *əwr* (and) which the older romanizers wrote *aur*.[4]

164. My last example is taken from the Tswana language. It is an instance where an incorrect phonemic analysis is reflected in current orthography, though fortunately without any untoward results. Tswana contains an ordinary ʃ which is pronounced with

---

[4] For particulars of the proposed All-India Romanic Orthography, see my paper on *The Problem of a National Script for India*, which incorporates Firth's discoveries.

spread lips; it also contains a strongly labialized ʃ which may be denoted by the symbol ʡ.[5] Both these sounds occur before the vowels i, ɩ, e, ɛ and a, and in consequence they constitute separate phonemes. Examples illustrating their phonemic use are ʃā (die), ʡā (burn), sɩʃeʃe (flower), ʡeū (white). Before the remaining vowels ɔ, o, ɷ and u, only ʡ occurs; the non-labialized ʃ is never used before these vowels by the native speakers I have heard. Examples are ʡɔka (twist), ʡɷtlā (harass, mock), ʡutā (move).

165. Some observers have treated ʡ as if it were not a separate phoneme. Before i, ɩ, e, ɛ and a they have taken it for a sequence of ʃ and w, and before ɔ, o, ɷ and u they have identified it with ʃ. This incorrect analysis is no doubt the origin of old spellings such as *sha, shwa, sesheshe, shweu, shôka, shotla, shuta*. Phonetic consistency would require writing *shwôka, shwotla, shwuta*.

166. It so happens, however, that the incorrect analysis leads in this case to the same style of orthography as that derived from the correct analysis. The orthographic forms given above, or their more phonetic equivalents ʃa, ʃwa, sɩʃeʃe, ʃweu, ʃɔka, ʃɷtla, ʃuta, are justifiable on grounds of practical convenience, though not on grounds of phonetic exactitude. It is convenient in Tswana to use *w* as a general symbol denoting labialization, and to use it in the representation of various labialized consonants. ʃw can thus be used as a digraph denoting ʡ. Then the *w* may be omitted by convention before ɔ, o, ɷ and *u*, to economize letters in the spelling, since no ambiguity is caused by doing this. It must be remembered, however, that though the result might be a convenient orthography on phonetic basis,[6] it is not an accurate phonetic transcription. For teaching a good pronunciation of the language an accurate phonetic transcription is required; this should be on phonemic basis and should consequently make use of either a special symbol for ʡ or the digraph ʃw, which should be employed before ɔ, o, ɷ and u as well as in such words as ʃwā, ʃweū.

---

[5] The labialization is of an unusual type. The lips are rounded, and the lower lip is so held that the upper teeth touch it at a place about three-quarters of an inch behind its edge. This kind of labialization gives a peculiar acoustic effect.

[6] In the new orthography proposed by A. N. Tucker the vowel representation would be different from that indicated here. See his article *Sotho-Nguni Orthography* referred to in §482, footnote 18.

CHAPTER XII

DIFFICULTIES IN IDENTIFYING SOUNDS IN SPECIAL SEQUENCES

167.   In the preceding chapter emphasis was laid on the need for the accurate analysis of sounds as an essential preliminary to attempting any phonemic classification.   Mention must now be made of the fact that sequences are occasionally such as to render a sound difficult to identify, with the result that there may be some uncertainty as to the appropriate phonemic grouping.

168.   Such cases may be classified under two heads: (1) where two sounds, though acoustically rather similar, are recognized as distinct by the speaker and therefore may have "distinctive" function, (2) where the sounds have acoustic similarity but are so placed that they do not have "distinctive" function.

169.   The English sounds s and voiceless z (z̨) furnish an illustration of these cases.[1]   There are, as is well known, certain phonetic situations in which both of these sounds can occur.   They can, for instance, both occur initially, as in si:l (*seal*) and z̨i:l (*zeal*)[2]; an English speaker can sound either of these syllables at will, and an English hearer will usually identify the consonants correctly in spite of their resemblance to one another.[3]   For this reason the sounds s and z̨ belong to separate phonemes.

170.   In some sequences, however, it is difficult to hear which sound is employed.   Instances of the first type (§168) are found in such words as *obstruct, abstinence, Beaconsfield*.   It is sometimes nearly impossible for a hearer to tell objectively whether a speaker

---

[1] These sounds differ from each other solely in the degree of breath force, s having strong force and z̨ being a similar sound uttered with weak force.

[2] The reference here is to the pronunciation of those numerous English speakers who do not use voiced z initially.

[3] In final position after a long vowel the identification is facilitated by the difference of vowel-length which accompanies these consonants.   Thus the u: in the sequence -u:s is easily heard to be much shorter than that in -u:z̨. (See §§188–190.)

is pronouncing əbˈstrʌkt, ˈabstinəns, ˈbekənsfiːld or əbẓˈtrʌkt, ˈabẓtinəns, ˈbekənẓfiːld; the speaker, however, knows by his subjective feeling, which pronunciation he is using.[4] English people who habitually pronounce these words in one of these ways are able, if they so wish, to pronounce them in the other way. The sequences bst, bẓt, nsf, nẓf are all familiar to him, though possibly he may use bẓt at word-junctions only; the "distinctive" function of the sounds is present at any rate in theory.[5]

171. An instance of the second type (§168) is afforded by the terminal consonant of such words as *puts, drinks, box*. The pronunciation usually transcribed is puts, driŋks, boks, and the pronunciation of these words with a normal s is usual. The case is, however, one where the degree of force of the s is immaterial, so that weak varieties of s are frequently used. In particular the use of ẓ (which = a weak s) is not by any means uncommon: putẓ, driŋkẓ, bokẓ. In this situation the distinction between s and ẓ is not "significant."[6]

172. The question therefore arises whether the ẓ in this pronunciation of these words should be regarded as a member of the z-phoneme, as it is in other connexions, or whether it should be assigned to the s-phoneme *in this particular case*. In other terms, is the ẓ in these words to be regarded functionally as a z, or are we to take account of the fact that organically it is merely a weak s?

173. It appears to me that this ẓ, like other ẓ's in English, should be regarded as a member of the z-phoneme. I feel this

---

[4] Speakers can doubtless be found who use voiced z in these words. With them the identification of the sound would present no difficulty to the hearer.

[5] It is doubtful if there exists any pair of English words distinguished solely by bst and bẓt. If there were such words, hearers would undoubtedly have difficulty in identifying them. Even at word-junctions differences of this sort are difficult for the hearer to perceive: *Bob struck* (ˈbob ˈstrʌk) and *Bob's truck* (ˈbobẓ trʌk) are very much alike to the hearer, as also are a *a good strain* (ə ˈgud strein, said with contrast emphasis on *good*) and *a goods train* (ə ˈgudẓ trein). nsf and nẓf occur only at word-junctions or in compound words such as ˈhensˈfoːθ (*henceforth*) and one pronunciation of *Beaconsfield*.

[6] Voiced z is not used by any English speaker in such a position. This fact is, however, not relevant to the present discussion.

to be necessary on the general ground that the assignment of a sound to two phonemes in the same language is inadmissible on principle, and that such a plan should only be resorted to if a case should arise where no other course is open (see §35, and Chaps. XIX and XX). This recommendation involves writing putz, driŋkz, bokz, etc., in a broad transcription of the speech of those who pronounce putẓ, driŋkẓ, bokẓ, etc.

174. It is worth noting that in my experience English students of phonetics not unfrequently write forms like putz, driŋkz, in their transcription exercises. In the past I have corrected these as errors, but I now think that such transcriptions may not always be erroneous. Often they are errors no doubt, but sometimes it may happen that a student uses the sound ẓ in such words because he subjectively feels the sound to be a z rather than a s. This experience may afford some additional support to the view expressed in §173.

175. It should be noted further that many English speakers have erratic pronunciation of words like *puts*, pronouncing sometimes puts and sometimes putẓ for no assignable reason. It is shown in Chapter XXVIII that erratic pronunciation cannot be reduced to phonemes. Phonemic classification of the final consonant of *puts* can only be made if the speech recorded is consistent. In the speech of a person who consistently uses a s-sound, that sound belongs to the s-phoneme even if it is a somewhat weakened form of the consonant; in the speech of one who definitely uses ẓ, and uses it consistently, the sound should, it seems to me, be assigned to the z-phoneme.

176. The following is an example from French of sounds which are difficult to identify in special sequences. In that language ǯ occurs as a member of the ʒ-phoneme; it is distinct from ʃ, and the two sounds may occur in similar situations. Thus *ne bouge pas* is commonly pronounced nə buǯ pɑ, and this is distinct from *ne bouche pas* (nə buʃ pɑ). When, however, ǯ occurs initially before a voiceless consonant, it is more difficult to distinguish from ʃ, and in fact ʃ is often substituted for it. Thus *je te crois* is pronounced ʃ tə krwɑ as well as ǯ tə krwɑ. Both pronunciations exist, and it is difficult to hear the difference between the sounds in this position. It will, I think, be generally agreed that, as in

the English case cited in §§170–173, when ӡ is used it should be assigned to the ӡ-phoneme.

177. The ӡ-like sound used by many English speakers in such expressions as *please yourself*, *Mrs. Young*, is sometimes difficult to identify. To determine its phonemic status it is necessary to make certain whether the speaker under observation uses a sound intermediate between z and ӡ ('pliːӡᶻ joː'self, misiӡᶻ 'jʌŋ) or whether he uses a real ӡ as in pres'tiːӡ (*prestige*). The use of a real ӡ identical with that in pres'tiːӡ means that in such an expression as *please yourself* the speaker substitutes the ӡ-phoneme for the z-phoneme ordinarily used in the word *please*. I should regard it as inadmissible to assign such a ӡ to the z-phoneme (see footnote 1 to §315). When, however, the sound in *please yourself* is near to ӡ but not identical with it, it cannot in my opinion be regarded as other than a subsidiary member of the z-phoneme.

178. Similar considerations apply to the terminal consonant of *dress* in *dress-shirt*. With many the pronunciation is 'dreʃ'ʃəːt, the ʃ being an ordinary one exactly like that at the end of fiʃ in 'fiʃʃop (*fish-shop*). The pronunciation 'dreʃ'ʃəːt is the result of a contextual assimilation by which the speaker substitutes his ʃ-phoneme for his s-phoneme. Others pronounce the first syllable of *dress-shirt* with a sound which is not definitely ʃ, but is a ʃ-like variety of s. Their speech exemplifies a similitude involving the use of a particular (ʃ-like) member of the s-phoneme. This pronunciation would be transcribed broadly as 'dres'ʃəːt.[7]

179. Instances of difficulty in identifying sounds are also to be found in Russian. In certain sequences it is difficult to hear whether a consonant is a "soft" (palatalized) or a "hard" (non-palatalized) one. This is the case, for instance, with the first sound of the groups stj, znj, slj, zlj when initial, as when the words stjix (стих, verse), 'zdjeʃnjij (здешний, local), 'sljiva (слива, plum) are said in isolation. On examination it is found that they are soft[8]; the best proof is furnished by the sounds of vowels immediately preceding these words in connected speech, for which see §183.

---

[7] For the difference between assimilation and similitude, see my *Outline of English Phonetics*, Chapter XXVI.

[8] The degree of softness is not the same in every case. For instance, the s is softer in stj than in snj.

CHAPTER XIII

IDENTIFICATION OF SOUNDS BY CHARACTERISTICS OF ADJOINING SOUNDS

(1) Recognition of Sounds through Subsidiary Members of an Adjacent Phoneme

180. It occasionally happens that the difference between two groups is made evident not so much by the sounds of the distinguishing phonemes as by special members of an adjacent phoneme. This occurs when the two distinguishing phonemes have members resembling each other and the adjacent phoneme has clearly distinct members which have to be employed in juxtaposition to those phonemes.

181. The case is illustrated by the Danish groups which would be written broadly -an' and -aŋ', to which attention has already been called in §92. In Danish, when a nasal consonant is in final position and pronounced with simultaneous glottal stop, a devoiced, or almost completely devoiced, variety is used. In the case of n and ŋ the resulting sounds ņ and ŋ̊ are acoustically very near to each other. Now, as we have seen, when the a-phoneme precedes the n-phoneme in Danish a front a is used, but when it precedes the ŋ-phoneme the vowel-sound is a back α. The above sequences could therefore be transcribed narrowly as [-aņ'] and [-αŋ̊']. It will be readily appreciated that these sequences are recognized much more by the vowel qualities than by the sounds of the consonants.

182. One cannot cite this case as a ground for assigning a and α to separate phonemes in Danish. It is clear from other considerations that the ņ and ŋ̊ must be regarded as the primary distinguishing sounds of such words as [saņ'] and [sαŋ̊']. In the first place the ordinary voiced n and ŋ are much commoner in Danish than the voiceless sounds used in the above special case, and instances such as 'onər ('oner, evils) and 'oŋər (unger, young ones) show that these voiced sounds must be held to belong to separate phonemes. Moreover, though the sounds n and ŋ require that special types of

a-sound should precede them, yet no analogous differences are found when other vowels precede.[1] It must be noted too that although there exist some varieties of ŋ in Danish, there is always a definite line of demarcation between the ŋ and n sounds. This cannot be said of the Danish a-sounds. Several varieties of these are used according to circumstances, and there is no line of demarcation between front varieties and back ones; the various shades merge imperceptibly into one another.

183. Certain of the Russian soft (palatalized) consonants are always quite distinct in quality from the corresponding hard (non-palatalized) sounds. This is the case more particularly with lj[2] and l. But there are some pairs, and notably nj[2] and n, sj and s, zj and z, which are heard as quite distinct sounds in some phonetic contexts but are much more alike in others. Thus the nj in 'njanja (няня, nurse), for instance, is a very different sound from the n of 'nada (надо, it is necessary). But when a consonant follows, and when therefore the sounds are deprived of their off-glides, the difference between them is by no means so clear; it would indeed be difficult to distinguish such sequences as njk and nk, were it not for the fact that vowels preceding soft consonants always have different shades of quality from vowels preceding hard consonants. For instance, the sequences in the words 'vanjka (ванька, diminutive of Ivan) and 'banka (банка, jar) are really recognized more by the vowels than by the qualities of the nasal consonants.[3] (The first a in 'vanjka is a fronter variety than that in 'banka.) Similarly, the softness of the s in 'pjesnja (song) and the hardness of the m in 'zjem-lji (lands) is heard chiefly by the closeness of the e in the first word and the comparative openness of the e in the syllable zjem-; narrow monographic transcriptions

---

[1] Thus the vowels in 'eŋə (*Inge*, proper name), 'lɛŋə (*længe*, long) and 'oŋər are not appreciably different from those in 'enə (*inde*, in), 'ɛnə (*ende*, end) and 'onər respectively.

[2] See footnote 15 to §95.

[3] The glides from the vowels to the consonants also help to show which type of consonant is used. There is always an i-glide between a vowel and a following soft consonant. The importance of glides in this connexion was, I believe, first pointed out by S. BOYANUS. See his article *Palatalization of Consonants in Juxtaposition in Russian* published in the *Transactions of the Philological Society*, 1943.

of these words would be ˈpe̞ʂɳə, ˈʐɛm|ʟ. Again, the fact that the
s and z of such words as stjix (стих, verse), ˈzdjeʃnjij (здешний,
local), ˈsljiva (слива, plum) are soft, is shown by the qualities of
the preceding vowels in such expressions as na ˈstjix (на стих, in
a verse), tje ˈsljivi[4] (те сливы, those plums). The a in na ˈstjix is
a distinctly fronter variety than that in, for instance, na ˈsontsi
(на солнце, in the sun), and the e in tje ˈsljivi is noticeably closer
than that in tje staˈli[5] (те столы, those tables).[6]

184. So also in Estonian. Such Estonian words as kɛʈtki
(cradle) and kɛttki (even the hand) are recognized mainly by the
variety of ɛ used and by the j-glide preceding the ʈ. See L. KRASS,
The Phonetics of Estonian, p. 90.

185. Cases of a similar nature are to be found in Arabic. The
pharyngalized consonants and the corresponding non-pharyngalized
consonants of the language are very distinct in sound when said
in isolation or when adjacent to i or e, but when adjacent to a or o
or u the difference between the consonants is less clearly audible.
In these cases the consonant differences are helped out by notable
differences in the shades of the vowels adjoining them. Thus
bass (only) and bass (bus) are probably recognized a good deal
more by the fact that bass has a forward a and bass a back a [ɑ]
than by the difference in the qualities of the consonants.

186. An illustration of a different kind has been discovered by
Professor IDA WARD in the Igbo language. The vowels u and ɷ
of that language are rather near to each other in sound, and the
distinction between them is often much facilitated by other vowels
occurring in the same words with them, as explained in §509.

(2) RECOGNITION OF SOUNDS THROUGH LENGTH OF AN ADJACENT SOUND

187. Sometimes a sound is recognized not so much by its
inherent tamber as by the length of an adjacent sound.

---

[4] Narrowly [tje ˈsljivt].

[5] Narrowly [tjɛ staˈłɨ].

[6] There are also audible i-glides before the s-sounds in na ˈstjix, tje ˈsljivi.
Many examples illustrating this point have been given by BOYANUS in the
article mentioned in footnote 3.

188. The case is illustrated by the English consonants p, t, f, s, etc., and ḇ, ḏ, γ, ẕ, etc., when they occur in final positions. Preceding vowels are much shorter in words like *seat, leaf, loose*, than in words like *seed, leave, lose*. The words might be transcribed narrowly as [si·t, li·f, lu·s, si:ḏ, li:γ, lu:ẕ], and I think there is no doubt that in such sequences the length of the vowel contributes more to the distinctions than the qualities of the consonants do.[7] (See also §169.)

189. The means of recognizing such sequences may be tested by a process of reversal, e.g. pronouncing groups like [si·ḏ] (with half-long i:) and [si:t] (with fully long i:), [li·γ] (with half-long i:) and [li:f] (with fully long i:). My impression is that [fi·ḏ], [li·γ] would be taken by the average English hearer to mean *feet, leaf*. And certainly the incorrect use of fully long i: by Germans when they pronounce such English words as *feet, leaf* gives to many English people the impression that they are saying the words with d and v.

190. There cannot be any question in a case like this of assigning ḏ and t to the same phoneme and treating the difference in vowel length as the essential distinguishing feature. One reason for this is that English speakers who use voiceless ḏ in final position as a rule use it also in initial position, and the numerous pairs of words like ḏen and ten show ḏ and t to belong to separate phonemes. Another is that numberless degrees of length of the English "long" i: are found in different phonetic contexts, with the result that it is impracticable to group them into more than one chroneme (§§390, 403).

191. Whether a final consonant is ḇ, ḏ, etc., or p, t, etc., is often shown in English by the length of a preceding consonant. Thus *pence* and *pens* are distinguished more by the length of the n than by the quality of the final consonant; the words may be written narrowly [peňs], [pen:ẕ]. Nevertheless, for reasons similar to those given above, it is necessary to regard the s and ẕ as constituting the primary means of differentiating the words.[8]

---

[7] Reference is here made to the pronunciation of the very numerous English speakers who do not voice final ḇ, ḏ, γ, ẕ, etc.

[8] It is interesting to notice that the sequence [pen:s] (with long n and normal s) gives the impression of something between *pence* and *pens*, while [peňẕ] (with very short n) gives the impression of *pence* rather than *pens*.

CHAPTER XIV

SOME DIFFICULTIES IN ESTABLISHING PHONEMIC GROUPINGS

192.   In Chapters X and XI it was shown that cases are sometimes found where an appropriate phonemic grouping is not immediately clear on account of some difficulty in recognizing the sounds used. The present chapter deals with difficulties in arriving at satisfactory phonemic classifications when sounds do not fall into obvious and natural groups, but have to be "assigned" to phonemes as the result of a more or less involved process of reasoning.   There are two causes of difficulties of this nature: (1) where there is a possibility of more than one method of grouping the sounds, and (2) where the controlling principles (§30) are complex or difficult to ascertain.

(1) POSSIBILITY OF GROUPING SOUNDS IN MORE THAN ONE WAY

193.   Circumstances occasionally arise in which there are, or would appear to be at first sight, two possible phonemic groupings of a sound—where in fact we can "assign" a sound to one of two phonemes, or where it seems possible either to group a sound into the same phoneme as other sounds of the language or to regard it as constituting a separate phoneme.

194.   Such possibilities are found in Korean, and may be exemplified by the bi-labial sounds occurring in that language. There are five non-nasal bi-labial sounds, namely, strongly aspirated p (ph), slightly aspirated p (p'), unaspirated (and perhaps glottalized) p, unexploded p (p̩), and b.   An examination of the situations in which these five sounds occur shows that they can be classed into three phonemes.   ph, p' and unaspirated p all occur initially and therefore belong to separate phonemes.   b occurs only medially; ph and unaspirated p also occur medially, but p' does not occur medially.   We find ourselves therefore under the unusual necessity of assigning b to the same phoneme as p', and of denoting this phoneme by the letter b.   Unexploded p̩ only occurs finally or preceding a consonant, while none of the other sounds occur in these positions.   p̩ may therefore be assigned ·to any one of the three above-mentioned phonemes.   As it has greater affinity to

unaspirated p than to ph or p', I think it should be assigned to the same phoneme as unaspirated p.[1]

195. Another instance where the appropriate phonemic grouping is not immediately obvious is the case of the Pekingese fricative consonant which may be written narrowly ɕ. In Pekingese ɕ only occurs before i and y, as in ´ɕi (practice), ‾ɕiŋ (star), ‾ɕiaŋ (box), ˋɕyn (teach), ´ɕye (learn). There are, however, three other fricative consonants occurring solely before vowels other than i and y, namely, x, s and ʃ. ɕ may therefore be assigned to the same phoneme as one of these. It has certain phonetic affinities to each of them, and doubt may well be felt as to which should be chosen. It would seem that those Chinese who have considered the matter feel ɕ to be acoustically nearer to ʃ than to x or s; if this is so, the sound may on that ground be assigned to the ʃ-phoneme.

196. But if there were to exist (as is quite possible) varieties of Chinese pronunciation in which the degrees of acoustic separation of ɕ from s and x and ʃ are definitely about equal, how should ɕ be phonemically classified? This would be a case where it would be immaterial which phoneme ɕ was assigned to. The choice could be made either arbitrarily, or by taking into account external considerations unconnected with the idea of the phoneme. One such external consideration would be the fact that in other varieties of Chinese the speakers apparently feel ɕ to have special affinity to ʃ. Another would be the history of the sounds. This latter would point to a different solution, for it is believed that some of the ɕ's of modern Pekingese are derived from an earlier s, while others are derived from an earlier x, but that none are derived from an old Chinese ʃ. ʃ might then be excluded for this reason. But even the history of the sounds does not furnish us with any reason for preferring s to x or vice versa. This hypothetical case is in fact one where, as far as I can see, no preference is possible, and it would be completely immaterial whether the ɕ were assigned

---

[1] The Korean phonetician, SHEON-GI GIM, thinks it better to regard unexploded p, as a separate phoneme, on the ground that being not plosive at all it is not sufficiently "related in character" to justify including it in the same phoneme with ph, p' (b) or p. See his *Phonetics of Korean* (thesis for the M.A. degree in the University of London).

to the s-phoneme or to the x-phoneme; the choice would have to be made arbitrarily.[2]

197. Instances where doubt may arise as to the best method of phonemic grouping, when the controlling principles offer no particular complexity, are also to be found in European languages. Notable is the case of the Southern English vowels in words like *bird*, *cup* and the first vowel of *along*. SWEET and most other English authorities have treated the vowel of *bird* as belonging to the same phoneme as the first vowel of *along*, but, as will be seen from what follows, there is a good case for regarding the vowels of *bird* and *cup* as belonging to the same phoneme. PAUL PASSY was in favour of so regarding it.[3]

198. That both courses have to be considered is shown by the fact that the vowel-sound of *bird* is always longer than both the other vowels in comparable phonetic contexts. Representing the quality of the vowel in *bird* narrowly by ɐ for the purpose of this discussion, we may exemplify the case as follows: the ɐ of bɐd (*bird*) is longer than the ʌ of bʌd (*bud*), the ɐ of hɐt (*hurt*) is longer than the ʌ of hʌt (*hut*), the ɐ of hɐˈbeiʃəs (*herbaceous*) is longer than the first ə of həˈbitjuəl (*habitual*), the ɐ of ˈreibɐn (*Raeburn*) is longer than the ə of ˈribən (*ribbon*), and so on.

199. If these examples represented the only facts to be considered, it would be immaterial which phoneme ɐ was assigned to. There are, however, other factors to be taken into account. In the first place "the vowel of *bird*" is an ambiguous expression. Different Southern English speakers use widely differing qualities of vowel in this and similar words, and it may well be that a classification applicable to one speaker is not necessarily suitable to the pronunciation of another.   The ɐ of some people is a rather open sound though quite distinct from ʌ. HENRY SWEET was one of these, and I remember well the quality of his vowel. He described the sound as "low-mixed-narrow";[4] it was quite different in quality from the ə he used in such a word as əˈloŋ, and distinct too from

---

[2] Another course would be to regard ɕ as a separate phoneme. It seems, however, unsuitable to do this in the case of a sound which so clearly lends itself to grouping with another sound.

[3] See his *Petite Phonétique Comparée*, §249, and the Southern English text on p. 127 of the same book.

[4] SWEET, *Primer of Spoken English*, p. 5.

his ʌ which was rather a-like. My ɐ is a much closer sound.[5] It is almost indistinguishable in quality from my ə in əˈloŋ, and may be regarded practically as this ə lengthened. With others the quality is near to ʌ. With others again the ɐ is rather ɯ-like in sound; this variety was observable, for instance, in the speech of the late Archbishop of Canterbury (Dr. Temple).

200. The existence of these varieties of pronunciation may explain in part the divergence of opinion regarding the phonemic status of ɐ, since the authorities undoubtedly do not all refer to the same sound. Those whose ɐ resembles ʌ might be expected to favour attaching it to the ʌ-phoneme, regarding it as "the long" of ʌ, while those who like myself use a sound almost identical in quality with the ə of əˈloŋ are naturally disposed to group these two together into one phoneme.[6]

201. A further complication arises from the fact that Southern English speakers use several varieties of unstressed ə depending upon phonetic context.[7] In particular it is customary to use a particularly open variety in final positions, as when such words as ˈtʃainə (china), ˈouvə (over) occur with a pause after them.[8] The existence of these varieties of short unstressed ə appears to me to tell in favour of assigning ɐ to the same phoneme as these ə's, since it is probable that most people's ɐ coincides in quality with one of their short unstressed ə's, just as my vowel of bird is practically indistinguishable from my ə of əˈloŋ. It is therefore

---

[5] *Outline of English Phonetics*, p. 86. See particularly Figure 51 (photograph of the mouth of my brother whose vowel in *bird* was similar to mine).

[6] SWEET, in spite of the openness of his ɐ, treated the vowel as belonging to the same phoneme as ə. He wrote it əə. He treated ʌ as "the short" of the vowel in *calm*, writing *calm* as kaam and *come* as kam. (He represented the ordinary short a by æ.)

[7] See *Outline of English Phonetics*, pp. 89–91.

[8] Some people use a sound indistinguishable in quality from their ʌ in words like *china*, *over*, *discover*, *colour*, when the words are said with a pause following (*Outline*, §§362, 363). I tend to do it myself when speaking loudly; the pronunciation is observable in gramophone records which I made before the days of electric recording, when one had to speak very loudly into a horn to obtain clear results. In this pronunciation these final ʌ's, which incidentally are often rather long, must be held to belong to the same phoneme as all the other ʌ's. The argument in §201 is concerned with the speech of those whose final vowel in *china*, *over*, etc., though rather open, is clearly distinguishable from ʌ.

logical to assign the two sounds to the same phoneme on the ground that it is undesirable to allocate one vowel quality to two phonemes.

202. I am disposed to think then that as long as the speaker's ɛ is distinct in quality, as well as in duration, from his ʌ, it is preferable that we should group it into the same phoneme as the short unstressed ə's. (This involves writing ɛ as ə: in broad transcription.) It must be admitted, however, that those who favour assigning ɛ to the ʌ-phoneme (a classification which would involve writing ɛ as ʌ: in broad transcription) also have a good case. They may adduce the fact that ɛ and ʌ are both stable in sound in the pronunciation of any given speaker—that there are no noticeable variants of either conditioned by sounds adjoining them in sequences. They are straightforward sounds to deal with; grouping them together as "long and short ʌ" would not cause inconvenience, were it not for the fact that ɛ is practically identical in quality with one variety of ə. The English unstressed short ə's are on the contrary elusive sounds, difficult to analyse, and subject to wide "variations" according to phonetic context. It may well be argued that it is convenient to keep them together in one phoneme separate from the longer and stressable ɛ. It may be remarked also that while ɛ and ʌ are very frequently found in similar phonetic contexts, these sounds rarely occur in the same phonetic context as ə.[9] These arguments, however, do not seem to me to be of sufficient cogency to outweigh the general principle that one sound-quality should not be assigned to two phonemes if it can possibly be helped. (See §35, also Chaps. XIX and XX.)

203. There are other types of English in which doubt may be felt as to the best phonemic classification of ʌ and ə for reasons different from those given in §§197–202. I refer to the pronunciation of those whose speech does not contain a long ə: at all, but who pronounce words like *burn, work* either with a sequence əɹ or with a monophthongal retroflexed or ɹ-coloured ə, thus bəɹn, wəɹk or bɹn, wɹk. Pronunciations of these types are common in the West and North-West of England and in America.[10]

---

[9] Some would say that they *never* occur in the same phonetic context as ə—that "weakly stressed" ɛ and ʌ in reality have a semi-strong stress. (See §204.)

[10] The usual American ɹ has a somewhat different quality from the Western English ɹ.

204. As in these types of English neither ʌ nor ə occurs long, the question arises whether the two sounds constitute separate phonemes or whether any grounds can be found for grouping them together in one phoneme. Personally, I take the view that both sounds occur in comparable phonetic contexts, such as those mentioned in §148, and therefore constitute separate phonemes. The opinion has, however, been expressed[11] that these contexts are not comparable, and that every so-called weakly stressed ʌ has in fact a semi-strong stress. Those who hold this opinion appear to consider that not only ʌ but also the English e, a and o sounds are incapable of being uttered with weak stress. It seems to me to be difficult to maintain such a proposition. To me it appears more logical to postulate that any vowel-sound can be pronounced with any degree of stress. The opener vowels, it is true, generally have greater *prominence* than sounds of the types ə, i and u; but this is probably accounted for by their greater inherent carrying power,[12] and sometimes also to extreme shortness of the ə, i and u sounds. Non-final ə is generally elidable in British English, i.e. its elision does not as a rule affect the meanings of words. Therefore its precise quality is, within limits, immaterial. Weakly stressed e, a, o and ʌ, on the other hand, are not elidable; they have to be long enough to make their qualities distinctly recognizable. They are thus more prominent (by length) than ə, but this does not necessarily mean that they have stronger stress.

205. I have explained elsewhere[13] that I take stress to be largely a subjective feeling of forcibleness or effort in the action of producing sounds, and I may add here that I am doubtful if it will ever be found possible to determine degrees of stress by

---

[11] E.g. by G. L. TRAGER and B. BLOCH. (See TRAGER and BLOCH, *The Syllabic Phonemes of English* in *American Speech*, Vol. XVII, No. 3, July, 1941, p. 227, and the transcriptions by TRAGER in *Le Maître Phonétique*, January, 1935, p. 11, and April, 1941, p. 17; also the note by BLOCH in *Le Maître Phonétique*, January, 1943, p. 4.)

[12] The term "inherent carrying power" has been objected to by some on theoretical grounds. I submit, however, that it is a justifiable term to use in linguistic work, since it is a matter of experience that close vowels can only be made to carry as well as opener vowels by uttering them with greater effort (e.g. in attempting to get comparable tone-volumes when making gramophone records of vowels). (See also §437.)

[13] §425 of this book. Also *Outline of English Phonetics*, §909 and footnote.

laboratory methods.[14]   Certain other features contributing to the
prominence of syllables can be investigated by laboratory methods,
and notably duration and, to some extent, intonation[15]; and I am
disposed to think that what is taken by some authorities to be
"semi-strong stress" on ʌ and certain other English vowels is in
point of fact merely prominence effected by these other means.
I would add further that in my speech there are constant relations
between intonation and what I judge to be stress, and that the
intonations used on syllables containing "weakly stressed" ʌ, a,
etc., are the same as those applied to similarly placed syllables
containing ə.

206.   Even if it could be proved that all the ʌ's which I take
to be weakly stressed have in reality a semi-strong stress, it is
still not certain that it would be advantageous to utilize this fact

---

[14] As far as I am aware the experiments carried out by J. W. JEAFFRESON
constitute the nearest approach yet made towards the determination of stress
by laboratory methods.   These experiments were based on the assumption
that degrees of stress are proportional to the amount of depression of the
lower jaw, allowance being made for the fact that the amount and manner of
lowering differs for different vowels.   (JEAFFRESON claimed that this is not
an assumption but a proved fact.   Incidentally, he was able to recognize
certain vowels by the shapes recorded by their jaw-movements.)   As the
Southern English ʌ is normally pronounced with considerable lowering of
the jaw, JEAFFRESON's experiments apparently tend to support the theory
of TRAGER and BLOCH.   On the other hand, although JEAFFRESON's premise
concerning the relationship of stress to jaw-movement may hold good in
most cases, we should not ignore the fact that it is possible to give strong
stress to sounds said with closed or nearly closed jaws.   How far strongly
stressed sounds of this description actually occur in speech I am not prepared
to say, but the fact that they can be made cannot but cast a certain doubt
on the validity of JEAFFRESON's theory.

Only a few of the results of JEAFFRESON's remarkable experiments have
ever been published.   These appeared in a paper entitled *Stress and Rhythm
in Speech* in the *Transactions of the Philological Society*, 1938, a work which
deserves close study.   Many other results were incorporated in his *Mensuration
of French Verse* (thesis for the London M.A., 1924) which has never been
printed.   This valuable work may be consulted in the Library of the University
of London.

[15] In my experience the actual intonations revealed by laboratory methods
often do not correspond either to the intention of the speaker or to the perception of the hearer.   For example, the effect of a fall from high to low
pitch is often produced by an intonation which can be shown by laboratory
examination to be only a fall from a high to a mid pitch.

for grouping ʌ and ə into one phoneme. The two sounds would be distinguished by a complex of quality and stress, and doubtless also of length, neither of these attributes predominating decisively over the other. When such is the case, either attribute can be regarded as the primary means of differentiation and the other considered subsidiary (see §491). Our choice might therefore be determined by some irrelevant external consideration. Such a consideration is the appearance and legibility of phonetic transcription. If the degree of stress were taken to be the primary means of differentiation, with the result that the letter ʌ could be dispensed with, we should have to use a mark (ˌ) to indicate semi-strong stress. The words 'hikʌp, 'hʌmdrʌm, 'katəpʌlt would then be written 'hiˌkəp, 'həmˌdrəm, 'kataˌpəlt, and the other three words quoted in §148 would be written 'sirəp, kə'nəndrəm, 'difikəlt. From the point of view of legibility I believe this system would be inferior to the equally justifiable system of using the separate and easily distinguishable letters ʌ and ə.

207. Another solution of the problem would be to regard the difference of *length* between ʌ and ə as the primary means of differentiation. We might in fact either write all ʌ's of the type of English under consideration as ə with a length-mark or all non-final ə's with a mark indicating extreme shortness. The first of these alternatives would be inconvenient, as it would mean using a length-mark in the representation of a sound which is not longer than the other short vowels. The second alternative, of writing say ə̆ in place of every ordinary ə, would impair both legibility and ease of writing, owing to the commonness of the sound.[16]

208. I regard it as necessary to bear in mind continually in phonemic investigations that one of the main objects of the phoneme theory is to establish a basis for the elaboration of simple and legible forms of writing (Chap. XXXI). Consequently, though I advocate the principle of writing by means of the bare minimum of letters, I feel that in the case we are now considering the best solution is to use the two letters ʌ and ə.

209. The foregoing discussion (§§197–208) relates to types of English in which ʌ and ə are clearly distinct in quality—where the two sounds said in isolation with identical stress and length are easily distinguishable. Other types exist (especially in the

---

[16] It occurs approximately 40 times in every 100 words.

North of England and in America) in which ʌ is very near in sound
to ə, and in these the TRAGER-BLOCH method of phonemic classification would presumably be the only appropriate one.[17]

210. The following is another example, this time from a European
foreign language, where doubt might at first be felt as to the proper
phonemic allocation of a sound. It is the case of the Italian final
weakly stressed o in such words as ˈɛkko (ecco), ˈkwattro (quattro).
In the pronunciation of many Italians this vowel is a rather open
one, nearer in quality to the ɔ of ˈskwɔla (scuola), ˈnɔtte (notte)
than to the close o of ˈdove, ˈsopra. Representing this final vowel
narrowly by the symbol ǫ for the purpose of this discussion, we
may express the case thus: ǫ is acoustically nearer to ɔ than to o,
and ǫ is always weakly stressed while ɔ is always strongly stressed[18];
such a state of affairs naturally tempts a foreign observer to assign
ǫ to the ɔ-phoneme. Further observations show, however, that
this allocation cannot be maintained. For if we examine a number
of words containing weakly stressed non-final o's, such as doˈmani,
dotˈtore, konˈtɛnto, orˈribile, forˈtissimo, ˈɛkkomi, ˈkredono, we
find that a whole series of vowel-sounds exists ranging by imperceptible degrees from nearly close o to the comparatively open ǫ
of final positions. In this series it does not seem possible to draw
any definite line of demarcation which would justify assigning
the final ǫ's to a different phoneme from the other unstressed o's.
The situation is probably about as shown in the accompanying
diagram (Fig. 5). Such being the case, it is necessary to assign ǫ
to the o-phoneme.[19]

---

[17] Many people in the North of England and in America do not have any
ʌ-sound in their speech. Where Southern English has ʌ, they use an ə of
the same quality as the ordinary weakly stressed ə; for instance, they
pronounce cup as kəp. The above discussion has naturally no application
to this pronunciation.

[18] Unless we take sentences into account, which is contrary to the principles
which in my opinion should be followed in investigating the nature of the
phoneme (see §§31, 34, and Some Thoughts on the Phoneme, pp. 127–132).

[19] If in the pronunciation of some Italians there is a clear line of demarcation
between the quality of non-final unstressed o's and that of final ǫ, it would
mean that ǫ need not necessarily be attached to the o-phoneme in their
speech. The case for attaching it to o would be no better than the case for
attaching it to ɔ. We should have to choose one of them. This could be
done purely arbitrarily, or by taking into consideration some external fact
unconnected with the idea of the phoneme. Such a fact would be the history
of the sound, which would naturally lead us to prefer the o-phoneme.

211. It may be mentioned here that in some cases of apparent difficulty the investigator should take account of the "linguistic sense" of speakers of the language under examination. I believe it to be a fact that the instinctive feeling of a native whose speech is unstudied is at times a better guide than the reasonings of the phonetician. Thus a phonetic expert might be disposed to reason that the Italian and Spanish ŋ should be assigned to the ɲ-phoneme since the tongue position of ŋ is nearer to that of ɲ than to that of n. But the "linguistic sense" of Italians and Spaniards leads them to consider ŋ as "a kind of n" and not as "a kind of ɲ." If a reason is assignable, it is no doubt that ɲ is always completed with an off-glide (a rapid j); ŋ has no off-glide in Italian and Spanish, and is therefore felt to be nearer to n which also occurs without an off-glide.

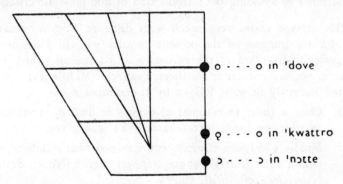

Fɪɢ. 5.   Positions of the Italian o and ɔ sounds.

212. Sometimes the natural "linguistic sense" of the native is difficult to ascertain, owing to prejudice created by orthography. A case in point is the labio-dental ɱ which is used in Italian to the exclusion of other nasal consonants before f and v, as in ['niɱfa] (ninfa), [iɱ'vetʃe] (invece). The circumstances under which this sound is used show that it must be grouped into the same phoneme as one of the other nasal consonants. Some might be inclined to assign it to the n-phoneme, but I think that this feeling would be mainly, if not entirely, due to the influence of the current orthography. I believe that if orthography could be disregarded, the natural linguistic sense would be found to be that the sound is "a kind of m." This is borne out by the fact

that children who have this pronunciation in English are liable to write *envelope* as *emvelope*. On acoustic and organic grounds I think too that the Italian ŋ should be assigned to the m-phoneme. It is worthy of note also that the same sound occurring in Greek is written with μ, as in 'simfoni ['simfoni] (σύμφωνοι, agreed).

213.   Further instances of the possibility of more than one method of phonemic grouping are given in Chapter XX.

(2) COMPLEXITY OF CONTROLLING PRINCIPLES

214.   The case of the French sound (or rather the set of shades of sound) known as "e moyen" or "middle e" affords an illustration of difficulties in establishing a phonemic classification by reason of complexity of "controlling principles" (§30). It also illustrates the importance of avoiding the introduction of non-phonetic criteria.[20]

215.   Usage varies very much with different French speakers, but for the purpose of the present enquiry we will examine the following distribution of the various e and ɛ sounds, which is, I believe, not uncommon in Northern France. (Middle e is represented narrowly in what follows by the symbol ẹ.)

(1)   Close e (near to cardinal e) occurs in final open syllables: te (*thé*), ne (*nez*), ʃāte (*chanter*), ke (*quai*), etc.

(2)   Middle ẹ (various shades) occurs in non-final syllables: ẹkla (*éclat*), sẹde (*céder*), rẹpẹte (*répéter*), bẹtiːz (*bêtise*), dẹsāːdr (*descendre*), ẹfɛ (*effet*), etc.[21]

(3)   Open ɛ (about cardinal) occurs
  (a)   in final open syllables: nɛ (*naît*), ɔbʒɛ (*objet*), vrɛ (*vrai*), etc.[22];
  (b)   in final closed syllables long and short: mɛːm (*même*), mɛːtr (*maître*), tɛːt (*tête*), mɛtr (*mettre*), dɛt (*dette*), ʃɛf (*chef*), etc.

---

[20] In §§215–229 most of the words quoted as examples are written in a narrow transcription. I have not thought it necessary to enclose them all in square brackets as is done in most other parts of the book (§45). The few cases in which the transcriptions are broad are evident from the context.

[21] Some speakers also pronounce with middle ẹ some or all of the words here grouped under 4 (*b*).

[22] Some Parisians use close e in all or many of these words.

(4) Open ε (cardinal or slightly less open) occurs

    (a) in non-final closed syllables: vεst5 (*veston*), εrmit (*ermite*), εktaːr (*hectare*), εkski (*exquis*), prεskri (*prescrit*), εspaːs (*espace*), εnmi (*ennemi*), etc.[23];

    (b) in non-final open syllables: εmabl (*aimable*), plεziːr (*plaisir*), εrœːr (*erreur*), mεle (*méler*), εde (*aider*), etc.[24]

216. Basing our enquiry on the above distribution of the e and ε sounds, we find that there are undoubtedly two phonemes and no more. These we represent naturally by the letters e and ε. Further we find that the middle ẹ's must be assigned to the e-phoneme and not to the ε-phoneme.[25] For it will be seen from §215 (1) and (2) that middle ẹ only occurs in situations where close e does not occur; whereas a comparison of (2) and (4) shows that middle ẹ may occur in the same situation as open ε.

217. It follows from this that the distinction between middle ẹ and close e can never be significant, but the distinction between middle ẹ and open ε is capable of being significant.[26]

218. The fact that there is so much variation in the pronunciation of different French speakers (see footnotes) illustrates well the necessity for establishing phonemic classifications from the speech of one individual, and taking no account of any other.

219. It will not do, for instance, to say that "the middle ẹ used by those who pronounce ẹmabl must belong to the ε-phoneme because other people pronounce εmabl." Such a manner of reasoning would cause the collapse of the whole theory of phonemes. We must simply observe that people do not all use the same phonemes in the same words.

220. Other non-phonetic criteria which are inadmissible are "root forms" or "the vowel which the syllable would have if strongly stressed." For example, the fact that bẹtiːz (*bêtise*) may be supposed to be a derivative of a root form bεːt (*bête*) does not

---

[23] Some speakers use middle ẹ in some of these words, e.g. ẹktaːr, ẹkski, ẹspaːs, ẹnmi, ẹskimo.

[24] Many speakers use middle ẹ in some or all of these words: ẹmabl, plẹziːr, mẹle, ẹde.

[25] Subject to the particular case noted in §§307, 312.

[23] Example: ẹlbœf (*et le bœuf*), εlbœf (*Elbeuf*).

provide a reason for assigning the ę to the ɛ-phoneme. This is simply a case where a derived form is said with a phoneme different from that of the root form. If we were analysing the pronunciation of those who pronounce męle, ęde, etc., many further examples would be found, since męle, ęde, etc., are pronounced by those speakers with phonemes different from those in mɛːl (*mêle*), ɛːd (*aide*), etc.

221. Similarly the fact that some speakers pronounce *est* (is) as ɛ in strongly stressed positions and ę in weakly stressed positions[27] does not mean that this ę belongs to the ɛ-phoneme in their speech; it is merely an instance of a word changing its phoneme according to the phonetic context.[28] *Mais* is another such word: some speakers pronounce mɛ when a pause follows, but mę in męn5 (*mais non*), etc.[29]

222. Two further facts that might strike some observers as constituting difficulties are (1) that there may be "overlapping" of the French e and ɛ phonemes and (2) that some French people have erratic pronunciation of particular words in a given context. These points are dealt with in Chapters XIX and XXVIII, from which it will be seen that they do not affect the conclusions arrived at here.

223. The phonemic classification of the German e, ɛ and ə sounds presents features of interest owing to a certain complexity in the controlling principles, and to the fact that conclusive examples are rare.

224. In the type of German described in VIËTOR's *Aussprache-wörterbuch* these sounds are used in phonetic contexts as follows:

e.[30]   Always long or half-long. Generally strongly stressed or medium stressed, but also occurs weakly stressed. Examples: (strongly stressed) 'eːrə (*Ehre*), 'neːmən (*nehmen*), fɛr'keːr (*Verkehr*), gə'beːt (*Gebet*), (medium stressed) eːvaŋ'geːliʃ (*evangelisch*, first eː), 'angəneːm (*angenehm*), 'zyŋkoːpe: (*Synkope*), (weakly stressed) eː'lɛktriʃ (*elektrisch*).

---

[27] As in wi, il l ɛ; n5, i n l ę pɑ (*oui, il l'est; non, il ne l'est pas*).

[28] Just as the English word *is* is pronounced z and s according to the phonetic context (e.g. hiː z 'gouiŋ, it s 'gouiŋ).

[29] This was PAUL PASSY's pronunciation.

[30] Narrow transcription is used in the course of this explanation.

ε. Occurs long and short. Both can have any degree of stress, but weakly stressed long ε is uncommon. Examples: (long, strongly stressed) 'eːrə (*Ähre*), 'eːnliç (*ähnlich*), (long, medium stressed) eːkviː'noktsjum (*Äquinoktium*), (long, weakly stressed) εː'raːr (*Ärar*), dεː'moːnən (*Dämonen*); (short, strongly stressed) 'gεltən (*gelten*), 'bεsər (*besser*), 'hεndə (*Hände*), (short, weakly stressed) bεr'liːn (*Berlin*), pεr'zoːn (*Person*), εnt'zεtsliç (*entsetzlich*), 'alεtʃ (*Aletsch*), 'eːlεnt (*elend*), 'εŋlεndər (*Engländer*), mεr'tseːdεs (*Mercedes*).

ə (an opener variety before r and a closer variety elsewhere[31]). Is always short and weakly stressed. Examples: 'bitə (*bitte*), 'oːnə (*ohne*), gə'vis (*gewiss*), bə'axtuŋ (*Beachtung*), 'bitət (*bittet*), 'untər (*unter*), 'hundərt (*hundert*), 'mindəstəns (*mindestens*), 'feːlənt (*fehlend*), 'feːləndər (*fehlender*), 'aːbənts (*Abends*).[32]

225. An examination of the foregoing examples shows that, in the style of speech under consideration, e and ε belong to separate phonemes, and that ə is assignable to the same phoneme as e. That e and ε belong to separate phonemes is shown by pairs such as 'eːrə, 'εːrə, 'zeːən (*sehen*), 'zεːən (*säen*). That ε and ə belong to separate phonemes is shown by pairs such as 'eːlεnt, 'aːbənt, 'εŋlεndər, 'feːləndər.[33] That ə is assignable to the e-phoneme is shown by the fact that in comparable phonetic contexts e is always longer than ə; the e of 'zyŋkoːpeː (*Synkope*) is longer than the final ə of 'ziŋkəndə (*sinkende*), and the e of eː'lεktriʃ is longer than the ə of gə'lεkt (*geleckt*).

226. In broad transcription we should therefore write 'eːre (*Ehre*), 'neːmen, eː'lεktriʃ, 'εːre (*Ähre*), 'εːnliç, 'gεlten, 'bεser, 'hεnde, bεr'liːn, 'eːlεnt, 'bite, 'oːne, 'mindestens, etc.

227. The phonemic status of these sounds is different in the speech of the numerous North Germans who do not use long εː, but who pronounce such words as *ähnlich*, *Ähre* with long close eː.

---

[31] Reference is here made to the pronunciation of those who sound vowel plus r. (See footnote 13 to §91.)

[32] In some styles of speech ə is also used in certain pretonic closed syllables, e.g. in words beginning with the prefixes *er-*, *ver-* (ər-, fər- instead of εr-, fεr-).

[33] Other examples occur in the speech of those who use ə in prefixes like *er-*, *ver-* (footnote 32 above), e.g. bεr'liːnər, fər'liːrən.

In their speech ɛ cannot be regarded otherwise than as a member of the same phoneme as e, since ɛ is always short and e always comparatively long. ə, on the other hand, must be held to constitute a separate phoneme in this type of German, since differences like those in 'eːlɛnt and 'feːlənt are not attributable to phonetic context.

228. A broad transcription of this type of German would not need the letter ɛ, but it would require the use of ə. We should write 'eːrə (for *Ehre* and *Ähre*), 'neːmən, eː'lektriʃ, 'eːnliç, 'geltən, 'besər, 'hendə, ber'liːn, 'eːlent, 'bitə, 'feːlənt, 'oːnə, 'mindəstəns, etc.

229. A curious point to note is that words like *elend*, containing weakly stressed ɛ in post-tonic syllable, are few in number and are seldom used. If they did not happen to exist, and if names were excluded from our enquiry as not belonging to the language proper, the three sounds e, ɛ and ə would apparently, in one type of German, be assignable to a single phoneme. (The type in question is the speech of those who pronounce *ähnlich*, *Ähre*, etc., with long close eː, and who use ɛ in the prefixes *er-* and *ver-*.) One might perhaps make out a case for ignoring such a word as *elend* on the ground that it does not belong to the normal spoken language. Whether proper names should or should not be taken into account in ascertaining the phonemic structure of a language is a question that must for the present be left open. It is one which needs investigation, since proper names sometimes contain sound-sequences alien to ordinary words (cf. §§284, 298).

230. There is some uncertainty as to whether the German consonants x and ç belong to a single phoneme or constitute separate phonemes. The conditions under which these sounds are normally found are clear enough. They are as follows: (1) x only occurs when an a, o or u sound precedes in the same syllable, (2) ç occurs in all positions other than these, namely (*a*) at the beginnings of syllables, (*b*) when a front vowel precedes in the same syllable, and (*c*) when a consonant precedes. Examples are: (1) bax (*Bach*), ʃpraːx (*sprach*), dox (*doch*), hoːx (*hoch*), brux (*Bruch*, breakage), buːx (*Buch*), (2) (*a*) çeː'miː (*Chemie*), 'çryːzaːlis (*Chrysalis*), ar'çaːiʃ (*archaisch*) and all the words ending with the suffix -çən (-*chen*), (*b*) iç (*ich*), 'tyçtiç (*tüchtig*), rɛçt (*recht*), (*c*) milç (*Milch*), durç (*durch*).

231. It will be seen from these conditions that it is possible to group ç and x into a single phoneme if we know where the beginnings and ends of syllables are. This is often a matter of word-division and sometimes a question of knowing whether a certain sequence of sounds is or is not a prefix or a suffix. Now North Germans appear to have a particularly definite feeling for word-division, and they seem to feel various prefixes and suffixes as word-like entities.[34] In particular, they seem to feel the suffix -çən (-chen) to be a sort of "word." They seem to take it for granted, for instance, that the x of ʹrauxən (rauchen) terminates a syllable and that the ç of ʹfrauçən (Frauchen) begins a syllable; in other words, they appear to have a clear perception of the morphological structure of the words. If, therefore, we consider the suffix -chen to be a word, our case for regarding x and ç as members of a single phoneme is all but complete.[35]

232. It would be quite complete were it not for the existence of the exceptional word vaʹxolder (Wacholder, juniper) and a few proper names such as vaʹxau (Wachau, district in Austria) in which x appears to begin a syllable. A case can, I think, be made out for excluding proper names from the materials upon which we base phonemic grouping in many languages (cp. §298), but it does not seem to me justifiable to ignore a reasonably common word like vaʹxolder in order to be able to establish a convenient phonemic system. For a similar reason I doubt the feasibility of the ingenious proposal made by J. L. M. TRIM in Le Maître Phonétique, July, 1951, p. 41, to assign ç to the same phoneme as h. The German words of Greek origin beginning with ç are surely too numerous to be ignored in a phonemic account of normal German.[36]

---

[34] It will be recalled that in my view a system of phonemes must be based upon the pronunciation of isolated words and not upon connected speech (§34). See also Some Thoughts on the Phoneme, pp. 127–132.

[35] The theory that German x and ç belong to a single phoneme was, I believe, first propounded by L. BLOOMFIELD (see Le Maître Phonétique, April, 1930, pp. 27, 28).

[36] I have heard from several sources that Wacholder is pronounced with a h in it (vaxʹholder) by some Germans. If this pronunciation could be taken as the standard form in this and all similar words, the establishment of x and ç as members of a single phoneme would apparently be demonstrated. As matters stand, however, the evidence in favour of the pronunciation vaxʹholder is insufficient. vaʹxolder is the only form recorded in SIEBS' Hochsprache and in VIËTOR'S Aussprachewörterbach.

CHAPTER XV

GLIDING SOUNDS AND COMPOUND SOUNDS

233. "Gliding sounds" and "compound sounds" (§§9–19), though audibly divisible into parts, have to be regarded for linguistic purposes as single entities. Like other sounds they belong to phonemes, and may occur either as principal or as subsidiary members. They are sometimes found in the same phonemes as "simple" sounds.

234. In the following paragraphs examples are given of phonemes comprising gliding sounds and compound sounds. In §§243–257 and §§270–272 will be found examples of simple sounds occurring in the same phonemes as gliding and compound sounds.

GLIDING SOUNDS

235. The English w is a phoneme the members of which are all gliding sounds. They are all formed by starting at or near an u position and immediately moving away in the direction of some other vowel. Thus the w of wet starts near the English short u (as in huk, *hook*) and immediately moves away in the direction of the e. The w of wo:k (*walk*) is different; it starts with a somewhat closer lip-position than the w of wet, and the gliding sound from this to the o: is evidently different both in tongue movement and in lip movement from the previous w. The w of wu: (*woo*) is again different; it starts with a much closer lip-position, and the passage from the initial position to the u: involves only a very slight movement.

236. The English j is a gliding sound showing similar characteristics. The initial position of the tongue is much lower in ja:d (*yard*) from what it is in ji:ld (*yield*). The nature of these two members of the phoneme is shown in Figure 6. Although these two sounds are so very different in formation, it would never occur to any ordinary English person that they were anything else than "the same sound"—meaning members of the same phoneme.

237. Diphthongs[1] must in my opinion be considered as indivisible gliding sounds. It is convenient to represent them in writing by

---

[1] For definition of the term "diphthong" see my *Outline of English Phonetics*, 8th edition, 1956 (Heffer, Cambridge), §219 ff.

digraphs, the first letter representing the starting point and the second indicating the direction of movement. In the following paragraphs are given some examples of diphthong phonemes which have subsidiary members differing notably from the principal members.

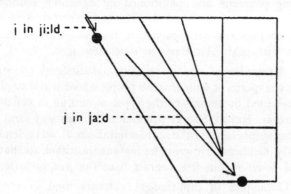

i in ji:ld

j in ja:d

FIG. 6. Movements of j in ji:ld and ja:d.

238.   One is the English ei.[2]   In my speech the principal member is a sound gliding approximately from a sound near to my e of beg towards my i of big.   This sound is used in final positions, e.g. in plei (*play*) when it occurs at the end of a sentence.   When a consonant follows, closer varieties are generally used.   Thus my ei in geim (*game*) has a higher starting point than my ei in plei. Before some consonants, and especially before t, s and ʃ, a still closer variety of ei is used; examples pleit (*plate*), pleis (*place*), 'steiʃn (*station*).

239.   A noteworthy instance of variant sounds which would appear at first sight to be two sounds belonging to a single diphthong phoneme is afforded by the sounds which may be written ʌi and ae in common varieties of Scottish pronunciation.   For instance in one type of Scottish, described in my book *The Pronunciation of English* (Cambridge University Press, 4th edition, 1958, p. 58), ʌi is used to the exclusion of ae when one of the consonants p, b,

---

[2] My pronunciation.   These observations do not apply to the nearly monophthongal ei (approaching ɛː) which is now very prevalent in the South of England.

t, k, g, m, n or l follows in the same syllable. Further examination of the occurrences of ʌi and ae (see §522) shows, however, that the idea of grouping the two diphthongs into a single phoneme cannot be maintained.

240. The above are examples where different members of a diphthong phoneme are conditioned by adjoining sounds in the words. Special members of diphthong phonemes may also be used in conjunction with particular degrees of stress or in conjunction with particular tones in tone languages.

241. Examples of special variants conditioned by stress are found in the speech of some English people whose ai and au phonemes are represented by sounds of the types əi and əu in syllables with weak stress. HENRY SWEET pronounced in this way, and in some of his transcripts he used the narrow notations əi, əu to denote these subsidiary members. He wrote for instance mistifəid, and həuevə (for *mystified, however*), but faiv, səpraiz, haus (for *five, surprise, house*).[3]

242. Examples of diphthongal variants used in conjunction with special tones are found in Pekingese. For instance, in that language distinct members of the au-phoneme are associated with different tones. In particular the diphthong used in association with the third tone, as in ˏxau (good), is a notably lower variety than that used in words with other tones, e.g. ˉxau (plant). It might be represented narrowly by ɑɔ.

GLIDING SOUNDS AND SIMPLE SOUNDS AS MEMBERS OF THE
SAME PHONEME

243. Gliding sounds and simple sounds sometimes occur as members of the same phoneme. An example is found in the French j. The common members of this phoneme are gliding sounds similar to the English j-sounds described in §236. Thus gliding sounds are commonly used in jø (*yeux*), jɔd (*iode*), mjɛt (*miette*), lj5 (*lion*), kaje (*cahier*), vjɛjaːr (*viellard*). In certain final positions, however, and particularly when the preceding vowel is i,

---

[3] SWEET, *Primer of Spoken English*, p. 78. In his *Elementarbuch des Gesprochenen Englisch* he wrote these sounds broadly, using ai, au in weakly stressed as well as in strongly stressed positions. The use of diphthongs of the əi, əu types in weakly stressed positions appears to be less prevalent in the Southern English of to-day than in SWEET's time.

Northern French speakers commonly use a simple sound, fricative j. It is usual, for instance, to hear such words as fiːj (*fille*), briːj (*brille*) pronounced with fricative j. There is no reason for considering this fricative sound as other than a special member of the French j-phoneme.

244. Other instances of simple sounds belonging to the same phonemes as gliding sounds are found in the case of various phonemes which have diphthongs as their principal members.

245. The case may be illustrated by the English ei-phoneme. Besides the diphthongal members mentioned in §238 it comprises a monophthongal member which is used when ə or l follows, as in pleiə (*player*) or feil (*fail*). [4] That the sound is monophthongal or approximately so is fairly easily heard in the group eiə. The monophthongal character is less noticeable in the sequence eil, but it may be demonstrated by whispering the syllable and listening to its whisper pitch. In ei, said alone, the whisper pitch is heard to ascend[5]; in eil it remains about stationary until it descends for the l.[6] The monophthongal variety of e heard in these syllables must evidently be held to be a member of the phoneme which has the diphthong ei as its principal member. It is apprehended by speaker and hearer as being "the same sound" as ei, i.e. it is the variety of ei which it is natural to use in these special phonetic contexts.

246. In broad transcription the words *player* and *fail* are written pleiə, feil. To show in writing the monophthongal character of the sound written ei would necessitate introducing a special symbol,

---

[4] Here again I refer to my own speech, which is I believe similar to that of a considerable proportion of Southern English speakers.

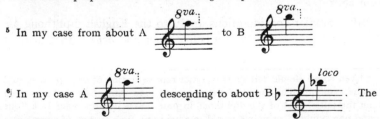

[5] In my case from about A   to B

[6] In my case A   descending to about B♮   . The

fact that the whisper pitch descends in the English syllable eil was first discovered by W. PERRETT; see his *Some Questions of Phonetic Theory*, Part I, p. 32 (1916).

say ε, to denote the short e-sound of lɛt, fɛl (*fell*), etc. *Play, player, pair, let, fell, fail* could then be represented more narrowly by the notation [plei, pleə, pεə, lɛt, fɛl, fel (or feːl)]. The transcription of *pair* could be still further narrowed by marking the ε so as to show that it is an opener sound than the vowel of *fell*, thus: [fɛl, pε̞ə].[8]

247. The treatment of the English diphthong phonemes ai and au when followed by ə may be cited here in connexion with the subject of monophthongs in diphthong phonemes.

248. In the speech of many English people words like *fire* and *hire* are pronounced with a sound which may be written aə. This is probably best regarded as a diphthong, though it may be taken to be a sequence of the two sounds a and ə.[9] If it is held to be a diphthong, it constitutes a separate diphthongal phoneme. If it can be treated as a sequence of an a-sound + ə, the a may either be assigned to the ordinary a-phoneme, which comprises the vowels in kat (*cat*) and haːf (*half*), or it may be considered as a monophthongal member of the ai-phoneme. The only reason for suggesting the latter course is an external one unconnected with the phoneme theory, namely, that other speakers use pronunciations of the types aeə, aεə in such words—that there exist in fact with different speakers various shades of pronunciation extending from a clearly disyllabic aeə to a monosyllabic or barely disyllabic aə. With those whose pronunciation shows any trace of tongue raising between the a and the ə, the first part of the sequence (ae or aε) cannot be treated as other than a member of the ai-phoneme. There is therefore a certain practical convenience in treating similarly the pronunciation of those who have a "level" pronunciation aə.[10]

249. Similar considerations apply to the English diphthong au. Some speakers pronounce words like *tower* and *hour* with a distinct disyllable which could be written narrowly aoə or aɔə. The ao

---

[8] Even so we should fall short of strict representation of one speech-sound by one symbol. The vowel of *fell* is opener than that of *let*, but less open than the initial part of the diphthong in *pair*. Stricter adherence to a "one sound one symbol" principle would involve some such system of representation as fel (*fail*), lɛt (*let*), fε̞l (*fell*), pæə (*pair*).

[9] It is difficult to distinguish between the diphthong and the sequence.

[10] For the occasional possibility of assigning a sound to a particular phoneme on grounds unconnected with the phoneme theory, see §§322 ff.

or aɔ in this form of pronunciation must without doubt be considered as a subsidiary member of the au-phoneme. Other speakers use a "levelled" form which is nearly or quite monosyllabic. Its value varies considerably according to the speaker's dialect, but it is more often a backer sound than the aə corresponding to aiə. This form may consequently be represented phonetically by ɑə. The ɑ in this pronunciation may be regarded as a monophthongal member of the au-phoneme. Alternatively the ɑə may be considered as constituting a separate diphthongal phoneme.[11]

250. Some English speakers who pronounce *fire* and *hire* as faə, haə use a disyllabic pronunciation with aiə in the words having the suffix -*er*, e.g. 'haiə (*higher*), 'flaiə (*flyer*), 'ʃaiə (*shyer*). In this style of speech the initial part of aə evidently cannot be considered as having anything to do with the ai-phoneme. If the aə of this style of speech sounds disyllabic, the a may be assigned to the ordinary English a-phoneme. If the aə is definitely monosyllabic it must be held to constitute a separate diphthong phoneme [aə̆]. Similar considerations apply to such words as *plougher*, *allowance*.

251. The West of England pronunciation of "long o" gives us a further illustration of the occurrence of a diphthong and a pure vowel in the same phoneme. Before ɹ the sound used is with many Western speakers monophthongal: moːɹ (*more*), 'poːɹiŋ (*pouring*), foɹs (*force*), etc.[12] But in other situations a diphthong of the ou type is used: sou (*so*), oun (*own*), etc.

252. It has been suggested that the so-called monophthongal o-sound often heard from English speakers in such words as *molest*, *obey*, *profound*, *November*, should be regarded as a member of the ou-phoneme. If it can be established that there are speakers who

---

[11] The phonemic status of the "level" forms of aiə and auə presents a singularly difficult problem. The values of the sounds vary from one speaker to another, and the differences of classification depend upon the starting points of the speaker's ai and au and upon the value of his long aː. The problem is complicated by the fact that many people use a still more "level" pronunciation than aə and ɑə, viz. varieties of long ɑː, in such words as *fire*, *tower*. These generally differ somewhat from the long aː of *half* as well as from each other. Moreover, the pronunciation of one and the same speaker may vary according as he is speaking rapidly or slowly. Consequently people's pronunciation of such words is often erratic and cannot be reduced to phonemes. Some further information on the subject is given in my *Outline of English Phonetics*, §§414, 415, 430, 431.

[12] Also pronounced moəɹ, 'poəɹiŋ, foəɹs, etc., by some.

use a really monophthongal sound which they employ to the exclusion of **ou** in definite phonetic contexts, e.g. in pretonic position, then it furnishes us with yet another example of the grouping of a simple sound and a gliding sound into one phoneme.

253. In my opinion, however, the conditions under which this **o**-like sound is used are not such as to make it groupable into the same phoneme with any other vowel. I do not think it can truly be said to be a sound of any consistent form of the English language. It is rather what may be called an "unstable" sound. Every word in which it is used has alternative pronunciations with one of the stable English sounds **ou** or **ə**, and I do not think any English speaker can be found who uses the sound in question consistently and to the exclusion of diphthongal **ou** in any particular phonetic setting. It is, I believe, always used in an erratic manner, that is to say, people sometimes use one pronunciation and sometimes another without adhering to any consistent principle. That such a way of speaking cannot be reduced to phonemes is explained in Chapter XXVIII.

254. We can, as it seems to me, only assign this monophthongal **o**-like sound to the **ou**-phoneme if we take as the form of English to be recorded the pronunciation of an imaginary consistent speaker who always uses it to the exclusion of diphthongal **ou** in pretonic position or some other definite phonetic context.[13]

255. Broad transcription of such a normalized form of speaking would involve using **ou** to denote both the diphthong **ou** and the special monophthongal **o**-sound, with the convention that the latter sound is meant in the particular contexts referred to in the last paragraph. We should thus write **mou'lest, ou'bei, prou'faund, nou'vembə**, etc., if our imaginary speaker is considered to use the special monophthongal **o**-sound in such words.

256. A case could, I think, be made out for regarding the monophthongal **o**-sound under discussion as a separate phoneme in the pronunciation of speakers (if there are any) who use it consistently in a particular set of words. To transcribe broadly the speech of such people would require that we should denote this sound by

---

[13] The pronunciation of such an imaginary speaker would be recognizable as perfectly "good" English.

the letter o and use a special symbol (ɔ) in the representation of the ordinary short o of *hot, long,* etc., and the long oː of *caught, fall,* etc. Thus we should write moˈlest, oˈbei, noˈvembə, moulesˈteiʃn, hɔt, lɔŋ, kɔːt, fɔːl. This manner of transcribing has been followed in many published texts.

257. A further case of the existence of a pure vowel and a diphthong in one phoneme, a case which if it can be established is a particularly striking one, is that of Pekingese u. In that language there is an u-phoneme, the sound of which is usually a rather open variety of monophthongal u. But when the phoneme is preceded by i and the syllable is said on the third or fourth tone, the sound used is diphthongal and sounds like əu. The case may be exemplified by the words ˉiu (sad), ´iu (oil) which have monophthongal u, and ˌiəu (have) and ˋiəu (right hand) which have the above-mentioned diphthong. If this analysis is correct, these latter words would be written ˌiu, ˋiu in broad transcription. J. P. BRUCE did in fact write them narrowly with əu in the "Tone Practice" examples on p. 40 of his *Linguaphone Chinese Course*[14]; in the following exercise and throughout the rest of the book he wrote them broadly with u.[15]

---

[14] First edition.

[15] An observation of the pronunciation of two Pekingese speakers leads me to think that the very marked diphthong used in these third and fourth tone words should perhaps not be considered as belonging to the u-phoneme at all, but to the ou-phoneme, and that in consequence the above four words should be transcribed ˉiu, ´iu, ˌiou, ˋiou. If this is the correct view, it means that the sequence iu never has the third or fourth tone, and the sequence iou never has the first or second tone. KARLGREN, however, appears to be in substantial agreement with BRUCE. He says (*Phonologie Chinoise*, p. 318) that with many speakers the "final" iu varies with the tone, and that many Pekingese pronounce iu on the first tone and a sound which he writes iəu on the other tones. It is worthy of note too that in the "Gwoyeu Romatzyh" (´kuoˌy ´luoˌmaˋtsə) system of writing, in which the tones are shown by means of spellings, this syllable is written with ou or ow: iou, you, yeou and yow. Iou and you are pronounced ˉiu and ´iu, while yeou and yow appear to me to be pronounced almost, if not quite, ˌiou and ˋiou. Similar considerations appear to apply to the syllable which appears in the first tone as ˉui (second tone ´ui, third tone ˌuei, fourth tone ˋuei). This point is noted by KARLGREN (*Phonologie Chinoise*, Vol. II, p. 732, footnote 2).

Pekingese pronunciation being rather variable, it is probable that the degree of diphthongization of the "diphthongal u" is greater with some speakers than with others, and that consequently the sound has phonemic affinity to u in the speech of some and to ou in the speech of others.

Compound Sounds

258. Phonemes comprising compound sounds (§9) are very common, and are found in all languages. When the sounds are of the second category (§§16-18) there are often a great many members. Such phonemes are the English t and k. Five members of the English t-phoneme were mentioned in §72. As for the k-phoneme, it has different members according to adjacent vowels (§21), and it has more or less aspirated members according to the degree of stress, less for instance in 'stokiŋ (*stocking*) than in kiŋ (*king*), and still less after s, as in 'biskit (*biscuit*), and so on.

259. When the sounds are of the first category (§16), there are not as a rule many members of the phoneme. The English tʃ-phoneme, for instance, has little in the way of subsidiary members beyond a variety somewhat less aspirated than the principal member, which occurs in weakly stressed positions. Thus there is a certain aspiration of tʃ in tʃin (*chin*), less in 'hatʃit (*hatchet*), and hardly any when another consonant follows, as in wotʃt (*watched*).

260. A difficulty of an unusual kind is encountered in connexion with certain compound consonants of colloquial Sinhalese.[16] This language contains two nasal consonant phonemes, m and n (the latter of which includes two subsidiary members ꞑ and ŋ[17]); they occur in various phonetic contexts, and in particular they may precede b and d, ḍ, g respectively. The language also contains four sounds which I write here as m̃b, ñd, ñḍ, ñg; they are regarded by Sinhalese speakers as single sounds, but analysis shows them to be of a compound nature—plosive consonants preceded by a very short nasal element. The nasal element is so short that the

---

[16] I refer here to the ordinary *spoken* language of the better educated inhabitants of Colombo, Ceylon. Formal Sinhalese differs from this in various respects; in particular, ꞑ and ŋ are phonemes separate from n in formal Sinhalese, since in that style of speech ꞑ occurs before vowels and n occurs finally. See PERERA and JONES, *The Application of World Orthography to Sinhalese*, in the *Bulletin of the School of Oriental Studies*, London, Vol. IX, Part 3, p. 705. Incidentally I have been informed by a Sinhalese that even the most highly educated Sinhalese find it difficult to speak for any length of time in the theoretically correct formal style.

[17] ꞑ is used when ṭ or ḍ follows. ŋ is used finally and when k, g or h follows. Ordinary n does not occur in these positions in the colloquial language. (It does occur finally in the formal language.)

word **kañdə** (trunk) has the same rhythmic pattern as **kadə** (shoulder pole carrying weights at each end); it is not at all like the English word *candour*.

261. A case of this nature raises the question whether one is at liberty to divide into two parts a sound which is regarded by native speakers as indivisible, and whether, if one does divide it, the parts can properly be assigned to other phonemes existing in the language.   Thus in the present case is it admissible to divide **ñd** into **ñ** and **d**, and to assign the **ñ** to the n-phoneme and the **d** to the d-phoneme?

262. I am disposed to think that in making a classification into phonemes the view of the native speaker as to what constitutes a "single sound" should be regarded as important, though not necessarily conclusive.[18] If the Sinhalese people regard **m̃b**, **ñd**, etc., as being indivisible, we should give their view serious consideration, even though it should conflict with the ideas we have derived from European languages; we should be open-minded enough at least to examine the possibility of regarding these sounds as constituting separate independent phonemes. My personal opinion is that they should be so regarded.

263. This does not mean that we must necessarily avoid using such letters as **m**, **n**, **b**, **d** in the representation of these sounds in phonetic writing. If a Sinhalese were attempting to devise a romanic orthography for his language, his first impulse would be, I believe, to represent the above sounds either by specially designed letters or by **b**, **d**, **ḍ**, **g** with a diacritic attached (e.g. **ɓ**, **d̃**, **ḍ̃**, **g̃**[19]). The use of completely new letters has much to be said in its favour, but against it must be set (1) the difficulty of devising four new letters which are sufficiently simple and which harmonize properly with the other roman letters, (2) the fact that in the view of many it is preferable to keep the alphabet as small as practicable (see §684).   The use of **b**, **d**, **ḍ**, **g** with diacritics attached is unsatisfactory for two reasons: (1) because all systems of diacritics are in themselves

---

[18] For instance, I have heard English people express the opinion that the **ks** of *box* is a "single sound."   Such a view cannot be maintained without regarding the **ks** of *locks* also as a "single sound." And if **ks**, why not also **ps**, **gz** and many other consonant groups?

[19] Using ˜ in the sense of a slight nasality preceding the plosion.

undesirable, and should be avoided if possible,[20] (2) because there are typographical difficulties in putting a diacritic above tall roman letters like b and d.

264. Fortunately it is easy to devise a system of phonetic writing which involves neither the introduction of new letters nor the use of diacritics. Let the sounds under discussion be denoted by the convenient digraphs mb, nd, nɖ, ng, and let the sequences m + b, n + d, etc., which have a prolonged nasal consonant, be represented by prefixing another nasal consonant, thus mmb, nnd, etc. This mode of writing the latter sounds may be interpreted either as long m + b, long n + d, etc., or as m + m̃b, n + ñd, etc. (since long m + b is indistinguishable in sound from m + m̃b, and so on).

265. The following are examples of Sinhalese words written phonetically by this system (which I will call System A):

ambə (mango)	gemmba (frog)
kandə (trunk)	kanndə (hill)
hanɖə (sound)	kannɖijə (moumd, embankment)
angə (horn)	anngə (limbs)

266. Another possible system (System B) would be to use the diacritic ˇ, in which case the long nasal sounds would be represented by one letter only, thus:

am̃bə	gemba
kañdə	kandə
hañɖə	kanɖijə
añgə	angə

267. I think this course is really less satisfactory than the other, firstly on account of the disadvantages inherent in diacritics, and secondly because m̃b is rather a cumbrous way of representing what native speakers regard as a single sound. The Sinhalese phonetician H. S. PERERA preferred, however, System B.

268. In Sinhalese, nasal consonants may precede consonants other than b, d, ɖ, g. In these cases they are fairly long and are naturally identified as m, n (ɳ, ŋ) by Sinhalese speakers. They therefore correspond to the sounds written mm, nn in System A. It would, however, not be necessary to write them double, since no confusion could ever arise if they were written with single m, n. Examples: ampitigə (name of a place), antimə (end),

---

[20] See footnote 7 to §277 (p. 84).

kəranʈə²¹ (to do), ankə²² (numbers), maːncu (fetters), sinhea²³ (lion). If System A were adopted, this would be a case where phonetic consistency might well be sacrificed to practical convenience. If System B were adopted, no inconsistency would arise.

269. The answer to the question propounded in §261 should then, in my opinion, be that the m̐b, n̐d, n̐ḍ, n̐g of colloquial Sinhalese are best regarded as separate single phonemes, but that it is convenient to represent these phonemes by digraphs made up of letters representing other phonemes with or without the use of the diacritic ˇ. The case is analogous to that of diphthongs.

COMPOUND SOUNDS AND SIMPLE SOUNDS AS MEMBERS OF THE SAME PHONEME

270. The "stop" elements of plosives are "simple" sounds. Not unfrequently these occur as subsidiary members of plosive consonant phonemes. Thus the k-phoneme is represented by stop only in the common pronunciation of such English words as akt (act), 'lektʃə (lecture).

271. A stop may also be a member of an affricate consonant phoneme, but apparently this only occurs in the first part of a doubling ("lengthening," §§360 ff.): e.g. in Italian 'fattʃa (faccia), 'mɛddzo (mezzo), Hindustani bəcca (child), həɟɟam (barber).²⁴

272. An example of a simple consonant phoneme which has a compound consonant as a subsidiary member is found in Tamil. In that language the phoneme which it is convenient to denote by c has for its principal member a sound resembling the Polish ɕ. This is the sound used initially before all vowels except i, e.g. in col (word). Intervocalically it is commonly voiced; thus acai (shake) could be written narrowly aʑai. But initially before i, and medially when doubled, an affricate c is used: examples, cinam (anger), peːccu (talk). For further details, see J. R. FIRTH'S Short Outline of Tamil Pronunciation, pp. xi, xii, from which the above examples are taken.

---

²¹ Narrowly [kəranʈə]. Also pronounced with ḍ (kərannḍə in System A).
²² Narrowly [ankə].
²³ Narrowly [siŋhea].
²⁴ When two affricates follow each other in English, the first is fully pronounced. The case only arises in compound words such as 'wotʃtʃein (watch-chain). Repeated affricates are occasionally found in Russian, and then too the first is fully pronounced; example: 'tʃtʃetnij (тщетный, vain).

CHAPTER XVI

COLOURED VOWELS

273. Sets of vowels can be pronounced which differ from common vowels by having one or more special "colourings." The chief kinds of colourings are

(1) nasalization, when vowels are said with simultaneous lowering of the soft palate,

(2) r-colouring, when vowels are said with a quality reminiscent of a frictionless ɹ,

(3) breathiness, when vowels are "aitchified," i.e. pronounced with "husky" or "breathy" voice, due to the emission of more air than is needed for ordinary vowels,

(4) creakiness, when vowels are pronounced with "creaky" or "intermittent" voice produced by a pharyngal contraction somewhat like that used in forming the Arabic consonant ٩,

(5) sulcalization, when vowels are said with a "throaty" voice-quality due to sulcal tongue position (raising the sides of the back part of the tongue and leaving a groove down the centre).

All ordinary vowels can be said with any of the above modifications and with combinations of some of them.

274. Vowels with the first four of the above colourings are not uncommon in languages, and the distinction between the coloured vowels and ordinary vowels are often significant. Thus, as is well known, nasalized vowels occur with significant function in French, Polish, Portuguese, Hindustani, Gã and other languages. r-coloured vowels are found with significant function in various types of American and British English. Urdu and other languages of Northern India contain vowels said with breathy voice. So also do some languages of the Sudan. Vowels said with creaky voice occur in languages of the Sudan and (sometimes in conjunction with special tones) in Vietnamese and cognate languages. Sulcalized vowels are easy to make,[1] but I have not heard of any language in which they are used side by side with ordinary vowels for making significant distinctions.

---

[1] The old-fashioned Polish ł (i.e. not the common modern sound which is a variety of w) is a sulcal sound. It resembles a sulcalized u.

275. The clearest method of representing coloured vowels phonetically is by means of digraphs, i.e. by denoting each coloured vowel by the letter for the ordinary vowel followed by a letter indicating the colouring. Thus nasalized vowels can almost always be denoted unambiguously by vowel letters followed by ŋ,[2] r-coloured vowels by vowel letters followed by ɹ, aitchified vowels by vowel letters followed by h, and so on.

276. Deviations from the digraphic notation may be found convenient in particular cases. It is, for instance, convenient and economical to write the r-coloured ə of ordinary American English simply with ɹ instead of with the digraph əɹ: ɹθ (*earth*), bɹd (*bird*), 'stɹɪŋ (*stirring*)[3] rather than əɹθ, bəɹd, 'stəɹɪŋ. And if there were a language containing a single nasalized vowel with a basic quality distinct from all the other vowels of the language, it would probably suffice to represent it either by ŋ alone or by an appropriate vowel letter without any indication of nasality.

277. As coloured vowels are single sounds, it would be possible to represent them in writing by special letters or letters with diacritic marks. This has hitherto been the usual practice in regard to nasalized vowels: they have generally been written with ˜ above the letter denoting the ordinary vowel, thus: ã, ẽ.[4] Similar devices might be adopted for other coloured vowels. Thus letters like a̡, ə̡, ɤ[5] or a diacritic ˙ (a̒, ə̒, etc.)[6] may be used to denote r-coloured vowels, and diacritics such as superposed ' and ' to denote vowels with breathy voice and creaky voice. Except perhaps in the case of

---

[2] Unambiguously as far as the particular language transcribed is concerned. According to J. R. FIRTH, Marathi is an exception in which nasalization must be denoted by a letter other than ŋ. See JONES, *The Problem of a National Script for India*, p. 14, footnote 3.

[3] Cp. strɪŋ (*string*).

[4] PAUL PASSY, however, used the diagraphs ɛŋ, ɑŋ, ɔŋ, œŋ to denote the French nasalized vowels in the 1917 edition of his *Premier Livre de Lecture*. The same system is followed in the proposed new romanic orthography for Hindustani; see JONES, *The Problem of a National Script for India*. Ordinary French spelling uses the digraph system (with *n*), and it works on the whole satisfactorily. It would be completely unambiguous if the letter for nasalization were *ŋ* instead of *n*.

[5] See *Le Maître Phonétique*, Jan., 1947, pp. 16, 17.

[6] ˙ was used by R. J. LLOYD in his *Northern English*.

creaky voice I feel that the digraph system is the better mode of representation.[7]

278. The following are examples of words containing uncoloured vowels compared with similar words having vowels with various types of colouring:

(1) nasalized vowels: French pɑ (*pas*), pɑŋ (*paon*),[8] mɛs (*messe*), mɛŋs (*mince*)[8]; Hindustani həʊ (is), həʊŋ (are);

(2) r-coloured vowels: American English ˈmanə (*manna*), ˈmanɹ (*manner*); South-Western British English ˈfaːðɹ (*father*), ˈfaɹðɹ (*farther*);

(3) vowels with breathy voice: Hindustani ka (of), kah (grass), ʝa (go), ʝah (high rank), bəʊr (revenge), bəʊhr (sea), ɖoɽa (rope), ɖohɽa (wooden spoon), kora (new), kohra (fog), tera (curtain), tehra (threefold), ʈona (enchantment), ʈohna (feel); in the Abua language spoken at Ahoada, Southern Nigeria, doɣ (to be sweet), dohɣ (to speak a parable)[9]; in Nuer kɔm (chair), kɔhm (insect)[10];

(4) vowels with creaky voice: Vietnamese ˇbe (basin), ˈbe (broken), ˇzai (belt), ˈzai (saliva), ˇda (to knock), ˈda (sign of past tense).[11]

279. Vowels may have two colourings simultaneously. Examples are seen in the Hindustani words mɒŋh (mouth), siŋh (hedgehog), koŋhɽa (sweet pumpkin), meŋh (rain), pəɒŋhcna (to reach), in which the vowels are both nasalized and pronounced with breathy voice.

---

[7] Diacritic marks are known to be unsatisfactory from the point of view of legibility, handwriting and printing. See *The Practical Orthography of African Languages*, revised edition, pp. 4–6 (International African Institute). Letters with two diacritics are particularly objectionable. They would be needed if the diacritic system of indicating nasalization were applied to such a language as Panjabi which makes use of essential word-tones. See GRAHAME BAILEY's *Panjabi Phonetic Reader*.

[8] More usually written pɑ̃, mɛ̃ːs.

[9] Example furnished to me by Professor IDA WARD.

[10] Example taken from A. N. TUCKER's description of Nuer in WESTERMANN and WARD's *Practical Phonetics for Students of African Languages*, p. 204, where a number of other instances are given.

[11] Examples furnished to me by Miss E. HENDERSON. ˇ has been suggested by her to denote a rising tone accompanied by breathy voice, and ˈ to denote a rising tone accompanied by a creaky voice. (See §587.)

280. Coloured vowels must, according to the principles suggested in this book, constitute phonemes separate from ordinary vowels occurring in similar phonetic contexts in the same language. Thus I think it necessary to regard the Hindustani sounds u, uh, uŋ and uŋh as four separate phonemes.[12]

CHAPTER XVII

VOWELS AND CONSONANTS AS MEMBERS OF THE SAME PHONEME

281. A vowel and a consonant occasionally occur as members of the same phoneme. This is the case, for instance, with the French vowel y and the consonant ў (more usually written ɥ). In ordinary Parisian speech these sounds are not found in identical positions in words. ў occurs (1) initially preceding a vowel, (2) after any consonant or consonant-group when i follows, (3) after single consonants when other vowels follow. It is used, for instance, in (1) ўit (*huit*), (2) nўi (*nuit*), plўi (*pluie*), brўi (*bruit*), kɔ̄strўiːr (*construire*), (3) tўɛ (*tuait*), nўaːʒ (*nuage*), nўɑ̄ːs (*nuance*), kwatўɔːr (*quatuor*). On the other hand the vowel y does not occur in these positions; it never occurs before i, and it only occurs before other vowels if two consonants precede, as in kryɛl (*cruel*), kryote (*cruauté*), ɛ̄flyɑ̄ːs (*influence*).

282. It is to be noted that if word-groups were to be admitted into the criterion for establishing phonemes, y and ў would have to be assigned to separate phonemes in French, on account of

---

[12] Some of those interested in the theory of phonemes have expressed the opinion that "colourings" can be regarded as phonemes, so that, for instance, a nasalized vowel may be looked upon as a group of two phonemes, viz. the vowel and the nasalization. It does not appear to me possible to maintain such a theory. One might as well treat as phonemes many other features of speech which are common to several sounds, such as voicing, dental and other articulations of consonants, lip-rounding of vowels. (One colleague has indeed suggested to me that the implosive character of the Sindhi voiced implosives should be regarded as a phoneme.) Such a view would involve an entirely different conception of the phoneme from that put forward in this book, and one which I think would have little practical value even if it could be worked out into a consistent system.

comparisons such as ty̆a *(tua)*, tya *(tu as)*. See §34, also *Some Thoughts on the Phoneme*,[1] p. 129.

283. For reasons similar to those given in §281, u and w appear to belong to one phoneme in one type of French. In this type w occurs to the exclusion of u initially, as in wi *(oui)*, wɛst *(ouest)*, wa *(oie)*, and after single consonants, as in lwe *(louer)*, mwa *(moi)*, but u is used to the exclusion of w after two consonants in such words as bruɛt *(brouette)*, klue *(clouer)*.

284. This type of French is that of speakers who make no difference in sound between pairs of words like *voua* and *voit*, *joua* and *joie* (vwa, ʒwa). There are, however, many Frenchmen who distinguish them as vua, vwa, ʒua, ʒwa. With them w is a phoneme separate from u. The same is true of those who use the sequence ua in various proper names such as *Touareg* (pronouncing tuarɛg and not twarɛg),[2] if it is considered impracticable to exclude proper names from the material required for phonemic analysis (§229).

285. The case of French i and j is different. These sounds must be considered as belonging to separate phonemes on account of the occurrence of j in final position: compare trai *(trahi)*, travaj *(travail)*.[3]

286. It would seem that in Italian the gliding consonant j must belong to the same phoneme as the vowel i. The controlling principles are not entirely clear, and probably vary from one speaker to another, but it seems likely that with many Italians the phoneme appears as j when it is weakly stressed, is followed by a vowel and is not preceded by r or certain consonantal groups, such as kl. Examples where the sound is j: jɛri *(ieri,* yesterday), 'pajo *(paio,* pair), 'sjamo *(siamo,* we are), i'talja *(Italia,* Italy), ita'ljano *(italiano,* Italian). Examples where the sound appears to be usually syllabic i, in spite of the weak stress: ori'ɔlo *(oriolo,* watch), 'prɔprio *(proprio,* one's own), riuʃ'ʃita *(riuscita,* success), kli'ɛnte *(cliente,* client),

---

[1] In the *Transactions of the Philological Society*, 1944.

[2] These speakers may be the same as those who distinguish *voua* from *voit*. The matter does not appear to have been investigated.

[3] It might be possible to make out a case for assigning i and j to the same phoneme in French on the ground of relations between the sound used and the incidence of the strong stress or the nature of the intonation. The conventions would, however, be difficult to formulate and inconvenient to work with in practice.

probably also 'grattsie (*grazie*, thanks), diskussi'one (*discussione*, discussion), inkwi'eto (*inquieto*, anxious). Similar considerations probably apply to Italian w.

287. It will be noticed that the use of *i* and *u* in ordinary Italian spelling conforms to this phonemic classification.

288. It is possible that in some types of German too the consonant j should be held to be a member of the i-phoneme on similar grounds. TRUBETZKOY was of this opinion.[4] He did not, however, give the evidence for his conclusion, and I am not at present able to produce conclusive arguments for or against the theory.

289. Certain details of transcription depend upon what is considered to be the phonemic status of j in such a language as Italian. If j is held to belong to the i-phoneme, and is therefore written broadly with the letter i, some indication must be given that it is weakly stressed as compared with the vowel following it. The transcription ita'liano, for instance, would be ambiguous: it might mean [ita'lja:no] or the non-existent [ita'li:ano]. Probably the best system is to retain the letter j; another plan would be to write ĭ in the relevant cases. In words like *discussione*, where usage is variable or doubtful, the position of the stress-mark would be a matter for consideration: one might write either diskussi'one or diskus'sjone.

290. Sounds so different as i and z occasionally occur as members of the same phoneme. This is found in Cantonese and other types of Chinese, where the i-phoneme following s has the value of a kind of z. Examples from Cantonese are ⁻si [narrowly ⁻sz] (four), ⁻tsi [⁻tsz] (most), ˌtshi [ˌtshz] (later).

CHAPTER XVIII
MANNER OF USE AS A CRITERION

291. Sometimes the manner of using a sound has to be taken into account in settling its phonetic status. A particular manner of use may on occasion render it necessary to class a sound as a separate phoneme, or to group it phonemically with another sound having the same manner of use, and to disconnect it from the same sound when used in a different manner. In other terms, identity

---

[4] *Grundzüge der Phonologie*, p. 64, footnote (in CANTINEAU's translation, p. 74).

in manner of use occasionally forms a stronger bond than phonic identity.

292. This appears to be the case with the Japanese syllabic ṃ, ṇ and ŋ̇.[1] These syllabic sounds occur in Japanese only before homorganic consonants. Thus, syllabic ṃ occurs only before p, b and non-syllabic m; examples: saṃpo (walking), siṃbuŋ (newspaper), seṃmoŋ (speciality). Syllabic ŋ̇ occurs only before k and non-syllabic ŋ, and exceptionally before -g in the word -go (five) (which is always treated phonetically as a separate word); examples: deŋ̇ki (electric power), saŋ̇ŋai (third storey), oŋ̇ŋaku (music), saŋ̇-go (three times five). Syllabic ṇ occurs only before consonants other than the above, including non-syllabic n; examples: seṇdo: (boatman), kaṇdjo: (account), koṇnaŋ (confusion), oṇna (woman). Non-syllabic m, n, ŋ occur only before vowels, as in nomu (drink), [kaŋo] (basket).[2]

293. It is natural to a Japanese to regard the syllabic ṃ, ṇ, ŋ̇ as being all "the same sound"—that their syllabic use (which involves a certain length and a lack of "off-glide") connects them with each other, and that they have, to a Japanese, more resemblance to each other than they have to the non-syllabic m, n, ŋ (which are short and pronounced with off-glide). A Japanese does not apparently look upon the syllabic ṃ of saṃpo as having any particular relation to the non-syllabic m of say samasu (cool); he considers it to be "the same sound" as the ṇ of seṇdo: and the ŋ̇ of deŋ̇ki.

294. He also finds it natural to identify these three syllabic sounds with their final nasal sound ŋ, which is heard in such words as saŋ (three), keŋ (prefecture).[3] Syllabic ṃ is to him "a kind

---

[1] A "syllabic" consonant is one that is used in the way that vowels generally are. It is made prominent (§§434, 435) enough to be reckoned in counting the number of syllables in a word or sentence. In most situations it gets its syllabic character by being pronounced with greater length than non-syllabic consonants. The Japanese syllabic consonants occupy approximately the same length of time as ordinary syllables which consist of a non-syllabic consonant plus a vowel.

[2] Non-syllabic ŋ may be a member of the g-phoneme in some forms of Japanese (see §122). It is not used by all speakers; some use g instead, and pronounce the word for "basket" as kago.

[3] The sound here written with ŋ is a peculiar nasal sound which appears to vary between ŋ and ỹ, and which involves partial or sometimes complete nasalization of the preceding vowel. It is written (adequately) with n in romanic orthography.

of ŋ," and not "a kind of m"; syllabic ṇ is likewise to him "a kind
of ŋ" (not "a kind of n"), and syllabic ŋ̍ is to him "a kind of ŋ"
(not "a kind of ŋ or g" nor a separate phoneme).[4]

295. Two phonemic classifications of the Japanese nasal sounds
are therefore possible. The first, which seems more natural from
the European standpoint, is to regard syllabic m̩, ṇ, ŋ̍ as members
of the m, n, g phonemes respectively, and to regard ŋ as a separate
phoneme. The second, which for some not easily definable reason
appears more natural to a Japanese, is to regard ŋ together with
syllabic m̩, ṇ and ŋ̍ as constituting one phoneme, and the non-
syllabic m, n, ŋ as belonging to phonemes separate from this.
Presumably one should accept in preference the Japanese viewpoint. A broad transcription of Japanese on this basis would
therefore require that we should write saŋpo, siŋbuŋ, seŋmoŋ,
seŋdo:, etc. For symbol economy n may be substituted for ŋ; this
gives the spelling used in the Kunreisiki Rōmazi orthography.

296. The expression "related in character" (§§31–33) has thus
to be taken occasionally to include "related in manner of use."

297. Manner of use must, I think, be advanced as the chief
reason for regarding the Parisian French ə ("e mute") as a phoneme
separate from œ, if indeed ə can be considered to be a phoneme
at all in that language.[5] The function of ə in Parisian speech is
a peculiar one. The sound appears to be merely a vocalic noise
which speakers insert here and there in order to prevent the
occurrence of certain sequences of consonants alien to their manner
of speaking. It is immaterial to the sense of all ordinary words
whether an ə is inserted at the place appropriate to it, or whether
it is omitted. This vowel is thus used in a different way from
other vowels. If a word said in isolation contains ə, that ə is often

---

[4] His identification of these sounds receives a certain support from the fact
that words compounded with a word ending in -ŋ have a pronunciation with
m̩, ṇ or ŋ̍ according to circumstances: compare saŋ (three), sampondo (three
pounds), sambeŋ (three times), sambjaku (three hundred), saṇdo (three
times), saŋkiro (three kilos). This consideration is, however, not conclusive,
since one must always make allowance for the possibility that the formation
of compound words may involve a change of phoneme.

[5] The remarks in this and the following paragraphs do not apply to types
of French in which all final "e mutes" are sounded as ə, e.g. where bout and
boue are distinguished as bu and buə. They probably apply to types of French
in which bout and boue are distinguished by length (bu, bu:).

omitted in connected speech, generally in accordance with rather complicated principles.[6] Moreover, the conditions under which ə is inserted or omitted differ in different parts of France and French-speaking Switzerland.

298. Proper names form exceptions. In them the sound ə is more stable than in ordinary words, and it seems to be this fact alone that causes ə to constitute a "speech-sound" of Parisian French. If it were not for the proper names, I doubt if it would be possible to regard the ə of Parisian French as a phoneme any more than we can regard the common sound ʔ as a phoneme of ordinary English.[7] The ʔ of ordinary English and the ə of ordinary words of Parisian French are so to speak accidental sounds. The ʔ of English is a sign of word separation, or is prefixed to vowels to give them emphasis; its presence or absence cannot affect the meaning of a word. The presence or absence of ə in ordinary Parisian French words is largely determined by the sound of neighbouring words in connected speech, and is not essential for the intelligibility of the word containing it. In proper names, however, its presence may be necessary to intelligibility. I do not know of any pair of words differing solely by the presence or absence of ə,[8] but a case like **kartərɛ** (*Carteret*) and **ekartrɛ** (*écarterait*) or **pɔrtrɛ** (*portrait*, *porterait*) suffices to show that such a distinction is a possible one.[9]

299. The quality of the noise which we are here representing by ə is intermediate between the French vowels ø and œ. Its precise value varies somewhat from speaker to speaker and to

---

[6] These are formulated in various books on the phonetics of French. See for instance ARMSTRONG'S *Phonetics of French*, Chapter XX.

[7] I refer here to the types of English usually described in books on phonetics. There are other types in which ʔ is an essential sound, "replacing" the t of **ˈlitl** (*little*), etc.; in these types it either constitutes a phoneme or is a member of the t-phoneme.

[8] Unless we take into account the exceptional word **dəɔːr** (*dehors*). It may, however, be held that this word contains a kind of h, or that its first vowel is a variety of ø or of œ. The case of **sərɛ̃** (*serein*, serene) and **srɛ̃** (*serin*, stupid person) is probably also inadmissible, since **sərɛ̃** belongs to formal speech and **srɛ̃** to the colloquial language.

[9] The proof afforded by this name is not absolutely conclusive. The sound of **kartərɛ** is hardly to be distinguished from **kartœrɛ**, so that it might reasonably be maintained that the sound used in this word is œ. I think it likely, however, that other proper names containing an undoubted ə exist which would demonstrate the proposition.

some extent according to phonetic context; it is, for instance, nearer to œ after r (ʀ) as in prəmje (*premier*), otrəmã (*autrement*), and nearer to ø in various other combinations, e.g. in bəzwɛ̃ (*besoin*), nəvø (*neveu*). The difference between ə and ø may be considered to be significant, though the conditions under which comparable contexts are found are always of a rather special nature: either the contexts are in word-groups, which strictly speaking do not count for the purposes of phonemic classification,[10] e.g. ʒə kuːr (*je cours*), ʒø kuːr (*jeu court*), or the distinction is helped out by the greater length of the ø, e.g. ʒənɛ (*genêt*), ʒønɛ (*jeûnait*). The difference between ə and œ is also supposed to be significant, but it is difficult to find examples, and such examples as there are are not conclusive. səlɛ (*celait*) and sœlɛ (*seulet*) are supposed to be pronounced differently, but the difference when any is made is slight, and it is certain that these rare words would be recognized in sentences by the verbal context and not by the difference of vowel. Other examples may be found in word-groups, which, as already mentioned, do not provide good evidence for phonemic grouping (§34). nəvø (*neveu*) is distinct from nœv ø (*neuf œufs*) and lə rtuːr (*le retour*) is supposed to differ in sound from lœr tuːr (*leur tour*).[11]

300.   The French sound ə is thus too near both to ø and to œ to be capable of effecting significant word distinctions by ordinary interchange with them.   In other terms, if ə were looked upon as an ordinary vowel, it could not be considered as a phoneme separate from both of these; it would have to be attached to one of them— presumably to œ.   In view of the special circumstances, and in particular of the facts that (1) ə is functionally different from ordinary vowels, and (2) though ə resembles œ in sound it cannot be grouped into the same phoneme as œ on·account of its particular manner of use·(§297), I think we are justified in calling it a phoneme for the reason given in §298.

301.   It has been suggested that the syllabic use of certain consonants in English and in colloquial German is a phonemic phenomenon, and that such "syllabic use" should be held to belong

---

[10] §§31, 34.

[11] This latter example is quoted from PASSY (*Les Sons du Français*, 7th and subsequent editions, §254).   Whether most Parisian speakers make any difference between these two sequences is doubtful.

to the same phoneme as short ə. Such a view may perhaps be upheld if a phoneme is taken to be an ideal or abstract sound (§20 and Chap. XXIX). On this hypothesis one may say that the abstract ə is manifested concretely as ə in such words as ˈbrekfəst (*breakfast*), ˈbulək (*bullock*), ˈmeθəd (*method*), but that its concrete manifestation takes the form of "syllabic use" in words like ˈmʌtn̩ (*mutton*), ˈpedl̩ (*pedal*).[12] Stated otherwise, the speaker "thinks" ˈmʌtən and ˈpedəl but utters ˈmʌtn̩ and ˈpedl̩. But I do not think the syllabic manner of using such consonants can be said to belong to a phoneme if the phoneme is defined in a physical way as in §31. Objectively, words like ˈmʌtn̩, ˈpedl̩ merely contain n's and l's which are somewhat longer than most non-syllabic n's and l's and which receive intonations in the same way that vowels do.[13]

CHAPTER XIX

THE OVERLAPPING OF PHONEMES

302. There may be rare cases where two phonemes contain a particular sound as a subsidiary member; the phonemes would be said in such a case to "overlap" or to "intersect." Two types of phonemic overlapping may be possible. The first would be when the common sound belongs to one phoneme in one context and to the other phoneme in a different context. The second type is when a sound occurring in one particular context may be assigned to either of two phonemes.

OVERLAPPING IN DIFFERENT CONTEXTS

303. When two phonemes comprise members differing considerably from each other, it may happen that a member of one of them used in one context is near to or possibly identical with a member of the other used in some other context.

304. This type of phonemic overlapping can generally be illustrated by means of diagrams. It will be recalled, for instance,

---

[12] The syllabic mark is generally omitted in simple transcriptions.

[13] TRUBETZKOY and others have regarded such syllabic consonants as "realizations of the phoneme sequences ən, əl" (*Grundzüge der Phonologie*, p. 56, CANTINEAU's translation, p. 64). See also G. L. TRAGER's article on *The Transcription of English* in *Le Maître Phonétique*, Jan., 1935, p. 12.

that the various members of a vowel phoneme may often be visualized as lying within an "area" in a two-dimensional vowel figure, as shown, for example, in Figure 2.   With most languages the "areas" corresponding to each vowel phoneme are fairly small and are separated from each other by relatively wide spaces.   Thus the vowel phonemes of Spanish lie in small "areas" like those shown in Figure 7, which indicates that no member of the a-phoneme is near to any member of the e-phoneme, and so on.   Where, however, the areas are large, it may happen that they overlap.

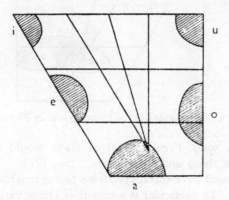

FIG. 7. Areas of the Spanish Vowel Phonemes.

305.   Such overlapping may be observed in the ɔ and œ phonemes of many Northern French people.   The "areas" covered by the phonemes used by such speakers are approximately as shown in Figure 8.   The backest member of the ɔ-phoneme is the one used before r followed by another consonant, as in pɔrt (*porte*).   A fairly back one is used before r only, as in kɔːr (*corps*).   Fronter members occur in other situations, e.g. in ɔm (*homme*), bɔn (*bonne*), etɔf (*étoffe*), klɔʃ (*cloche*).[1]   Retracted varieties of œ are heard when r precedes or follows, as in œrt (*heurte*), kœːr (*cœur*), ˈrœfeːr[2] (*refaire*), while fronter varieties occur in such words as ʒœn (*jeune*), œf (*œuf*), vœl (*veulent*).

306.   It will be seen from Figure 8 that the frontest French ɔ resembles the backest œ—that the vowel sounds in œrt and

---

[1] The frontness of the ɔ in such words is the cause of considerable difficulty in the acquisition of the pronunciation of such words by English learners.

[2] Emphatic form of rəˈfeːr.

klɔʃ, for instance, are very near to each other. The two areas overlap, and a detailed examination of all the distinguishable variants in each phoneme might well reveal at least one sound common to both of them.[3] (See also §309.)

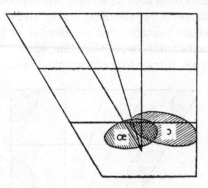

FIG. 8. Overlapping of the French ɔ and œ Phonemes.

307. With some French speakers there would appear to be overlapping of the **e** and **ɛ** phonemes. (See §215.) The shades of vowel sound used have certain relations to the neighbouring sounds in the words. In particular it seems that closer varieties are used by many before **s** and **t**, especially when these are followed in turn by **e** or **i**, and that opener varieties are used before **r**. Thus the **e** of **presi** (*précis*) is closer than that of **ero** (*héros*), and the **ɛ** of **ɛkski** (*exquis*) is closer than those in **sɛrvo** (*cerveau*) and **ɛrœːr** (*erreur*). Consequently there is little difference between the closest variety of **ɛ** and the openest variety of **e**. In fact it is probable that in the pronunciation of many, these sounds are identical, or that the closest **ɛ** is even higher than the openest **e**, e.g. that the

[3] It does not appear possible to connect the forms **ʒœli** and **apsœly**, which are so often heard in the North of France as alternatives to **ʒɔli** and **apsɔly**, with phonemic classification or with the overlapping of the French ɔ and œ phonemes. If, as is generally assumed, **ʒœli** and **apsœly** are modern pronunciations of *joli* and *absolu* replacing older forms with ɔ, they are merely examples of the replacement of one phoneme by another in the course of historical development (see §710). Why this change has been made is not clear. Vowel harmony has been suggested as an explanation, but this theory is not borne out by the pronunciation of other words which usually have ɔ in analogous positions, e.g. **pɔsibl** (*possible*), **pɔli** (*poli*), **ɔfis** (*office*), **mɔdifje** (*modifier*).

ε of εkski may be identical with or even closer than the e of ero. (See further, §312.)

308. In Russian there is probably a certain overlapping of the e and a phonemes. Both these phonemes cover considerable "areas." The e-phoneme has members ranging from about cardinal e (between two soft consonants, as in pjetj (петь, to sing)) to a very open and somewhat retracted sound well below cardinal ε (initially or preceded by ʃ or ʒ and followed by a hard consonant, as in 'etat (этот, this), 'ʒertva (жертва, victim)). The a-phoneme has members ranging on the outside of the vowel figure from a raised front a which might be denoted narrowly by a˔ or æ (between soft consonants as in pjatj (пять, five)) and a very back ɑ (preceded by a hard consonant and followed by l, as in 'palka (палка, stick)). In addition there are ə-like variants used in weakly stressed positions. There is thus in all probability an overlapping of the type shown in Figure 9.

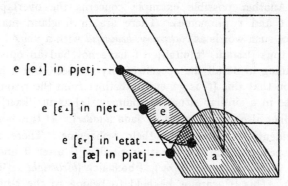

e [e˔] in pjetj
e [ε˔] in njet
e [εʳ] in 'etat
a [æ] in pjatj

FIG. 9. Overlapping of the Russian e and a Phonemes.

309. Overlapping of the type described in the preceding paragraphs does not interfere with phonemic grouping. The grouping presents no difficulty so long as the necessary degree of acoustic separation between phonemes occupying neighbouring "areas" is maintained in each phonetic context. In French, for instance, ɔ and œ are clearly distinguished in any given context: kɔːr (*corps*) is distinct from kœːr (*cœur*), and the ɔ's in vɔl (*vol*), etɔf (*étoffe*) are equally distinct from the œ's in vœl (*veulent*), œf (*œuf*). Similarly, in the pronunciation of those referred to in §307, the

low "e moyen" and the low "ɛ ouvert" are distinct from each other in ero (*héros*) and ɛrœːr (*erreur*), while the higher "e moyen" and the higher "ɛ ouvert" are equally distinct from each other in presi (*précis*) and prɛse (*presser*) and in ɛ̃besil (*imbécile*) and vɛstjɛːr (*vestiaire*). So too in Russian the distinction between the vowels in pjetj and pjatj is a very wide one, and the distinction between those in 'etat and sat (сад, garden) is equally so. The similarity between the French sounds in œrt and klɔʃ or between the Russian e of 'etat and the a of pjatj is immaterial to the phonemic analysis.

310. Overlapping of the type we have been considering is uncommon in consonants, and I am at present unable to quote any certain examples. It is, however, possible that overlappings of q and k might be found in languages containing q and ɯ. In such a language it would not be surprising to find that the q of the syllable qi had about the same articulation as the k of the syllable kɯ.

311. Another possible example concerns the overlapping of English t and r phonemes. There are in England many who pronounce such words as *Saturday*, *beautiful* with a voiced alveolar flap [ɾ], thus ['saɾədi, 'bjuːɾəfl]. I have not had an opportunity of examining in detail the speech of any of these, but I have the impression that this [ɾ] is generally distinct from the r-sound they would use in a similar situation, namely, [ɹ] as in ['kaɹi] (*carry*), and distinct also from their d in 'ladə (*ladder*). If this is so, their [ɾ] is evidently assignable to their t-phoneme. There are also English speakers who use a rather similar [ɾ] after θ and ð, i.e. in such words as [θɾiː] (*three*), ['bəːθɾait] (*birthright*), ['breðɾin] (*brethren*). This [ɾ] cannot be held to belong to the t-phoneme, because the sequence θt is a possible one[4]; nor can it be attached to the d-phoneme, since θd and ðd are also possible sequences.[5] The sound can therefore only belong to the r-phoneme, since the [ɹ] of other contexts is excluded from use after θ and ð.[6] If, as

---

[4] It is uncommon, but it is found in bəːθt (*berthed*) and əːθt (*earthed*) and in proper names like 'hiːθtən (*Heathton*), 'smiθtən (*Smithton*).

[5] They occur, for instance, in 'bəːθdei (*birthday*), beiðd (*bathed*), wiðˈdroː (*withdraw*).

[6] I refer here to those whose normal r-sound is [ɹ], and who use this in such words as ['kaɹi] (*carry*), ['veɹi] (*very*). What is said here does not apply to those who use [ɾ] in these words.

is possible, there are speakers who combine the two above-mentioned forms of pronunciation, their t and r phonemes would overlap in the sound ɾ.[7]

312.   The fact that the same sounds or two very similar sounds may occur in different phonetic contexts where there is overlapping does not mean that they should be written in phonetic transcription with the same letter.   On the contrary two separate letters should be used to distinguish the phonemes even if the sounds are barely distinguishable.   The values to be attached to the letters in phonetic transcriptions are not absolute but must always be interpreted in the light of the phonetic context.   Thus it may happen that in particular cases in the transcription of French the letter ε may have to denote a sound very similar to or even closer than that represented by e under other conditions.   (See §307.)

313.   It is possible to have overlapping of members within a phoneme.   Thus the l-phoneme of Southern English is usually represented as consisting of two important members, a "clear" l and a "dark" (velarized) l, which are used in the contexts described in §71.   There exist, however, shades of these.   When a clear l precedes a back vowel, the variety used is less clear than when a front vowel follows.   And similarly a dark l following a front vowel is less velarized than a final syllabic l or a dark l following a back vowel.   Thus with many speakers the l in lo: (*law*) is much less clear than that in li:f (*leaf*), while the dark l in bild (*build*)

---

[7] My attention was first called to the possibility of the overlapping of t and r phonemes by BERNARD BLOCH's article on *Phonemic Overlapping* in *American Speech*, December, 1941, p. 278.   At the time when BLOCH wrote the article he thought he had found instances of this overlapping in a certain type of Mid-Western American English.   He wrote to me, however, in September, 1942, saying that he had found it necessary to change his view, and that he considers the two ɾ's in cases such as those above-mentioned not to be identical.   And as I too have not actually found anyone whose speech exhibits the combination of the two features above referred to, it cannot be claimed that the example is a convincing one, though there remains the possibility that the case may be found to exist.

BLOCH also told me that he had come to the conclusion that "overlapping' of phonemes is everywhere and under all conditions inadmissible."   It must be conceded that it is difficult, and perhaps even impossible, to prove that two sounds occurring in different phonetic contexts are "identical."   Nevertheless, in the present state of our knowledge I hardly think it possible yet to maintain such a generalization with complete confidence.

is less velarized than those in **'dʌbl** (*double*) and **skuːl** (*school*).
Hence with some there is an overlapping, by which the clear **l**
in **loː** is about identical with the dark **l** in **bild**. This is the case in
my pronunciation. And I think it likely that some Southern
English speakers could be found whose **l** in **bild** was definitely less
velarized than their **l** in **loː**.

Overlapping in the Same Context

314. When a sound occurs in a certain phonetic context to
the exclusion of two nearly related sounds, it is possible, though
not necessarily suitable, to assign it to the phoneme of one of the
related sounds in some words and to that of the other related sound
in other words. If this course is adopted, the two phonemes
overlap, and the sound in question is shared between them. There
is some doubt as to whether this procedure is ever justifiable. The
question is discussed in §§321 ff., and examples are given there of
cases in which "di-phonemic" treatment of a sound might possibly
be resorted to.

CHAPTER XX

DI-PHONEMIC SOUNDS

315. Where there is no "overlapping" of the first type, as
described in §§303–311, it must I think be taken as axiomatic
that in all ordinary circumstances a given sound cannot belong
to more than one phoneme of a language.[1] Very rarely, however,

---

[1] I have heard it suggested by one phonologist that the phoneme should
be so defined as to allow **ŋ** to belong to the **n**-phoneme *in the English word*
iŋk, though admitting it to be a separate phoneme in such a word as **siŋ**.
The admission of such a possibility would, in my view, render the whole
phoneme theory unworkable. For if **ŋ** can belong to the **n**-phoneme in
words like **iŋk**, but not in words like **siŋ**, then **m** might with equal right
be classed as a member of the **n**-phoneme in words like **lamp**, though not
in words like **ham**. Or we might, with equal right, reverse matters and
assign the **m** of **lamp** and the **n** of **end** to the **ŋ**-phoneme. Moreover, on
the same principle, we might regard **s** as belonging to the **z**-phoneme in
stand and in **boks** (*box*), on the ground that **z** cannot occur in such situations.
It might likewise be maintained in French that the **g** of **anɛgdɔt** (*anecdote*)
should be assigned to the **k**-phoneme, on the ground that **k** does not exist
before **g** in the speech of those who pronounce in this way. And so forth.

I believe it would not be feasible to invent a definition of a phoneme which
would allow for such possibilities.

instances may occur where a certain justification can be found for assigning a sound to two phonemes. These exceptional cases are where strict adherence to the ordinary principles of phonemic grouping would lead to inconvenience in morphology, or would obscure unnecessarily the relationships between words.

316. If a sound is assigned to two phonemes, it may be termed "di-phonemic."

317. The cases of di-phonemic sounds fall under two heads: (1) when a sound occurs "incidentally" as well as "expressly," and (2) when there are equally good reasons for assigning a sound to either of two phonemes. In both cases the assignment of a sound to two phonemes should not be made without the strongest possible morphological or other grounds. If great care is not exercised we may easily find ourselves faced with impossible proposals such as those mentioned in footnote 1 to §315.

SOUNDS OCCURRING "INCIDENTALLY" AS WELL AS "EXPRESSLY"

318. The nasalized vowels of some Indian languages should, I believe, be regarded as di-phonemic on the ground that they occur incidentally as well as expressly. The Hindustani sound ẽ is a case in point. In this language vowels are regularly nasalized when a nasal consonant precedes. Thus the agentive suffix commonly written *ne* is usually pronounced nẽ, though Indians are not as a rule aware of the fact; they think they pronounce ne, and the pronunciation ne would be accepted as correct. The nasalization is "incidental." The sound ẽ occurs also "expressly" as a phoneme separate from e. It generally occurs after non-nasal consonants, e.g. in pẽ (singing), ghẽṭ (throat), ḍẽgi (boat). But it sometimes occurs "expressly" after a nasal consonant; it does so, for instance, in the word mẽ (in), and in the case of this word a Hindustani-speaking Indian will not accept me as a correct substitute.

319. It therefore seems advisable in Hindustani to assign the sound ẽ to the e-phoneme in some words where a nasal consonant precedes, but not in others. The words in which this treatment is necessary can often be recognized by analogy (as when the sound denotes the suffix -e and not the suffix -ẽ), or they may be ascertained by asking a Hindustani-speaking Indian to pronounce slowly, in

which case the incidental nasalization is with some speakers not complete. Essential nasalization is moreover shown in Indian writing.[2]

320. It seems that cases of a similar kind are to be found in various languages of West Africa. Thus, according to WESTER-MANN, the Ewe word ma (not) is indistinguishable in sound from mã (to divide); but in ma (not) the nasalization is incidental, whereas in mã (to divide) it is essential. In slow speaking the words would be distinguished. For this reason we may be justified in assigning the "incidentally nasalized" a to the a-phoneme. It must, however, be borne in mind that such a reason is only adduced for practical convenience; what is done in slow speech or any particular variety of speaking has in reality nothing to do with the phonemes of other styles of speaking.

SOUNDS ASSIGNABLE TO EITHER OF TWO PHONEMES

321. If a case were found in which there were equally good reasons for assigning a sound to either of two phonemes, an arbitrary classification would have to be made. There would be three possible solutions to the problem presented in such an event. (1) The sound might be assigned to one of the two phonemes chosen at random, (2) the sound might be treated as a separate phoneme independent of the other two phonemes, (3) the sound might be treated as di-phonemic, i.e. assigned to one phoneme in some words and the other phoneme in other words.

322. The first solution would no doubt be the better one, even if no grounds could be found for preferring one of the phonemes to the other. The second should, I think, be dismissed as un-practical; it would involve introducing an unnecessary letter into broad transcriptions. The third plan could not be justified on phonetic grounds, but it might be found to have a certain practical convenience from the linguistic point of view. It would involve taking into consideration external facts unconnected with the idea of the phoneme. Such are the history of the sounds, the sounds of related dialects, analogy, grammatical relationships and perhaps even conventional writing.

---

[2] It is noteworthy that the Hindustani word ma (*mother*) has a recognized variant form mã with essential nasalization.

323. Some difficulties in phonemic classification, possibly involving di-phonemic treatment of some sounds of Pekingese, were suggested in §196.

324. I had hoped also to be able to illustrate di-phonemicism by examples from Japanese. But on enquiry it seems that convincing examples are difficult or perhaps impossible to find, although the language presents several features suggesting that such treatment may be appropriate. The pronunciation, and therefore the phonemic system, has been undergoing a number of changes in recent years: I have been informed for instance that the syllable du [narrowly dzu] is no longer in general use, but has been replaced very commonly by the syllable zu. New sounds are coming into use owing to borrowing or tendencies to acclimatize foreign words (with their foreign sounds). Words which might at one time have served as examples have gone out of use. The Kana syllabic writing has been altered in some respects, so also have the newer systems of romanic writing. It looks as if such changes in the written and spoken languages are going to continue, so that anything one may say now about the phonetic or the phonemic systems of Japanese is likely to become out of date before long. One cannot illustrate phonemic phenomena in a language which is in such a changeable state.

325. To illustrate possible di-phonemicism in language I will therefore give now a simple hypothetical example suggested by Japanese. Let us suppose that a language exists in which every syllable is composed of a consonant followed by one of five vowels [i, e, a, o, u], and that among the consonants are a [d], a [z] and an affricate [dz], and that these sounds are used according to the following system:

[d] occurs solely before [i], [e], [a] and [o] (with almost imperceptible variants according to the vowel),

[z] occurs solely before the same vowels (also with almost imperceptible variants according to the vowel),

[dz] occurs solely before [u].

326. In this hypothetical language the [d] and [z] sounds obviously belong to separate phonemes, which we may call the d-phoneme and the z-phoneme. As the sound [dz] occurs only in a phonetic context from which [d]-sounds and [z]-sounds are excluded, it does not "constitute" a phoneme separate from these, but it must be grouped either into the d-phoneme or into the z-phoneme, or perhaps di-phonemically into both. And as the nature of the sound [dz] can be such that there are no phonetic grounds why it should belong to one rather than to the other, we may find ourselves in the position of having to "allocate" it suitably.

327. It is in this sort of case that it may be considered justifiable or even advisable to settle the allocation by taking into account non-phonetic criteria such as those suggested in §322.

328. A historical possibility might be that at one period in the history of the hypothetical language the syllable [dzu] was non-existent, but that some of the words now containing it used to be pronounced with [zu] while others used to be pronounced with [du].   A change of pronunciation subsequently took place by which the [zu] and [du] fell together and both came to be replaced by the analogous syllable [dzu]. Such a development might well leave a tradition (possibly supported by archaic writing) that [dz] had a relationship with [z] in some words and with [d] in others. This tradition might well be sufficient to suggest that the present day [dz] should be treated di-phonemically, i.e. assigned to the z-phoneme in some words and to the d-phoneme in others.

329. I have been informed by a Japanese scholar that a development of this type is believed to have occurred in the Japanese language.

329 (a). If there should exist present day dialects of the hypothetical language in which the syllable [dzu] does not occur, but the words containing [dzu] in the standard language fall into two categories, one set of words being said with [zu] in the corresponding words of those dialects, and the remainder having [du] in the same dialects, it would no doubt be advisable to treat the dzu of the standard language di-phonemically in a manner corresponding to the dialectal forms.

329 (*b*). It appears that examples of this type are to be found in Japanese. I have been informed, for instance, that the two words [midzu] of standard Japanese (meaning "water"and "not see" respectively) are distinguished as [midu] and [mizu] respectively in dialectal speech of Shikoku where the sound [dz] does not occur. (These two words also differ in tone: midzu [.·] (water) but midzu [·.] (not see).)

329 (*c*). If there were to exist as cognates to words containing [dzu] words having [z] or [d] with vowels other than [u], it would no doubt be found advantageous to assign to the z-phoneme those [dz]-sounds which have cognates with [z], and to the d-phoneme those which have cognates with [d]. There would be no phonetically valid reason for such allocations. They would, however, afford a means of distinguishing some of the homophones in a practical orthography for the language.

329 (*d*). The following are examples of this procedure which may possibly apply to some Japanese. In [kadzu] (number)[3] it is desirable to assign the [dz] to the z-phoneme, since the word is cognate with kazoeru (to count). On the other hand it might be considered advisable to assign the [dz] of the classical verb [idzuru] (go out) to the d-phoneme on account of its kinship with the corresponding colloquial deru.

330. The following is probably an example from substandard Japanese which may be treated as a case of di-phonemicism. In this dialectal form of speech there exists a consonant of the [ɕ]-type which occurs before [i] to the exclusion of the [h] of standard Tokyo pronunciation (which is a weak variety of [ç]) and also to the exclusion of [s].[4] If anyone desired to make a phonemic transcription of this dialectal form of speech, this [ɕ] might be assigned

---

[3] Referring to the speech of such Japanese as there may be who pronounce [kadzu] consistently with [dz] and do not use a variphone (Chap. XXVIII) comprising [z].

[4] This pronunciation is common "in the popular speech of the Kantō [Tokyo, etc.] region, and probably beyond it" (H. E. PALMER, *Principles of Romanization*, p. 85). It accounts for the difficulty that many Japanese have in distinguishing *he* from *she* when learning to speak English.

to the h-phoneme or to the s-phoneme, or alternatively for an external reason the unusual course might be followed of treating the sound di-phonemically, allocating it to the h-phoneme in some words and to the [s]-phoneme in others.

331. The "external reason" would be that the speech of those who confuse [h] and [s]-sounds is not considered good by the education authorities, and the modern official writing distinguishes the two sounds by separate symbols.

332. It has been suggested that the Russian sounds of the ι-type might be treated as di-phonemic, belonging to the i-phoneme in words which have cognates with stressed i, or where ordinary spelling has и, and to the e-phoneme in words having cognates with stressed e or where ordinary spelling has e or ə or я.[5] The suggestion would involve assigning the varieties of ι to the i-phoneme in such words as [zjι'ma] (зима, winter),[6] [ljι'la] (лила, she poured),[7] ['ljudjι] (люди, people), [pjιsj'mo] (письмо, letter), but to the e-phoneme in such words as [djι'la] (дела, affairs),[8] [sjιmjι'na] (семена, seeds),[9] [pjι'ro] (перо, pen), [ι'motsɨjə] (эмоция, emotion), [mjι'dvjetj] (медведь, bear), [jιj'tso] (яйцо, egg).

333. I feel it to be most unsatisfactory to resort to non-phonetic criteria such as derivation and spelling, and fortunately a detailed

---

[5] Reference is here made to the (apparently older) style of Russian in which weakly stressed и and e or ə are pronounced with precisely the same variety of ι in similar phonetic contexts, i.e. the style in which the ι's of [pjι'rok] (пирог, pie) and pjι'ro (перо, pen) are identical. (It appears that at the present day a differentiation is generally made between the two classes of words, a variety of e and not ι being employed in the words written with e, ə and я. This style of speech does not illustrate the point under consideration.)

[6] Compare 'zjimɨ (зимы, winters).

[7] From ljitj (лить, to pour).

[8] From 'djela ['djɛlə] (дело, thing).

[9] From 'sjemja ['sjemjə] (семя, seed).

examination of the circumstances under which i and e and the related sounds are used in Russian leads to the conclusion that we can manage well without such criteria. We can, in fact, show that there is no reason to depart from the fundamental principle that a sound cannot belong to two phonemes, and we can make out a good case for assigning every ɩ[10] to the i-phoneme. It is true that from some points of view it seems immaterial whether we assign ɩ to the i or to the e phoneme, since it occurs to the exclusion of both the i and the e sounds in weakly stressed positions, and is probably about equidistant acoustically from the openest stressed i (as in bjil) and the closest stressed e (as in pjetj). On the other hand there is a circumstance which tells in favour of considering ɩ as a member of the i-phoneme, namely, the existence of a sound ᵻ— a kind of ə which is more i-like than the ordinary Russian ə of such a word as ['domə] (дома, at home). This sound ᵻ may be regarded either as a lowered ɨ or as a retracted e; it would seem, however, to be definitely nearer to ɨ. It is used in weakly stressed positions in surroundings similar to those in which ɨ is found in strongly stressed positions, that is to say, after hard consonants and ʃ, ʒ and ts. Examples are ['gorᵻ] (горы, hills), [krᵻ'lo] (крыло, wing), ['sontsᵻ] (солнце, sun), [ʃᵻ'stoj] (шестой, sixth), [ʃᵻ'pjetj] (шипеть, to hiss). ɩ is treated similarly in respect to i. It is used, to the exclusion of ᵻ, in weakly stressed positions in the same surroundings as those in which i occurs in strongly stressed positions, that is to say, initially and when preceded by soft consonants. Examples are those quoted in §332. These parallel relationships of ᵻ to ɨ and ɩ to i seem to me to constitute an adequate reason for classing the sounds phonemically in a similar manner. ɩ should therefore be considered as belonging to the same phoneme as i, just as ᵻ falls into the same phoneme as ɨ. And since ɨ belongs to the i-phoneme (§97), so also must ᵻ and ɩ.

334. It will be observed that this manner of classification shows a symmetrical use of the vowels. The i, a and u phonemes occur under all conditions of stress, but the use of the e and o phonemes is confined to strongly stressed syllables. I am disposed

---

[10] In this paragraph the symbol ɩ is to be taken to mean "the various Russian ɩ-sounds." The shade of sound used depends upon the adjoining consonants: thus the ɩ's of [pjɩsj'mo] and [mjɩ'dvjetj] are closer than that in [djɩ'la].

to regard this symmetry as additional evidence in favour of the above classification of ι.

335. The phonemic grouping of all these sounds, as I see it, is shown in Figure 3 (p. 27).

336. If this is the correct way of classifying them, the broad (and digraphic) transcription of the words quoted in §332 would be as follows: zji'ma, lji'la, 'ljudji, pjisj'mo, dji'la, sjimji'na, pji'ro, i'motsija, mji'dvjetj, jij'tso.[11]

337. Some have expressed the opinion that for similar reasons the English short ə might be regarded as a member of two or even more of the English "strong vowel" phonemes, such as a and ʌ. It has been said in favour of this course that short ə only occurs with completely weak stress, but that such sounds as ʌ and short a always have either a strong or a medium stress. It has in fact been suggested that all the opener English short vowels overlap in the sound ə. Personally I do not think that this view can be maintained, and that for three reasons. Firstly, as explained in §§197–202, it seems to me best to assign the ordinary Southern English short ə to the same phoneme as the long əː. Secondly, as explained in §204, it does not appear to me admissible to postulate that such sounds as ʌ and short a are incapable of receiving weak stress. And thirdly, even if that postulate could be shown to hold good and at the same time a reason were found for not grouping short ə with əː, I think the sound should not be considered di-phonemic but should be assigned to the ʌ-phoneme, since the principal ə is nearer in sound to the principal ʌ than to any other of the short "strong" vowels.

338. The examples given in §§323–333 show then that when there are grounds for assigning a sound to either of two phonemes, it may perhaps be occasionally convenient to treat that sound as di-phonemic, but that di-phonemic grouping of such a sound is never a necessity. It is always possible to assign it arbitrarily to one of the phonemes, and as a rule this is probably the best course.

---

[11] It is noteworthy that if this classification of ι is correct, Russian exhibits a treatment of words containing *e* similar to that found in English. Compare English di'fəː (*defer*) but 'defərəns (*deference*), ris'tɔː (*restore*) but restə'reiʃn (*restoration*), 'trʌmpit (*trumpet*, from French *trompette*, now pronounced trɔ̃pɛt and doubtless also pronounced with ɛ when introduced into English in the fourteenth century), 'daːknis (*darkness*, formerly probably deɹk'nɛsə), etc.

CHAPTER XXI

FUNCTIONS OF LENGTH, STRESS AND VOICE-PITCH

339. Every speech-sound (phone) has tamber, duration, stress and (if voiced) voice-pitch. These attributes are usually distinct from each other, but it must be remarked that in exceptional cases a tamber has to be held to contain a duration, stress or pitch element. The chief of these cases are: plosive consonants (where the plosion is "instantaneous"), semi-vowels such as w, j, ỹ (ɥ) (which have to be very short), voiceless ƀ, ɖ, etc. (which differ only in degree of force from unaspirated p, t, etc.), the Arabic ʕ (which necessarily has a very low voice-pitch).

340. In the preceding chapters we have been concerned mainly with tamber. It is now necessary to turn our attention to length, stress and voice-pitch and their functions, when these attributes are separable from tamber (as is usually the case).

341. It will be found that groupings of lengths and voice-pitches can often be made which are comparable to the groupings of tambers into phonemes. But before entering into the theory of such grouping, attention must be called to an important difference of function between tambers and the other attributes. Differences of tamber are employed in language chiefly for the purpose of distinguishing "words" from one another.[1] In some languages degrees of length are likewise used for differentiating words; in some the kind of stress or the position of the strong stress (in words of more than one syllable) serves the same purpose; and in "tone languages" voice-pitches are similarly used. On the other hand there are languages in which length, stress and voice-pitch play no part in word-differentiation. These attributes have, however, other functions which tambers have not. They are made use of constantly and in all languages for giving *emphasis* to particular words in a sentence, for indicating *contrasts*, for reflecting *emotional states* of the speaker, or for suggesting other *implications* which cannot conveniently be expressed by means of words at all. These uses are exemplified in the following paragraphs (§342 ff.).

---

[1] Exceptions being differences between tambers found in the same phoneme.

342. Emphasis of particular words may be for "intensity" or for "contrast." The following are some instances of the use of length, stress and voice-pitch for purposes of *intensity*. The meaning of the English word iˈnɔːməs (*enormous*) can be "intensified," so that the word denotes "particularly large," by giving extra prominence to the already prominent second syllable; this extra prominence is effected by an increase of stress coupled with an increase in the length of the vowel² and the use of a special intonation. *Splendid* can be similarly treated, except that it is the consonant n which is lengthened in the emphatic pronunciation.³ The meaning of *absolutely* (in the sense of 'very much,' 'completely') may be intensified by putting an additional stress, coupled generally with a high pitch, on the third syllable (ˈˈabsəˈˈluːtli). So also in German (e.g. ˈˈfaːbəlhaft with a very long aː, ˈˈvundərbaːr or ˈˈvundərˈˈbaːr with lengthened n), and in Russian (e.g. udjiˈˈvjitjiljna with the i of the third syllable longer than usual and the two preceding syllables on higher pitch than usual⁴).

343. Stress may be used to express intensity in languages where it is not employed for word-distinctions. A noteworthy case is that of French, where intensity is shown by putting a special strong stress on the first or second syllable of various long words (e.g. ˈˈfɔrmiˈdabl, ˈˈpartikyljɛrmã, aˈˈbɔmiˈnabl or ˈˈabɔmiˈnabl, apˈˈsɔlymã or ˈˈapsɔlymã). In some French words intensification may be effected by a stress coupled with a lengthening of an initial consonant (e.g. ˈˈmːalœˈrø).

344. In emphasis for intensity the special attributes are applied to the particular words requiring intensification. *Contrast*, on the other hand, generally involves a special type of intonation spread over the contrasted word and all the following words in the sentence. Its nature depends largely on whether the contrast is with what has preceded or with what may be presumed to follow.

345. The following are some examples from English.

(1) Contrast with what precedes⁵:

---

² Also sometimes of the n preceding the vowel.

³ Not the vowel. The l preceding the vowel is also sometimes lengthened.

⁴ удивитильно (*wonderful*); intonation [˙ ˙ \ . .].

⁵ Intonations are represented here and elsewhere by the line and dot system. Thick lines and dots indicate the stressed syllables.

(bət) !'ai wont tə bai it [＼ ....]

(bət) "'ai dount wont tə bai it [＼ .....]

(bət) ai "wont tə bai it [·＼ ...]

(bət) ai 'dount "wont tə bai it [.·˙＼ ...]

(bət) ai wont tə "bai it [.·˙＼.]

(bət) ai 'dount wont tə "bai it [·˙.·˙＼.]

(bət) it 'woznt in"tenʃənl [·˙·.＼..]

(bət) it s "main [·＼]

(bət) it 'səːtnli iznt "main [.·˙·˙..＼]

(2) Contrast with what follows:

"'ai dount wont tə bai it (bət ....) [⋀.·˙˙]

ai 'dount "wont tə bai it (bət ...) [.˙⋀.·˙]

ai 'dount wont tə "bai it (bət ....) [.·˙.⋀⁄]

ai "wont tə bai it (bət ....) [·⋀.·˙]

it 'woznt in"tenʃənl (........) [·˙·.⋀.⁄]

it 'iznt "main (......) [·˙·⋀]

346. The following are similar examples from French:

(1) Contrast with what precedes:

(mɛ) "mwa ʒ ɛmrɛ l aʃ'te [＼....] or [˙.·˙.]

(mɛ) "mwa ʒə n vø 'pɑ [＼...] or [˙.·.]

(mɛ) ʒ e ã"vi d l aʃ'te [·˙＼..]

(mɛ) ʒə n e pɑz ã"vi d l aʃ'te [..·˙＼..]

(mɛ) ʒə vø 'bjɛ̃ l aʃ"te [.·˙·＼]

(mɛ) ʒə n vø 'pɑ l aʃ"te [.·˙·＼]

(mɛ) ʒə n l e 'pɑ fɛ ɛks"prɛ [..·˙.＼]

(mɛ) il ɛt a "mwa [..·＼]

(mɛ) i n ɛ 'pɑz a "mwa [.·˙·＼]

(o kɔ̃trɛːr) il ɛ tu"ʒuːr ã rtaːr [.·˙＼..]

(2) Implied contrast in context of situation:

(tjɛ̃), i fɛ 'bo oʒurdyi [·˙＼...]

(3) Contrast with what follows:

"mwa ʒə n vø pɑ l aʃ'te, (mɛ ....) [＼.·˙˙]

ʒə n e 'pɑ ã"vi d l aʃ'te, (mɛ ....) [·˙˙·＼·˙]

In many other cases the intonation is the same as when the contrast is with what precedes, e.g.

ʒə n vø ˈpɑ | aʃˈˈte, (mɛ . . . .) [· · · ◥]

347. A great number of special meanings may be given to sentences by means of intonation. A notable case is when a sentence in statement form is pronounced so as to mean a question requiring the answer "yes" or "no." Examples:

Statement	Question
English	
ju ə ˈkould [· ◥] (*you are cold*)	[·◢] (= are you cold?)
juː ˈsed sou [· ◥ .] (*you said so*)	[. .◢] (= did you say so?)
French	
i ˈvjɛn [ˈ◞] or [· ◥] (they are coming) (*ils viennent*)	[. ·] (are they coming?)
German	
ɛr ist ˈɛŋlɛnder [. · ◥ . .] (he is English) (*er ist Engländer*)	[. .· · ·] (is he English?)
Russian	
xaraˈʃo [· · ◞] (it is right) (хорошо)	[. ·◢] (is it right?)
kraˈsjiva [ˈ ◞ .] (it is pretty) (красиво)	[·◢.]⁶ (is it pretty?)
ˈxoladna [◞. .] (it is cold) (холодно)	[◢. .]⁶ (is it cold?)
vi tam ˈbilji [· · ◞.] (you have been there) (вы там были)	[· ·◢.]⁶ (have you been there?)
Hindustani	
t̪hik həʊ [ˈ .] (it is right)	[. ·] or [.◥] (is it right?)

348. The numerous other meanings that can be suggested by intonation in non-tone languages have been described in various

---

⁶ With the intonations [· _ ·], [_· ·], [· · _ ·] these expressions would suggest surprise and doubt: "do you mean to say you think it's pretty?"; "do you mean to say it's cold?"; "do you mean to say you have been there?"

books and articles, and readers are referred to them for further examples.[7]

349.   Languages do not all employ the same type of intonation for suggesting a given implication. And conversely a particular intonation may suggest one implication in one language and a different one in another.

350.   I have noticed for instance that some Russians when speaking English continually give (to the English hearer) the impression of impatience or querulousness or protest when in reality they have no such sentiments. The effect is produced by a frequent use of pitches much higher than those an English person normally uses. If an Englishman says ai 'wontid tu iks'plein it tə ju (*I wanted to explain it to you*), he would normally pronounce the expression with an intonation of the type [· ˙ · · ❭ . . .]. Some Russians, however, while saying the sentence with a somewhat similar tone-pattern, will use much higher pitches on wont and plein; they adopt in fact an intonation which an Englishman might employ when speaking impatiently.[8]

351.   Another instance is seen in the above-mentioned intonation of the type [· ❭] used by many Hindustani-speaking Indians to express a question requiring the answer "yes" or "no," as in ʈhik həʊ [· ❭] (is it right?). This is markedly different from the type [· · ʹ] or [· · ˙] commonly used for this purpose in such languages as English and French. In English the intonation [· ❭] is used to

---

[7] ARMSTRONG and WARD, *Handbook of English Intonation*; PALMER, *English Intonation*; Chapter on Intonation in JONES' *Outline of English Phonetics*, eighth and subsequent editions; KLINGHARDT und KLEMM, *Übungen im Englischen Tonfall*; COUSTENOBLE and ARMSTRONG, *Studies in French Intonation*; KLINGHARDT und OLBRICH, *Französische Intonations-Übungen*; KLINGHARDT, *Übungen in Deutschem Tonfall*; BOYANUS, *Russian Pronunciation*, Chapter XII and texts; BOYANUS, *Spoken Russian* R. KINGDON, *The Groundwork of English Intonation*, also his article *Tonetic Stress-marks for English* in *Le Maître Phonétique*, October, 1939, and articles on intonation by him in *English Language Teaching*, Vol. II, Nos. 4, 5, etc.

[8] Compare the Russian i 'on 'dumal ʃta 'eta at'kritjja [· · ❭ . . · ˙ ❭ .] with the English hiː 'θoːt it wəz ə dis'kʌvəri [. ˉ · . . . ❭ . .]. A Russian man often uses pitches such as F or G above middle C, or even higher, on the high stressed syllables of ordinary sentences. An Englishman rarely raises his voice as high as middle C in ordinary conversation, unless he is showing emotion or suggesting some special implication.

indicate astonishment, e.g. ꞌriəli [.\ ]. In Welsh the same intonation is used in the termination of ordinary statements; it does not
suggest any particular implication: a Welshman will say ꞌnevər
[·\] where an Englishman would say ꞌnevə [\.].

352. The methods of suggesting implications in tone languages
are naturally different from those in use in non-tone languages.
In Tswana, for instance, a statement cannot be converted into a
question by applying a rising intonation; it is done by *shortening
the vowel of the penultimate syllable of the sentence.* Thus when
ō *batla nama* is a statement (he is looking for some meat) it is
pronounced ō̄ batla naːma,[9] the vowel of the syllable na being
long; when it is a question (is he looking for some meat?), the
pronunciation is ō̄ batla nama,[10] the vowel of na being short.
Similarly, phāːxɛ[11] means "(it is) a cat," but phāxɛ[12] with short a
means "Is it a cat?"

353. I have been informed by Professor IDA WARD that in
Igbo and other languages of West Africa notable alterations in
tone -patterns have to be made in order to convert a statement
into a question. But here again the alterations are quite different
from those prevalent in non-tone languages such as English and
French. Example: Igbo aɲi ga ɛjɛ [.ˑ . . .] (*anyi ga ɛjɛ,* we
shall go), [. . . . ·] (shall we go?).[13] And L. E. ARMSTRONG has
noted a number of remarkable interrogative tone-patterns in
Kikuyu.[14]

354. In Cantonese, where the tones are so numerous as to
restrict considerably the possibility of making words prominent by
pitch, emphasis of particular words is effected mainly by length.
The syllables to be emphasized are made longer than adjoining
syllables, the length being spread over the vowel and final consonants

---

[9] With more precise tone-marking: ō̄ batla ṇ̱aːṃ̱a. The low-falling tone
(marked ꞏ̣) and the lowest level tone (marked ‿) are members of the ordinary
low toneme (left unmarked).

[10] With more precise tone-marking: ō̄ batla naṃ̱a.

[11] With more precise tone-marking: phàːxɛ̱.

[12] With more precise tone-marking: phāxɛ̱.

[13] From WARD, *Introduction to the Ibo Language,* p. 120.

[14] See her *Phonetic and Tonal Structure of Kikuyu,* pp. 72, 75, and elsewhere.

(if any) of the syllables; syllables of little importance are said very short.[15]

355.   But even in tone languages there is such a thing as sentence-intonation which can be used for suggesting implications or reflecting emotional states of the speaker.   The essential relationships between the word tones are as a rule preserved, but certain types of sentence-intonation can be superimposed on the tonal patterns of sentences to suggest the special meanings.

356.   The foregoing examples (in §342 ff.) illustrate the uses of length, stress and voice-pitch when these attributes are not "significant" in the usual linguistic sense of the term, i.e. when they are not used for distinguishing one "word" from another. In the following four chapters we shall examine the manner of using these attributes when employed as word-distinguishers. When so used, they are called by some writers "prosodic" elements of speech, as distinguished from the phonemic or qualitative elements.

CHAPTER XXII

SIGNIFICANT LENGTH

357.   Speech-sounds require time for their utterance; in other words, they have "duration," or "quantity" as it is often called. Some sounds are by their nature of limited duration, as already mentioned in §339.   In particular the plosions of plosive consonants and the flaps of flapped consonants are necessarily extremely short; sounds of a gliding type are susceptible of a certain degree of lengthening but they cannot be held on indefinitely.   Other sounds, namely those termed "continuants," can if desired be held on as long as the speaker's breath lasts.

358.   In connected speech the durations of continuant sounds and of the "stops" of plosive consonants vary greatly, and their differences of duration are attributable to a variety of circumstances. There are, for instance, quick speakers and slow speakers.   Those

---

[15] Examples of this method of effecting word-prominence will be found by referring to the *Cantonese Phonetic Reader* by JONES and WOO.   In many of the texts in that book the most prominent syllables are shown in black type and the least prominent in italics.

who talk fast use shorter sounds than those who talk slowly. There are also "drawlers"—people who are in the habit of making many of their continuant sounds (especially vowels) unusually long. Again the same speaker does not always pronounce words at the same rate, so that the sounds he uses in a given sequence are not always of the same length.

359. Then there are conventional usages as to duration in particular languages. These usages vary from language to language. There may be (1) duration used as a means of distinguishing one word from another, (2) variations of duration according to phonetic context, (3) special uses of length in the sentence, or for purposes of emphasis. It is with the first of these that we are chiefly concerned in this chapter. The second is dealt with in the chapter on "chronemes" (Chap. XXIII). The third has already been referred to in §§342, 352, 354, and further mention is made of it in §§383–385.

LENGTH AND DOUBLING

360. As we are here concerned with "true" or "indivisible" length and not with "doubling" or repetitions of sounds, and as the acoustic difference between a "long" sound and a "doubled" sound is often difficult to perceive, it is necessary to preface this account of duration by some remarks on the difference between these. By "true" or "indivisible" length is meant a "long" duration which is not felt by the speaker as a repetition of a sound, and which cannot be replaced by doubling. In most languages lengthenings are found which have to be considered disyllabic and which may be pronounced disyllabically (i.e. as repeated or "double" sounds); they are or may be divided into two parts by a diminution of intensity in the middle. Such are the double short i of such English words as ˈemptiiŋ (*emptying*), ˈbeibiiʃ (*babyish*), the doubled vowels in the French reeliːr (*réélire*), saara (*Sahara*), kɔɔpere (*coopérer*) and the double vowels in Tswana words such as lɩʊbana (young pigeon), lɩʊbāna (squall), maabāɲane (evening).[1] For examples of double consonants, see §§365 ff.

---

[1] In these Tswana examples the two vowels have the same tone. Other examples of repeated vowels occur very frequently in this language with two vowels having different tones. When the tones differ, the disyllabic character of the sequence is always very clear. Instances are ɟāakā (like), ɟāanɔ̄ŋ (now).

361. It is probable that the distinction between single and double sounds is always potentially significant. The distinction between short sounds and sounds pronounced with true length is, on the other hand, not of necessity significant, though in many languages it happens to be so.

362. Although the difference between doubled vowels and single long vowels may often be inappreciable to the ear, and may be even objectively non-existent to listeners, yet the difference would seem to be in most cases subjectively perceptible to the speaker. Long vowels which are subjectively double may always be pronounced double, but with true long vowels a pronunciation with double sounds is not a possible alternative: thus it is not possible to pronounce the French mɛːtr (*maître*) as mɛ-ɛtr or the German baːn (*Bahn*) as ba-an.

363. Whether a vowel heard as long is to be considered double is a matter to be decided by the feeling of the *speaker*, which in its turn is determined by reference to the structure of the language. If a given long vowel is separable into two, and if therefore in precise speech it could be pronounced double, it is convenient to regard it always as double. If, however, a certain long vowel is never separable into two, and cannot be replaced by a sequence of two in precise speech, then the case must be considered to be one of true length. The distinction between a lengthened vowel and a doubled vowel has not yet, as far as I know, been found to be significant in any language; the difference is probably insufficient for this.

364. If the difference between lengthening and doubling is difficult to perceive in vowels, it is still more so in the case of consonants. I cannot imagine that the difference between a long consonant and a doubled one could ever be significant.

365. In practice it is convenient to regard all intervocalic long consonants as double, on the ground that it is usually possible in precise speech to separate them into two by a diminution of force in the middle, attaching the first part to the first syllable and the second part to the second syllable. That long consonants are divisible in this way is obvious in the case of compound words and words formed with prefixes or suffixes,[2] as in the following

---

[2] These are the only cases where long consonants are found in English, French, German and Russian.

examples: English ˈbukkeis (*book-case*), ˈpennaif (*pen-knife*), ˈwʌnnis (*oneness*), ˈdʒenjuinnis (*genuineness*), ˈsoulli (*solely*);[3] French døzjɛmmã (*deuxièmement*), ɔnɛtte (*honnêteté*); German fɛrˈraist (*verreist*), ˈappaken (*abpacken*); Russian ˈstrannij (странный, strange), attaˈvo (оттого, therefore), adˈdatj (отдать, to give away); Hindustani bənna (to be made), janna (to know).[4] So also in Arabic where cognate words often have a vowel between the two consonants, e.g. dikkaːn (shop), the plural of which is dakaːkiːn (shops), or the Syrian mille (religion) which has plural milal.

366. When long consonants occur intervocalically with no such obvious derivations, it matters little whether they are regarded as double or merely as long. To me it seems preferable for practical purposes to regard them as double, one part being apportioned to each syllable.[5] The following are illustrations of the class of words referred to: Hindustani, gəlla (flock), pətta (leaf), rəssi (rope), pʊlla (large tablet)[6]; Somali báːddai (she searched).[7]

367. As to initial long consonants, they are best regarded as double whenever there is reason to consider the first part as a prefix or as an element of a compound. This is the case, for instance, in Russian words like ʒʒatj (сжать, reaped)[8] and in Tswana words such as mmetli (carpenter), mmilã (road). The same applies no doubt to the initial long consonants of Luganda, as in tta (kill), ggwa (be finished),[9] which in inflected forms occur intervocalically and therefore presumably double. But in instances

---

[3] Compare ˈhouli (holy).

[4] Compare bəna (made), jana (knew).

[5] Some transcribers of Italian have used length-marks to indicate the long consonants of that language: see, for instance, PANCONCELLI-CALZIA, *Italiano*. Others have repeated the consonant letter; see, for instance, CAMILLI, *Italian Phonetic Reader*. Those accustomed to use the Swedish Dialect Alphabet show the long consonants of Swedish by a length-mark; these consonants might equally well be indicated by doubling the letter, at any rate in intervocalic position. Most transcribers of Hindustani, Tamil, etc., show consonant length by doubling the letter, though the late Dr. GRAHAME BAILEY used a length-mark for this purpose in his *Panjabi Phonetic Reader*.

[6] Compar gəla (throat), pəta (address, sign), rəsi (juicy), pʊla (cooked rice).

[7] Compare báːdai (I searched) (ARMSTRONG, *Phonetic Structure of Somali*, p. 138).

[8] Compare ʒatj (жать, to reap).

[9] Compare ta (let go), gwa (fall).

like the emphatic pronunciation of the French word "mːizerabl (*misérable*) with a long m there is no reason to regard the sound as other than merely long.

368.   Final long consonants are conveniently regarded as double in all cases where there is reason to think that the native speaker feels them to be double, and more particularly when the latter part can be regarded as syllabic.   It is thus clear that they should be regarded as double in such cases as the German 'kønn, be'zinn (contracted forms of 'kønen, *können*, be'zinen, *besinnen*), since it is possible to pronounce them double; they are doubtless felt as double by German speakers even if objectively they sound merely long.   The same applies in the case of compounds such as 'zonnʃain (*Sonnenschein*).

369.   So also the final consonants of such Arabic words as dakk (sandhill), laðð (to be sweet), darr (abundant), or the colloquial ħaʔʔ (truth), ħubb (love) are doubtless felt by native speakers to be double rather than merely long on account of the existence of cognate forms such as dakaka, dikaːk (sandhills), laðiːð (sweet), midraːran (abundantly), ħaʔiːʔa (truth), ħabiːb (beloved).

370.   In languages where no such special conditions have to be taken into account there is no reason to consider final long consonants as double.   This applies not only to languages like English, French and Swedish where the lengths of final consonants are linked with the lengths of preceding vowels (§§548–553), but also to languages like Hungarian and Estonian where the lengths of final consonants are not so linked.

371.   Thus since the long final consonants used in English when short vowels precede, as in hil (*hill*), pen (*pen*), are never pronounced double, they need not be regarded other than merely long.   And as length is invariably applied to final consonants when the preceding vowel is short it is not necessary to mark it in transcription.   The same applies to the final consonants of French words like vil (*ville*), dɛt (*dette*).   In Swedish, although the principle is the same, the reverse notation is probably preferable on account of the frequent occurrence of long ("double") consonants medially.   The case is illustrated by the Swedish words kall (*kall*, cold), tɔpp (*topp*, top), lamm (*lamm*, lamb), sill (*sill*, herring), which may be compared with lam [laːm] (*lam*, paralysed),

sil [siːl] (*sil*, sieve) which have long vowels and short final consonants.[10]

372. In Hungarian and Estonian differences of duration in final consonants are significant, and accordingly the lengths must be shown in transcription. The following are some examples from these languages with words ending in single consonants for comparison. (Although there is no reason to consider the long consonants as double, it is nevertheless advantageous from the standpoint of legibility to write them with doubled letters.)

Hungarian: hall [hall] (*hall*, hears)   hal [hal] (*hal*, fish)

lapp [lapp] (*lapp*, Lap-   lap [lap] (*lap*, sheet of
lander)   paper)

'veːgett ['veːgɛtt]   'veːget ['veːgɛt] (*véget*,
(*végett*, on account of)   end, acc.)

føːtt (*fött*, cooked)   føːt (*föt*, chief thing, acc.)

Estonian: siːtt (*siit*, from here)   siːt (*siid*, silk)

saːːkk (*saak*, booty)   saːːk (*saag*, a saw)

373. There are cases where a long consonant preceding or following another consonant in medial position has to be considered truly long and not double. They would, however, all appear to be cases where particular conditions apply, and which consequently do not illustrate any principles of general application. Such are the long nasals preceding voiced plosives in Sinhalese (see §260, 264, etc.) and the long consonants in such Tamil words as maːttru (change), arttam (meaning), tirppu (sentence). These Tamil consonants are not ordinary instances of doubling since in that language the length of medial p, t, etc., is associated with the presence or absence of voice. Short consonants in the above positions would be voiced; thus the word written broadly ontru (one) is pronounced [ondru]. It is possible that the native Tamil speaker does not think of the above tt, pp as being doubled, since the sounds may be considerably shortened, as long as their voicelessness is maintained.[11]

---

[10] The phonemic system of Swedish is, however, obscure in several points, and I am not at present prepared to suggest a definite scheme for transcribing that language broadly. It might turn out that a broad transcription should show the lengths of vowels as well as of consonants. To ascertain this would require an investigation of the lengths of vowels in weakly stressed positions.

[11] See FIRTH's *Short Outline of Tamil Pronunciation*, pp. iii, v.

374.   In the case of various medial and final consonant groups in Swedish, the first consonant is long, e.g. the l in ˅vellja (*välja*, choose), the n in ˈinnrə (*inre*, interior), the k in ˈakksəl (*axel*, shoulder) or ˅akksəl (*Axel*). These clearly have to be regarded as having true length and not as being double. (Transcribers using the Swedish Dialect Alphabet habitually write them with a length-mark.)

375.   It is to be understood then in what follows that the terms "long" and "length" are used only in reference to sounds having "true" or "indivisible" length as explained in the preceding paragraphs. Any lengths which can be regarded as doubling or repetition do not come within the scope of this enquiry.

WORD DIFFERENTIATIONS BY DURATION

376.   As already mentioned in §§54 and 59, differences of duration are sometimes employed for the purpose of distinguishing one word from another. Some examples of differentiations by lengths of consonants were given in §372. Differentiations solely by lengths of vowels are exemplified in the following paragraphs (§§377–379). But where vowels are concerned, differentiations by length are very often accompanied by differences in some other attribute as well, generally tamber. Word distinction effected by duration in conjunction with other attributes is discussed in Chapter XXVI.

377.   Scottish English makes a limited use of distinctive length. In that type of English when inflected forms are constructed by the addition of -d or -z to a word ending in a vowel, the vowel is normally long. But in non-inflected words containing the same sounds the vowels are short. Thus, while *brood, greed, road, freeze, use, rose* have short vowels (broadly **brud, grid, rod, friz, juz, roz**), *brewed, agreed, rowed, frees, ewes, rows* have long ones (**bruːd, əˈgriːd, roːd, friːz, juːz, roːz**).

378.   Examples of foreign languages in which significant use is made of differences in the duration of vowels unaccompānied by perceptible differences of any other kind are Japanese, Finnish, Somali, Kikuyu, Luganda. Examples of words so differentiated are: Japanese **isso** (rather), **issoː** (more), **soko** (bottom), **sokoː** (conduct) Finnish **tule** (come!), **tuleː** (comes), **tulle** (might come), **tuːle** (it

blows), etc.; Somali kul (hot), kuːl (necklace), lab (male), laːb (chest); Kikuyu kōra (grow up), kōːra (root out), igɔko (bark of tree), igɔːko (thick thatching grass), hɛni (lightning), hɛːni (lies); Luganda okusona [. ˙ · ˙] (to sew), okusoːna [. ˙ ¯ ˙] (to take by surprise), okutuma [. . ˙ .] (to send), okutuːma [. . ¯ .] (to heap up), bagenda [˙ . .] (they go), baːgenda [¯ . .] (they went).

379. French too makes a certain limited use of significant vowel length with little or no accompanying distinction of tamber. Examples are mɛːtr (*maître*), mɛtr (*mettre*), bɛːl (*béle*), bɛl (*belle*), tuːs (*tous*, all of them, us, etc.), tus (*tousse*).[12]

380. In some varieties of English it would appear that no difference is made between the sounds of final *d* and *t*, both being pronounced ḓ. In the speech of those who pronounce in this way words like *heed* and *heat* (narrowly hiːḓ, hiḓ) are distinguished solely by the length of the vowel. H. J. ULDALL, a reliable observer, considered this pronunciation to be common in America,[13] but the point does not seem to have received much attention from American phoneticians.[14]

381. Languages which make use of duration for word distinctions, with or without the assistance of other attributes, may be called "chrone languages" (see Chap. XXIII). In chrone languages there are as a rule only two significant degrees of duration, "short" and "long." Estonian appears to be an exceptional language having three significant degrees of duration (see §§399, 419).

382. Though the duration of vowels is a feature of speech which is easily capable of distinguishing words, there exist many languages in which it is not employed at all for this purpose. Such are Spanish, Russian, Polish, Greek, Persian, Bengali, Marathi, Tswana; also the type of English described in §519.

---

[12] These distinctions are not made by all French people. In the speech of some who distinguish long and short ɛ there is a slight accompanying difference of tamber. Some do not distinguish tuːs and tus, but use a short vowel in both words.

[13] *Le Maître Phonétique*, October, 1934, pp. 97, 98.

[14] H. A. ROSITZKE has produced kymographic tracings showing that the sounds of final *d* and *t* differ (*Le Maître Phonétique*, October, 1938, pp. 64–66). He adds that "ULDALL's remarks should be taken to apply only to General American and Southern speakers, and even then not to all sections and speakers of the region."

SEMANTIC LENGTH IN THE SENTENCE

383. Languages exist in which differences in the duration of vowels distinguish one kind of sentence from another but not one word from another. The Tswana language of South Africa is one of these. In this language the vowels (or syllabic consonants) of penultimate syllables of complete *statements* are always very long. When the penultimate syllable of a complete sentence is short, it means that it is a *question* or a *command* or an *exclamation*. A statement can be converted into a question by shortening the vowel (or syllabic consonant) of the penultimate syllable. And in unfinished statements or non-final parts of sentences all syllables up to and including the penultimate are short, the ultimate being generally somewhat lengthened.

384. The following are some examples illustrating the use of length in Tswana. They are given here with precise length and tone-marking.[15]

Long penultimate: ō a̠: ꞁa̠ [˙ ⸜.] (he is eating)

ō a ꞁà: ɸa̠ [˙ · ⸜ ⸝] (he is eating here)

ō ꞁā na̠:ma̠ [˙ ˙ ⸜.] (he is eating meat)

ō a ba̠:tla̠ [˙ ·⸜.] (he is searching)

ō a batla̠: ɸa̠ [· · ⸝ ⸜] (he is searching here)

ō batla phà:xɛ [· · ⸜.] (he is looking for the cat)

ō batla kxɔ:mō [· · ·⸜·] (he is looking for the cow)

xω bɔ:na̠ [· ⸜.] (to see)

xω bɔnà:la [· ˙ ⸜ ·] (to be evident)

Short penultimate: ō a ꞁa̠ [˙ · .] (Is he eating?)

ō a ꞁā ɸa̠ [˙ · ˙ .] (Is he eating here?)

ō ꞁā nama̠ [˙ ˙ · .] (Is he eating meat?)

ō batla phāxɛ [˙ · · ˙ .] (Is he looking for the cat?)

ō batla kxomō [˙ · · · ˙] (Is he looking for the cow?)

---

[15] The tone-marks are as follows: ˉ high-level, ⸝ high-fall, ‗ low-level, mid falling to low; unmarked syllables have mid-level tone.

ȷā [˙] (Eat!)

ȷā nama̱ [˙ ·̣] (Eat the meat!)

batlā [·˙] (Search!)

batlā kxomō [·˙·˙] (Look for the cow!)

nanō̄xa̱ [·˙·̣] (Raise yourself!)

385. In this language then length is applicable to a certain syllable of the sentence, the penultimate, and is not in any way attached to particular words or to particular syllables of any words. *Batla* (is searching), for example, may have the first vowel lengthened or the second vowel lengthened or may have both vowels short.

RELATIONSHIPS BETWEEN DURATION AND STRESS IN NON-STRESS LANGUAGES

386. It is interesting to compare the case of Tswana with that of French, since neither language makes use of significant stress, but in both there are relationships between duration and stress. The usage in Tswana is as follows. There is strong stress on the two final syllables of every *statement*, except when these syllables bear the tone pattern [❭ ·]; and, as already mentioned in §383, the penultimate syllable of a statement is always long and the ultimate always short.[16] Thus if the words phāxɛ (cat), nama (meat), kxomō (cow) occur at the end of a statement both syllables receive strong stress, and the vowel of the first syllable is long.[17] In fact any syllable which in other positions in the sentence would be pronounced short has to be given length in the penultimate position in a statement. Usage in French is almost the opposite of this.

---

[16] The ultimate syllable is less objectively prominent than the penultimate owing to the shortness and frequent devoicing of its vowel, but strong stress is without doubt subjectively present and is shown objectively by the gestures (especially of the hands and head) which native speakers employ.

[17] With precise tone and length marking phà:xɛ [❭.], na̱:ma̱ [❭.], kxɔ:mɔ [❭·]. The exceptional tone pattern which is associated with strong stress on the penultimate and weak stress on the ultimate is exemplified by *khukhu* (beetle), which at the end of a statement is pronounced khù:khu [❭·].

When not final, Tswana words have other tone patterns, for which see JONES, *The Tones of Sechuana Nouns* (published by the International African Institute) and JONES and PLAATJE, *Sechuana Reader*.

Final syllables in French sentences generally bear a strong stress, while (in the absence of special emphasis) non-final syllables have weaker stress. Final syllables may have long vowels, but when a syllable requiring a long vowel in final position occurs in penultimate or other non-final situation, its vowel is short. Thus, when such words as fœːj (*feuille*), fɛːr (*faire*) occur at the end of a sentence, their vowels are long; but in non-final positions, as in fœj də lety (*feuille de laitue*), fɛr paːr (*faire part*), their vowels are short.

CHAPTER XXIII
CHRONEMES

387. In languages where differences of duration are employed for differentiating words, those differences are naturally considerable. But in such languages the "longs" are not always of the same duration, nor are the "shorts." Durations are also variable in languages where length has no significant function.

388. The chief factors associated with variations of duration are (1) the nature of the sound itself, (2) the nature of sounds adjoining it in the sequence, (3) the degree of stress, (4) the number of syllables intervening between one strong stress and the next, and occasionally (5) intonation. Illustrations of variations of length in accordance with these factors are given in the following paragraphs.

389. (1) In English the close i and the back a, though both "long" vowels, are not as a rule of the same length in the same phonetic context; the aː is generally longer than the iː. It is easy to hear for example that the vowel in haːt (*heart*) is longer than that in hiːt (*heat*).

390. (2) Variations in accordance with the nature of adjoining sounds are particularly frequent and noticeable in cases where there are associations of duration with quality (§§511 ff.); this can be readily understood, since when the differentiation between words is partly by tamber, the greater the tamber difference the less need is there for stability of length. Several of the vowels in my type of English illustrate such variations. Thus my vowels in

see, seed, seen, seat, seating, are all "long," but they have not all by any means the same degree of length when said in isolation; and further degrees of length are found when the words occur in connected speech.

391. It is easy to estimate roughly by ear the relative length of vowels in many cases of this sort, e.g. those in *seed, seen, seat* said in isolation. Accurate measurements of such lengths have also been made experimentally by many observers; see §403–406.[1]

392. The following is an example of degrees of length observable in a consonant. In Italian when t is preceded by a strongly stressed vowel + n, it is noticeably longer than a single t preceded by a strongly stressed vowel only. Thus the t in ˈdante (*Dante*) is longer than that in ˈdate (give)[2]; it is in fact almost as long as the long ("doubled") t of ˈfatto (made).

393. (3) In stress languages vowels are usually shorter in non-final weakly stressed positions than in strongly stressed positions.[3] Thus in English the weakly stressed "long" oː in koːˈzeiʃn (*causation*) is not so long as the strongly stressed vowel in koːz (*cause*).[4] Similarly hiː (*he*) has a shorter vowel in hiː ˈdʌznt (*he DOESN'T*) than in ˈhiː dʌznt (*HE* doesn't).

394. Many examples of shortening in conjunction with weak stress are found in French. For instance, as already mentioned in §386, *faire* said by itself has a long vowel (fɛːr), but in *faire-part, faire savoir,* where the syllable is weakly stressed, the vowel is short (fɛrˈpaːr, fɛr saˈvwaːr).

395. (4) In stress languages there is usually a tendency to make the strong stresses follow each other at fairly equal intervals, whenever this can conveniently be done. This tendency produces the effect commonly termed "rhythm." It often determines the

---

[1] The first measurements of this kind were made, I believe, by E. A. MEYER, and were published in his *Englische Lautdauer* (1903). It was he who first pointed out that the vowel in haːt can be heard to be longer than that in hiːt.

[2] Narrower transcription ˈdaːte.

[3] Especially in weakly stressed positions immediately preceding a stress. *Final* weakly stressed vowels are often rather long (see the example *city* in §405).

[4] Said in isolation or at the end of a sentence (see §395).

lengths of sounds. Thus if a number of weakly stressed syllables intervene between a strong stress and the next following strong stress in the sentence, various shortenings may take place in the unconscious endeavour to make the "stress bar" equal in length to other "stress bars." Thus, though the oː of the English word koːz (*cause*) is very long when the word is said by itself, it is much shorter in such a sentence as ðə ˈkoːz əv it wəz ˈnevə disˈkʌvəd (*the cause of it was never discovered*). It is for this reason that in such words as iˈmiːdjətli (*immediately*), inˈdjuːbitəbl (*indubitable*) the long vowel is much less long than that of such words as miːn (*mean*), djuː (*due*) said in isolation. (See my *Outline of English Phonetics*, §§886–890.)

396. (5) Lengthening of sounds appears to be a usual accompaniment of the English falling-rising intonation when this intonation is applied to a single syllable. Thus I should normally pronounce the trai in *I'll try* [· ‿] (implying "though I don't suppose I shall succeed") with a longer diphthong than in the plain statement *I'll try* [· ❨]. Moreover there are tone languages in which special lengths accompany significant tones (see §§557–565).

397. The lengths of sounds may be modified for purposes of emphasis. Emphatic lengthening must be regarded as belonging to a special form of the language. It is outside the scope of the present chapter.

398. Any particular degree of duration may be termed a *chrone*. For instance, the duration of the vowel in *see* said in isolation in a normal way, is an example of a chrone. The durations of the vowels in *seed* and *seat* (which are different from this) are examples of other chrones. The relative values of different chrones may often be estimated roughly by ear. Their absolute values may be measured accurately, if desired, by apparatus in any convenient units of time, e.g. hundredths of a second. Thus in my normal pronunciation the chrone of *see*, said in isolation, has been found to measure on an average[5] 0·317 sec., while the chrones of *seed* and *seat* have been found to measure on an average[5] 0·252 and 0·124 sec. respectively.

399. As the actual lengths of sounds are often conditioned by phonetic contexts, the various durations (chrones) can be grouped

---

[5] Average of four recordings.

together into what may be called *chronemes*, in the same sort of way as qualities (phones) may be grouped into phonemes. They differ from the latter, however, in that though there are many distinguishable chrones in most languages, there are seldom more than two chronemes. The actual lengths occurring in a particular chroneme may be called its "members" or "allochrones."

399a. Languages like Spanish and Russian where vowel duration is not "distinctive," contain only one vowel-chroneme. The languages in which vowel-duration is distinctive (with or without accompanying quality differences, §§510 ff.) contain for the most part two chronemes only. This is doubtless because it is difficult for people with ordinary powers of perception to distinguish with certainty more than two degrees of length in a given phonetic context. The existence of three chronemes is, however, a possibility, and has in fact been stated to be found in Estonian, where three chronemes are applicable to both vowels and consonants (see §419); it is possible also that Japanese contains more than two vowel-chronemes.

400. When there are two chronemes and they are not associated with quality-differences, there must naturally be a condition for intelligibility that the ratio between "long" and "short" should not fall short of a certain minimum.[6] Intelligibility is improved by increasing this ratio, as is no doubt often done.

401. Examples of the grouping of absolute lengths into chronemes are given in the following paragraphs (§§402–417). §§402–416 exemplify the principle in languages employing two chronemes; §417 contains illustrations from languages with only one chroneme.

402. The type of Southern English which I speak is an example of a language where the differences of length included within the chroneme are particularly striking. In this type of English two chronemes are employed, a "long" and a "short." Each of these comprises a number of chrones, some of which differ very considerably from each other. When the long chroneme is applied to the i-phoneme, a relatively close variety of i is used and the differences of chrone in different phonetic contexts are particularly noteworthy. In narrow transcriptions it is generally considered sufficient to indicate two of these chrones only, namely, "fully

---

[6] What this minimum is has not, as far as I am aware, been determined.

10

long" and "half-long"[7]; it is, however, not difficult to hear degrees of these, and it would theoretically be possible to mark them in very narrow transcriptions.

403.   The actual average lengths of the chrones used by me in the words mentioned in §390 have been measured and found to be as follows: siː 0·317 sec., siːd 0·252 sec., siːn 0·199 sec., siːt 0·124 sec., ˈsiːtiŋ 0·087 sec.[8]

404.   The following have been found to be the lengths of my long aː in similar conditions[9]: kaː (car) 0·406 sec., kaːd (card) 0·338 sec., kaːm (calm) 0·305 sec., kaːt (cart) 0·254 sec., ˈkaːtiŋ (carting) 0·187 sec.   It will be noticed that the chrones vary in somewhat the same way as those of iː, but that they are all a little longer and the ratios between them are somewhat less than the corresponding ratios for long iː.

405.   When the short chroneme is applied to the English i-phoneme, opener types of vowel are used, the variety employed in any given case depending upon the phonetic context and particularly upon the stress.   These opener sounds may be represented in narrow transcription by the letter ι.   Several chrones can be distinguished, but the differences between them are naturally less than between those found in the long chroneme.   The actual average lengths of the chrones used by me in the words lid, sin, sit, sitting, city were calculated in June, 1939, to be as follows: lid 0·135 sec.,[10] sin 0·077 sec., sit 0·085 sec., ˈsitiŋ (first i) 0·052 sec., ˈsiti (first i)

---

[7] And that only for the English pure or nearly pure vowels.   It is not customary to mark the lengths of diphthongs, though they vary in the same manner as the lengths of pure vowels.   (It is inconvenient to mark the lengths of diphthongs in writing.)

[8] These measurements and those in §§404–406 were calculated from kymographic tracings by Dr. D. B. FRY and Miss E. T. ANDERSON (now Mrs. H. J. ULDALL) in the phonetics laboratory at University College, London, in June, 1939.   The figures show the average of four recordings of each word.

Other kymographic tracings of similar words were published by me in the first and second editions of my Outline of English Phonetics (Leipzig, 1918, 1922), p. 179, and in the Proceedings of the Royal Institution, Vol. XXII, 1919, pp. 8–18 (report of a lecture on Experimental Phonetics and its Utility to the Linguist delivered on 9th Feb., 1917).   The measurements of the vowels there recorded were as follows: biː (bee) 0·47 sec., biːd (bead) 0·325 sec., biːn (bean) 0·304 sec., biːt (beat) 0·147 sec., bid (bid) 0·15 sec., bin (bin) 0·11 sec., bit (bit) 0·068 sec.

[9] Including the aspiration of the k.

[10] See §421.

0·054 sec., (second i) 0·175 sec.[11] These measurements show relationships similar to those found in the long chroneme, except in sin
where the vowel is somewhat shorter in proportion. It is not usual to
indicate any of these differences of chrone in narrow transcriptions.

406. Similar chrones are found in other cases of the short
chroneme in my type of English, e.g. ʌ and short o. Thus the
average lengths of ʌ in my pronunciation of *thud, shun, shut,
shutting* have been found to be as follows: θʌd 0·1405 sec., ʃʌn
0·110 sec., ʃʌt 0·0928 sec., 'ʃʌtiŋ 0·065 sec. These measurements show relationships similar to those of long i.[12]

407. Stage German also has chrones applicable to vowels which
can be grouped into two chronemes, a long and a short. There are
accompanying quality relationships in the case of all the vowels
except ɛ.[13] Thus the following pairs of long and short vowels
occur in German: iː i (narrowly ɩ), eː e (narrowly ə),[14] ɛː ɛ, aː a
(narrowly ɑ), oː o (narrowly ɔ), uː u (narrowly ѡ), yː y (narrowly ʏ),
øː ø (narrowly œ).

408. The chrones found within these chronemes are in one respect
similar to those occurring in corresponding situations in English.
In German, as in English, the chrones used in unstressed pretonic
syllables are notably shorter than those in comparable stressed
syllables: the eː of leː'bɛndiç (*lebendig*) is shorter than the eː of
'leːben (*Leben*), just as the aː in the English aː'tistik (*artistic*) is
shorter than that in aːt (*art*).

409. In other respects, however, the usage in German differs
from that in English. In particular there is little difference between
the chrones used in German before voiced and breathed consonants:
the lengths of the vowels in 'biːtə (*biete*) and 'biːnə (*Biene*), 'ʃtraːsə
(*Strasse*) and 'naːzə (*Nase*) are not perceptibly different.[15]

---

[11] It will be observed that final weakly stressed short i is longer than any of
the others. It is, however, shorter than final weakly stressed long iː, of such
words as 'koutiː (*coatee*), 'pedigriː (*pedigree*).

[12] The two chronemes are not applicable to all the English vowels. In
my pronunciation they are not applicable to the a-sounds, and there is some
doubt as to whether they can properly be applied to ə. (See §§197–202.)

[13] I refer to the type of German in which words like *spät, ähnlich* are said
with a long ɛ.

[14] The short e [ə] only occurs in syllables with weak stress.

[15] A constant source of mispronunciation for English learners of German
and German learners of English.

410. French makes a limited use of two chronemes. They are applicable only to certain vowels and to those only in certain situations. Moreover variations of usage are found with different French speakers. In one common type of French the two chronemes are applicable only to ɛ before final p, t, m, n, l, s, ʃ and j, to u before s and j, and to œ before j. Examples: gɛːp, djɛp (*guêpe, Dieppe*); ʒɛːm, ʒɛm (*j'aime, gemme*); bɛːl, bɛl (*bêle, belle*); abɛːs, abɛs (*abaisse, abbesse*); tuːs, tus (*tous* meaning "all of us," "of them," etc., *tousse*); nuːj, fənuj (*nouille, fenouil*); fœːj, rəkœj (*feuille, recueil*).[16] It is probable that the two chronemes are applicable to ɑ, but there appear to be no conclusive examples to prove this; pairs like ɑːt (*hâte*), drwɑt (*droite*) are perhaps a sufficient indication.[17]

411. The two chronemes are not applicable to the other French vowels. ə is always short, and the remainder (i, e, a, ɔ, o, y, ø, ɛ̃, ɑ̃, ɔ̃, œ̃) always have lengths determined by phonetic context.[18] Nor are the two chronemes applicable to ɛ, u and œ before consonants other than those mentioned in the preceding paragraph; before other consonants the vowels are long or short according to "rules."[18]

412. In the situations where the two chronemes are applicable in French there is not much variation of chrone within each chroneme. Thus the long ɛ's are approximately of the same length in bɛːt (*bête*), ɛːm (*aime*), bɛːl (*bêle*), bɛːs (*baisse*), frɛːʃ (*fraîche*); and the short ɛ's are approximately of equal length in bɛt (*bette*), ʒɛm (*gemme*), bɛl (*belle*), sɛs (*cesse*),[19] mɛʃ (*mèche*).[19]

413. In the circumstances where the two chronemes are not applicable in French certain notable differences of chrone are to

---

[16] Some French speakers do not make these differences in the length of u and œ. With others, on the other hand, the two chronemes are applicable to i and y in some situations: fiːs, vis (*fils, vis*), ɔmnibyːs, pys (*omnibus, puce*). With others again the two chronemes are not applicable to ɛ before n, s and ʃ, all the words ending in these sounds having ɛ's of equal length.

[17] On the assumption that the shortness of the ɑ in drwɑt is not in any way conditioned by the presence of the rw.

[18] See the "rules of length" formulated in the books on the phonetics of French (e.g. PASSY, *Sons du Français*, pp. 62, 63; ARMSTRONG, *Phonetics of French*, pp. 151–153; NICHOLSON, *Introduction to French Phonetics*, pp. 175, 176).

[19] The vowels in *cesse* and *mèche* are lengthened by some.

be found within the single chroneme. The length of i, for instance, follows the well-known rule that the long chrone is used in final syllables terminating in v, vr, z, ʒ, r or j, as in riːv (*rive*), iːvr (*ivre*), biːz (*bise*), tiːʒ (*tige*), fiːj (*fille*); a short chrone is used in all other situations, e.g. in vi (*vit, vie*),[20] vit (*vite*), vis (*vis*), viɲ (*vigne*), vil (*ville*), fig (*figue*), vid (*vide*).[21]

414. The distinctive long chrones of such words as gɛːp, ɛːm, bɛːl (§410) are approximately equal to the non-distinctive long chrones in such words as rɛːv (*rêve*), ʃɛːz (*chaise*), nɛːʒ (*neige*), pɛːr (*père*); and the distinctive short chrones of djɛp, ʒɛm, bɛl, etc., are approximately equal to the non-distinctive short chrones of such words as ʃɛf (*chef*), ɑ̃sɛɲ (*enseigne*).

415. French is thus a language in which the distinction between long and short chrones is sometimes significant and sometimes not. Another such language is colloquial Sinhalese. In that language all the vowels with the exception of ə are subject to two chronemes: examples piːli (gutters), pili (clothes), βeːlə (half-day), βelə (field), ɛːtə (distant), ɛtə (there is), maːlə (necklaces), malə (flower), poːrə (manure), porə (quarrels), suːdu (gambling), sudu (white). In final position it is usually immaterial whether a vowel other than ə is pronounced long or short: the word for "white" is pronounced indiscriminately as sudu or suduː, and the words for "eye," "small," "more" are pronounced ɛhɛ, poɖi, βaɖa or ɛhɛː, poɖiː, βaɖaː without any apparent system.[22] There are, however, a certain number of Sinhalese words in which the length of a final vowel is essential. Thus ridiː (silver), nɛː (not), gonaː (bull), koː (where, interrog.) cannot have their vowels shortened.

416. In final positions therefore two chronemes are applicable, (1) a long chroneme and (2) what might perhaps be termed a

---

[20] Reference is here made to the type of French in which feminine endings do not involve length of vowel. In some types of French, *vit* and *vie* are distinguished as vi and viː.

[21] With some speakers, final b, d, g are also associated with a long chrone on the preceding vowel.

[22] If there is any system governing the length of these final vowels it is probably to be found in the position of the word in the sentence, and in the nature of the sentence. This would be a phenomenon in length corresponding to sentence stress in stress languages and sentence intonation in tone languages.

"varichrone,"[23] the chrones of which vary from quite short to a duration equal to that of the long chroneme. There is in fact a kind of "overlapping" of chronemes here.

417. In the preceding paragraphs we have dealt chiefly with length in languages where two chronemes are found. The grouping of chrones into a chroneme may, however, also be exemplified from languages having only one chroneme. In Russian, for instance, it is probable that, other things being equal, the vowels in syllables closed by consonants have a somewhat shorter chrone than the vowels of open syllables. Thus the vowel of **rost** (рост, height) is probably a little shorter than the **o** in **sto** (сто, hundred).[24] In Spanish, according to NAVARRO TOMÁS, vowels have fairly long chrones when final (strongly or weakly stressed) and when strongly stressed and followed by a single consonant followed in turn by another vowel. Vowels in other situations (e.g. when strongly stressed but preceding two consonants or when weakly stressed and not final) have shorter chrones. Measurements are given on pp. 155, 156 of NAVARRO TOMÁS's *Pronunciación Española*.

418. From the linguistic point of view the differences of vowel length occurring in non-chrone languages are immaterial. One result is that length-marks need not be used in practical phonetic writing for such languages. Another is that (within limits)[25] though the use of incorrect vowel lengths by a foreign learner of such a language may cause him to speak with a foreign accent, it will not render him unintelligible.

419. The use of three chronemes in a language is very rare. Three chronemes have, however, been stated to occur in Estonian. They are exemplified in **jama** (*jama*, nonsense), **ja:ma** (*jaama*, of the station), **ja::ma** (*jaama*, to the station). Three degrees of consonant length are also believed to occur, and are exemplified in **lina** (flax,

---

[23] See "variphones" (Chap. XXVIII).

[24] Reference is here made to words said in isolation. In connected speech the lengths of words are often modified. It is, however, not possible to take account of variations of length in the sentence in order to arrive at a theory of chronemes, any more than it is possible to take into account variations of sound occurring in connected speech in grouping sounds into phonemes (§34).

[25] I.e. provided that the lengths are not so much altered as to give prominence to syllables which should not be prominent.

sheet), linna (of the town), linnna (to the town).[26]   These and many
other examples have been given by L. KRASS in her thesis on *The
Phonetics of Estonian* (1944) which may be consulted in the Library
of the University of London.[27]

420.   It is probable that in languages which make use of three
chronemes there is not much variation of chronc within each
chroneme.[28] Miss KRASS has, however, called attention to some cases
in which the extra long chroneme is not quite as long as usual.[29]

OVERLAPPING OF CHRONEMES

421.   It will be observed that in languages which make use of
more than one chroneme the lengths belonging to the chronemes
are liable to overlap a good deal.   This is especially the case when
differentiations are effected by duration in combination with
tamber or some other attribute.   Thus it will be seen from §§403
and 405 that my short i in lid has a longer duration than my long i
in si:t.   And I think it probable that the German long a in weakly
stressed pretonic position, as in da:'ne:ben (*daneben*), va:r'ʃainliç
(*wahrscheinlich*), would be found to be at least as short as the
stressed German short a in some positions.[30]   It must be emphasized
that the whole idea of the chroneme is based not on absolute lengths,
but on relative lengths in similar phonetic contexts.

DIFFERENCES OF CHRONE ACCORDING TO TYPE OF SENTENCE

422.   It will be seen from what was said in §§383–385 about
length in Tswana that that language illustrates a very unusual
type of chronemic usage.   There is a chroneme of one kind for
statements, and a chroneme of quite a different nature for questions,
commands and exclamatory sentences.   It is as if statements

---

[26] The case of Estonian words like *kabi* (hoof), *kapi* (near the cupboard),
kappi (into the cupboard) is similar.   The orthographic *b* represents a voiceless
consonant, unaspirated p; the *p* of *kapi* represents a lengthening of this, and
the *pp* of *kappi* a further lengthening.   The words might be written phonetically
kapi, kappi, kapppi.

[27] Professor L. POSTI, in his article, *On Quantity in Estonian* (*Jour. Soc.
Finno-ougrienne*, LIV, Helsinki, 1950), expressed the opinion that by a special
classification of the lengths in Estonian the number of chronemes is reducible
to two.   Miss Krass maintains her opinion that there are three chronemes.

[28] Except possibly in a language where two of the chronemes are associated
with notable distinctions of tamber, if such a language exists.

[29] Thesis on *The Phonetics of Estonian*, pp. 107, 110.

[30] Weakly stressed pretonic short a, as in ta'ni:n (*Tannin*), pa'si:va:
(*Passiva*), va'lo:niʃ (*wallonisch*), would be shorter still.

constituted a special variety of the language different from these other types of sentence.   In the chroneme applicable to questions, commands and exclamations there are no perceptible variations of chrone, except that if sentences of these kinds are divisible into two or more sense-groups, the final sound of each non-final sense-group is generally rather longer than the other syllabic sounds.   In complete statements, on the other hand, there is likewise a single chroneme but it comprises three very distinct chrones, a very long, a half-long and a short.   The very long chrone is used in the penultimate syllable of every sentence, the half-long at the end of non-final sense-groups and the short in all other situations.

Representations of Chronemes in Writing

423.   The theory of chronemes forms the basis for the marking of length in broad phonetic writing.   No indications of duration are needed in writing non-chrone languages.   In languages which make use of two chronemes the long chroneme has to be shown in writing; this may be done either by a mark or by doubling the letters denoting the sounds which have the long chroneme.   In languages like French or Sinhalese in which use is made both of significant and of non-significant length, it is not necessary to mark the non-significant lengths, even though these lengths may be equivalent to those found in the long chroneme.   It may, however, be found convenient to mark these lengths for the sake of consistency; this does not narrow the transcription.   Languages which make use of three chronemes require marks for two of them; alternatively, and perhaps preferably, the chronemes may be represented by single, double and treble letters.   This latter plan is followed by L. Krass for Estonian (§419).

CHAPTER XXIV
STRESS, PROMINENCE

The Nature of Stress

424.   It is possible to pronounce a given syllable with various *degrees* of force (strong, medium, weak, etc.) and with various *kinds* of force (level, crescendo, diminuendo or crescendo-diminuendo).

425.   Force of utterance, abstracted from the other attributes of speech-sounds, is termed *stress*.   Stresses are essentially subjective activities of the speaker.   A strongly stressed syllable, for instance, is one which he consciously utters with greater effort than other neighbouring syllables in the word or sentence. Special visible gestures, and especially movements of the head, arms and hands, often accompany the utterance of strongly stressed syllables. The application of strong stress involves in fact a special effort of the whole body; it is not confined to the speech mechanism.

426. To the hearer degrees of stress are often perceived as degrees of loudness. If a sound or syllable is said several times with varying degrees of stress in similar phonetic contexts, it appears to be less easy for the hearer to compare the degrees of its loudness than it is for the speaker to compare the degrees of effort he uses.

427. In actual language it is often difficult, and may be impossible, for the hearer to judge where strong stresses are. One reason for this is that the loudness or carrying power of a sound is largely a matter of its inherent quality (tamber),[1] and that in consequence a sound pronounced with strong stress may be less loud than another sound pronounced with weaker stress. Another reason is that in practice strong stresses are usually accompanied by one or more other speech attributes which contribute towards making the syllable more clearly heard (see §§446, 450, 456, 457).[2]

---

[1] Thus, if vowels of the u and ɑ types are pronounced with what the speaker feels to be the same degree of effort, the ɑ is found to be much louder than the u; it can be heard at a greater distance, and it comes out more clearly over a microphone. (See also §437, and footnote 12 to §204.)

Loudness must be distinguished from "penetration." A sound is said to be "penetrating" when it can be heard when other sounds are going on simultaneously. It "penetrates" those other sounds. Penetration is not an attribute of the sound itself; it is dependent upon the nature of the other sounds through which it is heard. Very soft sounds may penetrate loud sounds of a very different quality, that is to say, they may be clearly audible as separate sounds while the loud sounds are in progress. Thus, a weak s can be heard while an organ of considerable power is being played, although the same sound could not possibly be heard in the neighbourhood of an escape of steam from an engine. Conversely, the qualities of many organ flue stops, though loud and distinctive when played alone, do not "penetrate" the qualities of other organ stops. They blend with them and alter the quality of the total sound, but are not heard separately by ordinary people. It needs an expert to tell what stops are employed when a flue tone is being produced by the use of several stops.

[2] See my *Outline of English Phonetics*, footnote to §909, where it is pointed out that a strong stress may occur on a sound incapable of receiving any noticeable increase of loudness.

428. Languages in which meaning depends in any degree upon types of stress or upon the location of strong stresses in sequences of syllables are termed "stress languages." They fall into three categories, (1) those in which the location of strong stresses in words of more than one syllable is an integral part of the pronunciation of words, (2) those in which the use of special types of stress is an integral part of the pronunciation of words, and (3) those in which strong stresses are used in sentences but do not have fixed positions in particular words.

429. Stress languages of the first category are numerous. Among them are English, German, Russian, Spanish, Provençal, Danish, Hungarian, Icelandic, Welsh, Greek, Swahili. In these languages a given word always, or generally, has strong stress on a particular syllable. In some of them words of more than one syllable may be differentiated by the position of the strongest stress.

430. Languages of the second category are Serbo-Croat and (probably) Somali.

431. The best known language of the third category is French. In this language, all the syllables of groups containing no emphatic word have approximately equal stress except the last of the group which has a somewhat stronger stress than the others.[3] Tswana is another such language. As was pointed out in §386, the usage there is that the two last syllables of every complete statement are strongly stressed, except when these syllables have the tonal pattern [＼ ·], in which case the penultimate only is stressed.

432. In stress languages emphasis, whether for intensity or for contrast, is generally shown by means of special strong stresses. In languages of the first and second categories emphasized words of more than one syllable generally receive a stronger stress than usual on the syllable normally stressed, and emphatic monosyllabic words receive strong stress in comparison with other words near them in the sentence. In French, which is a stress language

---

[3] It is difficult, or perhaps impossible, to prove this statement. It is, however, common experience that good results are obtained in teaching French pronunciation if the teaching is based on this assumption.

of the third category, words requiring emphasis for *intensity* have a strong stress; if they are of two or more syllables, the stress falls on the first or second syllables according to well-known principles which we need not recapitulate here.[4] French words of more than one syllable requiring emphasis for *contrast* generally have a strong stress on the last syllable.[5] I have had no opportunity of making precise observations on emphatic words in Tswana, but it seems likely that the effect is produced by increasing the tonal intervals and not by any special stress.

433. Many languages exist in which stress variations can hardly be said to exist at all. They may be called "stressless languages." Such are Japanese, Hindustani, Marathi.

STRESS AND PROMINENCE

434. In all languages, including those in which the speakers make no conscious use of stress, syllables occur here and there in connected speech which are heard to be more "prominent" than others—syllables which stand out from other syllables near them in the word or sentence. Prominence is an effect perceived objectively by the hearer. It is thus quite a different thing from stress, which is a subjective activity on the part of the speaker.

435. Prominence of a syllable may be due to strong stress, but it may also be due to other features of pronunciation and particularly to the inherent quality of sounds, to the length of syllables (which may be occasioned either by the length of sounds in them or by their number) or to intonation. Different ways of effecting prominence are exemplified in §§436–447.

PROMINENCE BY STRESS

436. To appreciate the degree of prominence which can be given by stress alone one must pronounce a sequence of similar syllables on a monotone or in a whisper, putting the strong stress first on one syllable and then on another. A sequence such as ninininin serves the purpose, thus 'ninininin, ni'nininin, nini'ninin, ninini'nin, or pairs of English words like bi'gin (*begin*), 'bigin (*Biggin*),

---

[4] They are set out particularly clearly in Chapter XIX of COUSTENOBLE and ARMSTRONG'S *Studies in French Intonation*.

[5] See COUSTENOBLE and ARMSTRONG, *Studies in French Intonation*, Chapters XXIII, XXV.

riˈmit (*remit*), ˈlimit (*limit*). Experimenting thus it will be found that the positions of the strong stresses are always clear to the speaker, but are not always unmistakable to the hearer if the speaker is careful to make the stressed and unstressed vowels as nearly as possible of the same length. The fact that an English hearer perceives, or thinks he perceives, the chief prominence to be on the second syllable in riˈmit and the first syllable in ˈlimit, is, I believe, largely due to the fact that he knows the words and knows how he would pronounce them himself. It does not necessarily follow that foreign hearers would regard the same syllables as being prominent. Indeed, in my experience, many foreigners fail to perceive English stress correctly. This applies more particularly to those whose mother tongue is a stressless language such as Japanese or Hindi.

Prominence by Tamber

437.   Prominence effected by vowel quality may be illustrated by the following experiment, which was devised by A. Lloyd James. The English word miˈkanikəli (*mechanically*) has strong stress on the second syllable and weak stresses on the others. If one whispers the word (to eliminate intonation) and pronounces it in an artificial manner with strong stresses on the mi and ni and weak stress on ka, thus ˈmikaˈnikəli, it has been found that hearers still think they hear "stress" on the ka. (I have often tried this experiment.) Actually what the hearers perceive is the prominence of the syllable ka. The prominence of the English short a quality so outweighs that of the short i that it is well-nigh impossible to render an i more prominent by stress alone.[6] I believe that this prominence of the English short a as compared with the short i is inherent, and would therefore be observed by foreigners unfamiliar with the word as well as by the English hearers with whom the experiment is tried.

Prominence by Length

438.   Prominence effected by length may be observed in stressless languages like Sinhalese and Tamil. Let the reader say aloud the following Sinhalese words on a monotone with as nearly as possible

---

[6] In voiced speech the syllables mi and ni could be made more prominent than ka by means of stress coupled with intonation, e.g. by applying the subjective intonation [\ . \ . .].

equal stress on each syllable, but observing carefully the vowel lengths and the double consonants. It will be found that hearers will easily perceive the prominence of the long syllables.

saːgətə (famine)	palaːtə (district)
ekkenek (one person)	hɛdiːmə (the making)
piṭipasseŋ (behind)	iːṭəpasse (afterwards)
barəkaratte (cart drawn by two bulls)	nidaːgannəβa (I sleep)
attorəloːsuə (watch)	aːrassaːkərənəβa (I protect)[7]

Similar examples from Tamil[8] are:

aːlamaram (banyan tree)	vipattu[9] (calamity)
viːṭu[10] (house)	paṭeːn[11] (I did not endure)
palli (lizard)	irukkiraːn (he is)
paṭittukkol[12] (read)	

439. The prominence which causes consonants to be syllabic is generally produced by length. That this is so is shown by a comparison of such English words as ˈmedlə (*meddler*) and ˈmedlə (*medlar*), ˈkodliŋ (*coddling*) and ˈkodliŋ (*codling*), ˈbʌtn̩iŋ (*buttoning*) and ˈpʌtni (*Putney*). The l's and n̩ of ˈmedlə, ˈkodliŋ, ˈbʌtn̩iŋ are weakly stressed, but the sounds are much longer than the l's and n of the other words. It is this length that makes them prominent enough to strike the ear as forming syllables.

PROMINENCE BY INTONATION

440. Syllables are sometimes rendered prominent by special sequences of voice-pitches. Such a sequence is [-\\ _], in which the second syllable is liable to sound more prominent than the others. The extent to which intonation alone is capable of rendering

---

[7] These examples are taken from PERERA and JONES, *Colloquial Sinhalese Reader.* I have come to the conclusion that the view expressed by me (in 1919) on page 14 of that book, that there is a tendency to put stress on long syllables of Sinhalese words, is incorrect. I believe I mistook prominence for stress, and am now very doubtful if there are any real stress distinctions in the Sinhalese language.

[8] Examples taken from J. R. FIRTH's *Short Outline of Tamil Pronunciation.*

[9] Narrowly vibattɯ.

[10] Narrowly viːɖɯ.

[11] Narrowly paɖeːn.

[12] Narrowly paɖittukkol.

a syllable prominent without the aid of stress or some other attribute is a subject which merits detailed investigation. Here I am only able to give some preliminary notes on it (§§441–445).

441. Experiments appear to show that, within limits, no particular voice-pitch is inherently more prominent than another; for instance, it cannot be laid down as a general principle that high pitches are more prominent than lower ones. The reader may test this for himself by experiments such as the following. Pronounce a syllable, say la, on alternate moderately high and moderately low level pitches, thus [˙ . ˙ . ˙ .], keeping the lengths and stresses as equal as possible. A listener will find it quite easy to "hear" the higher pitch to be the more prominent. On the other hand he will find it equally easy to perceive the lower pitch as the more prominent. It is possible indeed that people of different nationalities may differ in their perception of the prominence of high and low pitches, attributing prominence to syllables which would have stress if a particular sequence of intonations were to occur in their native language. If the speaker wishes to give unmistakable effects of prominence in the above intonation sequence, he must either stress certain syllables, e.g. [• . • . • .] or [. • . • .] or [• . • . •], etc., or lengthen them, thus [¯ . ¯ . ¯ .] or [. _ . _ . _] or [¯ . ¯ . ¯], etc.[13]

442. So again, if a sequence of three syllables, say an invented word **barana,** is said with equal lengths of the vowels and equal stresses and with such an intonation as [· ˙ .], it does not seem that any one of the syllables is more prominent than any other; in fact, it is not difficult to "perceive" any one of the syllables as the most prominent. Nevertheless a French hearer might well think he perceived prominence on the final syllable of this sequence, while an English or German hearer would be more likely to attribute prominence to the second syllable. The same kind of thing is found if **barana** is pronounced with other sequences of level intonations such as [˙ ..], [. ˙ ˙], [˙ . ˙]; any syllable may be perceived as prominent, and hearers of one nationality may draw conclusions different from those of another nationality.

---

[13] In this graphic system large dots represent syllables pronounced with stronger stress than those represented by small dots. The horizontal lines represent long syllables pronounced with the same degree of stress as those indicated by small dots.

443. It seems, however, that rhythmic repetitions of a particular pitch give to most hearers the impression of prominence of that pitch under certain conditions. When, for instance, a high pitch is repeated at equal intervals of time and there are several intervening mid and low pitches, the high pitch may appear prominent, and it may require a certain effort of imagination to "perceive" prominence on one of the low syllables unless it is made prominent by length or stress. The following sequence of tones furnishes an example: [· · . · ¯ · · . · · etc.]. The same appears to apply to low-pitched syllables occurring at equal intervals of time among high syllables, e.g. [. · ¯ · ¯ · . . · etc.]. It needs a still greater effort to perceive prominence on mid-pitched syllables surrounded by rhythmically placed high and low syllables.[14]

---

[14] Prominence of mid-pitched notes situated between higher and lower pitched notes is often required in music. Thus, if the passage

is played on an organ legato and without any phrasing, it appears to be easier to perceive it

as

or

than as

(The passage is taken from Bach's Partita in E minor for violin, where the actual rhythm is the last of these three.)

Similarly it needs much concentration to keep in mind the rhythm indicated in the writing of such a passage as the following from Kreisler's Praeludium and Allegro for violin

on account of the prominence of the high pitches occurring on every third

444. Falling and rising tones appear to have a certain inherent prominence. This can be tested by saying a sequence of long and equally stressed syllables, say baːraːnaː, with intonations such as [\\ --], [- \\ -], [-- \\ ], [- \\ ⁻], [／ ⁻⁻], [⁻ ／ ⁻], [⁻⁻ ／], [⁻ ／ -]. To me, and no doubt to others, the falling and rising tones in these sequences have a certain prominence as compared with the level tones. Concrete examples of such tone sequences are to be found in such a language as Burmese, where successions of long and equally stressed syllables are common. Thus in the Burmese expression ‿pjã: ꜚpjɔ: ‿le: ‿ði: (he thus replied) the syllable ꜚpjɔ: appears more prominent than the others.

445. Summarizing what has been said in the preceding paragraphs we may say that prominence by intonation alone is rare in speech, and is perhaps confined to falling and rising tones on single syllables and to cases where level tones occur in some sort of rhythmic pattern. If a syllable has to be made prominent in other circumstances, the intonation used must probably be accompanied by some different reinforcing attribute.

PROMINENCE BY COMBINATIONS OF ATTRIBUTES

446. As syllables can have prominence through any one of the means mentioned in §§436–444, so they can be and often are rendered prominent by combinations of them. A common combination is, for instance, strong stress together with special intonation; this is the usual means of giving prominence in stress languages.[15] Sometimes the combinations serving to effect

---

note, which are liable to give the hearer the impression of a passage in triplets. The passage is one where, if it is played exactly as written, the prominences indicated in the printed music can hardly be otherwise than subjective. I believe it to be impossible for a listener unacquainted with the passage to perceive them. The prominences which are presumably intended can in fact only be apprehended by those who know beforehand where they are supposed to be.

Performers often give indication of the correct prominences in such passages by means of *rubato* or slight prolongation of some of the notes intended to be prominent. I have noticed, however, more than one eminent violinist who does not give any such indication in the above passage. In fact this passage is so rapid that it would hardly be possible to do so.

[15] See various works on English intonation, e.g. KINGDON'S *Groundwork of English Intonation*, ARMSTRONG and WARD'S *Handbook of English Intonation*, or Chapter XXXI of my *Outline of English Phonetics*.

prominence are very subtle, and it is difficult to determine what attribute, if any, is the dominating one. Languages in which significant distinctions are made by such means are Somali (see §§580–582), Serbo-Croat (§§466, 558–560, 583) and, perhaps, Hindustani.

447. A syllable which is prominent by reason of one attribute may be less prominent than one would expect on account of some other kind of prominence in a neighbouring syllable. Examples may be observed in many words of the Estonian language, such as **'puhatta** (*puhata*, to rest), **'kahekksa** (*kaheksa*, eight, m. sg.), **'vapastap** (*vabastab*, he sets free), **'vapantamisessse** (*vabandamisesse*, apology, inessive sg.). The first syllable of these words, as of nearly all Estonian words, has strong stress, and Estonian speakers feel these syllables to be the most prominent in the words. Some of the subsequent syllables have, however, a certain prominence by reason of the number of sounds in them and their consequent length. To me as an outsider unfamiliar with the language, but listening to the words objectively, the prominence of these other syllables often seems greater than that of the stressed syllables which are really the most prominent to the subjective feeling of an Estonian speaker.

NEED FOR DISTINCTION BETWEEN PROMINENCE AND STRESS

448. Syllables rendered prominent otherwise than by stress are liable to be mistaken for strongly stressed syllables by foreign hearers unfamiliar with the words. It is, for instance, very easy for an Englishman to imagine that Sinhalese speakers put strong stresses on the long syllables of the words quoted in §438. (Readers are recommended to try experiments with them.) Likewise some sequences of voice-pitches are liable to give to English observers the effect of strong stress on a syllable, when they are such as would be associated with strong stresses in English. English hearers would be liable, for instance, to form the opinion that the syllable ˋpjɔː in the Burmese example in §444 is stressed, which I do not think it is.

449. The following is an example where a combination of tones with lengths gives to the English hearer the impression of stresses. There are prominences, but my observation is that the first two prominences have no stronger stress than the less prominent

syllables adjoining them. The example is from the Tswana language, a language which I find to be stressless except for the two final syllables of statements (for which see §§386, 431). The last clause of the Tswana version of the Lord's Prayer is kāā bɷ sīna bɷkhutlɔ. With precise tone and length marking this would be written kāā bɷ sīna bɷkhʉːtlɔ. The length of the vowels of kāā[16] and -khʉː- and the rhythmical placing of the high-toned -sī- give a certain prominence to these three syllables, and the effect to English hearers is that they are stressed. The fact that kāā and sī are not stressed can be demonstrated by the experiment of saying this phrase with strong stresses on the first bɷ and on na, while keeping the correct tones and lengths. However much stress one puts on the bɷ and na, English listeners will continue to "hear stresses" on kāā and sī, unless they see the speaker's gestures.[17]

DIFFICULTY OF DETERMINING STRESS

450. From what has been said it will be seen that it is often difficult, if not impossible, to compare objectively by ear the stress of one syllable with that of another. In the first place, as has been pointed out in §437, a sound pronounced with strong stress is often less loud than another sound pronounced with weaker stress. Secondly, as in practice strong stress is almost always accompanied by a special intonation or some other attribute, one often cannot say for certain how much of the prominence is to be attributed to the stress. I therefore do not anticipate that it will prove possible to determine degrees of stress experimentally from sound records. It is conceivable that they might be determined experimentally from the movements of a speaker (muscular contractions of the chest wall, etc.) but little has hitherto been achieved in this direction as far as I am aware.

451. It will be seen further that to ensure correct phonetic analysis of foreign languages it is essential that the observer should differentiate correctly between strong stress and prominence effected by means other than stress. It is a natural tendency of English people and speakers of other stress languages to attribute all prominences to stress alone. As most observers have hitherto

---

[16] This doubled vowel is indistinguishable acoustically from a long vowel.

[17] These gestures indicate the ordinary strong stresses on the two final syllables, -khʉː- and -tlɔ, as well as the special stresses on bɷ and na.

not been on the look-out for the distinction between stress and prominence, it is necessary to be careful in accepting statements as to stress in non-European languages, and we must be ready to review them in the light of what is now known of prominence.

STRESS AS A SIGNIFICANT ATTRIBUTE IN WORDS

452. One function of stress is to give emphasis to words, as already mentioned in §341 ff. This is a use of stress in the *sentence*, strong stress being employed to make a word or part of a word stand out in order to give special intensity to its meaning or to show that it is in contrast with something. It is probable that this use of stress is to be found to a certain extent in stressless languages as well as in stress languages. The employment of stress for purposes of emphasis does not come within the purview of this book. We are here only concerned with the other functions of stress, namely, as an essential feature of the pronunciation of words and as a means of distinguishing one word from another, as is done in stress languages of the first and second categories mentioned in §§428–430.

453. English, as is well known, is a language in which stress is used in this way. When I say the word 'limit (*limit*) I consciously put strong stress on the first syllable, and when I say ri'mit (*remit*) I consciously put it on the second. Various pairs of English words are distinguished by the position of the strong stress. Such are 'inkriːs (*increase*, n.), in'kriːs (*increase*, v.), 'impoːt (*import*, n.), im'poːt (*import*, v.), 'insʌlt (*insult*, n.), in'sʌlt (*insult*, v.), 'toːment[18] (*torment*, n.), toː'ment (*torment*, v.), 'riːfʌnd (*refund*, n.), 'riːfʌnd[19] (*refund*, v.), 'bilou (*billow*), bi'lou[20] (*below*).[21]

454. Examples from other languages of distinctions of words by stress alone are: German 'viːderˌhoːlen (fetch back), ˌviːderˈhoːlen (repeat) (both words written *wiederholen*), 'yːberˌblike (plural of *Überblick*), ˌyːberˈblike (1st person present of *überblicken*); Spanish 'aʎa (*halla*, he finds), aˈʎa (*allá*, there), 'termino (end), terˈmino

---

[18] Pronounced by some 'toːmənt. With them the pair is not a case in point.

[19] Pronounced by some ri'fʌnd. With them the pair is not a case in point.

[20] Pronounced by some bəˈlou. With them the pair is not a case in point.

[21] Pairs of words, such as those written *present, subject, recount*, are not cases in point since they show differences of sound quality as well as stress: 'preznt, pri'zent, 'sʌbdʒikt, səb'dʒekt, 'riːˈkaunt, ri'kaunt.

(I finish), termi'no (he finished); Provençal[22] 'laŋgi (sorrow), laŋ'gi (to languish); Greek 'poli (city), po'li (much), 'ennja (worry), en'nja (nine).

455.   It will be observed that in all such languages the words distinguished by the position of strong stress alone are comparatively few in number, and that a substantial proportion of those that exist have such meanings that they would not be liable to be confused in any ordinary context.   This peculiarity is, I believe, attributable to the fact that stress alone, without the accompaniment of some other distinguishing feature does not constitute a very effective means of differentiating words.   The effort of pronouncing syllables with strong stress is clearly felt by the speaker, but the resulting prominence is not always easily perceived by hearers.

456.   Such experiments as have been carried out support this view.   Thus N. C. Scott's experiments described in his article *An Experiment on Stress Perception* in *Le Maître Phonétique*, July, 1939, p. 44, tend to show that when intonation is eliminated, stress distinctions are difficult for the hearer to recognize.   He concludes: "there seems to be a strong indication that stress, unaided, is not very efficient as a distinguishing feature in English."   (See also §436.)

457.   In practice strong stresses are nearly always accompanied by intonations which help to render the syllables prominent.   If, for instance, a Southern English speaker is asked to say the words 'impo:t and im'po:t in a normal manner with a falling intonation, he will in all probability distinguish them by intonations of the types [＼.] and [· ＼].   If asked to say them in a questioning manner, he will probably distinguish them by intonations of the types [·／] and [· ／].   And when such words occur in connected speech, they likewise nearly always have distinctive intonations. (These are sentence intonations, not word-tones.   See §§571, 572.)

458.   The combination of stress with appropriate intonation is a particularly effective means of rendering syllables prominent, and often gives prominence outweighing that of neighbouring syllables which have considerable length or other attributes making for prominence.   In the word 'pedigri:, for instance, said with a falling intonation [＼.－], the strong stress coupled with the high-

---

[22] Dialect of Arles, as described in H. Coustenoble's *Phonétique du Provençal Moderne*, where other examples will be found (p. 137).

falling intonation renders the first syllable much more prominent than the last syllable which has a vowel several times as long as the e of the first syllable. (Nevertheless cases are sometimes found where the combination of strong stress and prominent intonation does not give unmistakably the effect of greatest prominence to the syllable affected. See §447.)

459. The linking of stress with special intonations in English is so frequent and so necessary that the opinion has been expressed by some that stress is immaterial, or at least negligible, and that all necessary prominence is given to syllables by intonation only. The language was recorded on this assumption in H. E. PALMER's book *English Intonation*. My practical experience in teaching English to foreign learners has shown me that there is much to be said in favour of this view. I find that a foreign learner can almost always acquire a pronunciation recognizable as normal English by learning the intonation only and ignoring the stress. I find too that the reverse is not the case: a really good accent cannot be acquired by a foreign learner who pays attention to stress but ignores intonation. But I do not find it possible to ignore stress altogether. There are rare cases where an English intonation without the needful stress would give an un-English effect. An example is where a word stressed on the first syllable is given the common intonation [.\ ] denoting surprise or incredulity, e.g. 'riəli [.\ ] (*Really?*), 'jelou [.\ ] (*Yellow?*), etc., or one form of emphasis, e.g. 'veri [.\ ] (*Very*). Here the stress on the first syllable is so strong as to overpower the prominence produced by the high-falling intonation on the final syllable. Other instances are to be found where strong stress occurs in the middle of a continuous intonation, rising, falling or level; it is the case dealt with by N. C. SCOTT in the article referred to in §456. Insistence upon stress is also necessary in teaching the rhythm of English to foreign learners. (See further, §§570, 571.)

460. It would seem that in other stress languages, such as Italian, Spanish, Russian and Greek, differences of stress are likewise almost always accompanied by special intonations. In Russian differences of stress appear to be always accompanied by differences of sound-quality as well as by special intonations (see §536).

461. Owing no doubt to the elusive character of stress from

the point of view of the hearer,[23] most stress languages employ only two degrees of stress ("strong" and "weak") for effecting word-distinctions. I have only heard of one language, Serbo-Croat, which employs three degrees ("strong," "medium" and "weak") for this purpose. In this language words may be distinguished by the position of the strong or medium stresses relative to the weak ones; thus ˌveseli (gay, nom. pl.) and veˌseli (he entertains) ·are different words. Words may also· be distinguished according as a syllable has strong or medium stress: compare ˈgora (worse), ˌgora (wooded hill), ˈpretvori (he changes), ˌpretvori (he changed). Even monosyllables in this language have appropriate· degrees of force when emphasized. Thus when some words, e.g. ˈsad (now), ˈtsar (emperor) have to be emphasized, strong force is used, but when other words, e.g. ˌrad (voluntarily), ˌzar (then), ˌpas (dog), have to be emphasized, they are said with only medium force.[24] Presumably there exist some monosyllabic words in the language which are distinguished from each other solely by the degree of force used when they are emphasized.

462. In ordinary stress languages, i.e. those in which the location of strong stresses is an essential feature, it is generally considered possible to distinguish and locate "secondary stresses," i.e. degrees intermediate between the strongest and weakest stresses. I think, however, that the so-called intermediate degrees of "stress" are as a rule degrees of *prominence* due to tamber, sound-groupings, length or voice-pitch, or combinations of these, with or without the accompaniment of stress. However that may be, it would seem that in languages like English or German words are never distinguished by the· positions of secondary stresses alone,[25] and

---

[23] Stress being, as already observed in §425, mainly subjective and only partially perceived as loudness. (See my *Outline of English Phonetics*, §909.)

[24] The above information concerning Serbo-Croat was given me by Professor D. B. FRY.

[25] I looked out for cases of this while preparing my *English Pronouncing Dictionary*, but I discovered only one instance, and that a very doubtful one, namely, the two meanings of *certification*. It is barely possible that in the sense of "granting a certificate" the word might be pronounced səːˌtifiˈkeiʃn by some, thus distinguishing it from ˌsəːtifiˈkeiʃn meaning "act of certifying"; I have, however, only heard ˌsəːtifiˈkeiʃn for both senses. It is, moreover, probable that speakers, if any, who put a secondary stress on the second syllable would pronounce səˌtifiˈkeiʃn with short ə, in which case the word would cease to be a case in point.

that therefore we need not concern ourselves with them here. The semantic function of more than two degrees of stress in English appears to be confined to sentences, or to compound words of a type that cannot in my view be taken into consideration in the investigation of phonemic distinctions,[26] any more than the functions of English intonation can be. The position of secondary stress has a certain minor importance in that in a relatively small number of words a displacement of it may give an unnatural though not an unintelligible pronunciation.[27]

KINDS OF STRESS

463. There exist, as mentioned in §424, different kinds of stress as well as different degrees of stress. They are

(1) *level stress* within the syllable, i.e. where the same degree of force is sustained throughout the greater part of the syllable,

(2) *crescendo stress*, i.e. where the force increases during the course of the syllable,

(3) *diminuendo stress*, i.e. where the force diminishes during the course of the syllable,

(4) *crescendo-diminuendo stress*, i.e. where the force increases and then diminishes within the syllable.[28]

Each of these kinds may be uttered with different degrees of force, but the difference between the kinds of stress can only be made clear when the degree of force is considerable, i.e. "strong" or at the least "medium." If the degree of force is "weak," differences in the kind of stress cannot as far as I know be made perceptible to hearers.

464. The above terms, though fairly intelligible, contain elements of vagueness. We know how many syllables there are

---

[26] Such as *movie-auditorium*, which was quoted by TRAGER and BLOCH in their article *The Syllabic Phonemes of English*, or *elevator-operator* quoted in TRAGER and SMITH'S *Outline of English Structure*, p. 39, as words containing four essential degrees of stress.

[27] Even the common foreign pronunciation ˌeksamiˈneiʃn for the English igˌzamiˈneiʃn (*examination*), which contains an error of sound as well as of stress, is not unintelligible, though it is not our way of saying the word. (See *Outline of English Phonetics*, §942.)

[28] There cannot be a *diminuendo-crescendo* stress within a syllable. Such a type of stress necessarily produces a sequence of two syllables.

in a word by counting its peaks of prominence, but we cannot define with precision the points at which the syllables begin and end. Still less can we define the limits of the portions of syllables which are to be considered as bearing the strong stress.[29]   And if we often cannot tell what the whole of a syllable is, it evidently cannot be stated as a general principle that stress affects entire syllables. Moreover syllables often contain consonantal sounds which are by nature weak and can hardly be said to be capable of receiving degrees of stress.[30]   However, in spite of this lack of precision, the general meaning of the terms used in the last paragraph is sufficiently clear to justify using them in practical phonetic work.

465. The most usual kind of stress would appear to be the diminuendo type.   English strong stress is generally considered to be of this type, though it might be maintained that crescendo-diminuendo stress is used in syllables such as ja:d (*yard*), wel (*well*) which begin with a weak consonant; it depends upon where one considers the point of incidence to be.   The same applies to German, Russian and other stress languages.

466. It seems that level stress, crescendo stress and crescendo-diminuendo stress all occur in Serbo-Croat and its dialects.   Professor FRY has informed me that in normal Serbo-Croat the difference between crescendo and crescendo-diminuendo stress is used for word-differentiations in conjunction with special tones (the rising and rise-fall respectively) and with length (moderately long and very long respectively). The words for "young" and "bride" are examples of this given by FRY and KOSTIĆ in their *Serbo-Croat Phonetic Reader* (p. 8).   They write them phonetically with the notation mla·da and ˌmla:da respectively; this denotes that the first syllable of the first word has a rising tone, a moderately long vowel and crescendo stress, and that the first syllable of the second

---

[29] I.e. where the "incidence" of the stress is, and how long the stress lasts. Tapping experiments with a kymograph appear to show that if a strongly stressed syllable consists of a strong consonant followed by a vowel, people more usually feel the stress to begin at some point in the consonant at any rate in English.   But there are exceptions.

[30] Sometimes an increase of force with which a consonant is pronounced may convert it into another consonant   E.g. it is force only that distinguishes voiceless b (ḅ) from unaspirated p.   Semi-vowels, such as j and w, would appear to be essentially unstressable.

word has a rise-fall tone, a very long vowel and crescendo-diminuendo stress.[31] G. L. TRAGER has also noted the existence of the two kinds of stress in Serbo-Croat; he calls them "rising" (= crescendo) and "falling" (= diminuendo).[32] He also remarks that the crescendo stress may have level stress as a variant.[33] He has found similar stresses in a Serbo-Croatian dialect.[34]

467. It is doubtless the case that in such a language as Serbo-Croat the amounts of decrease and increase of force in the diminuendo and crescendo stresses vary to some extent according to the phonetic context, e.g. according to the types of stress used in adjoining syllables. If this is so, we shall on investigation find a state of affairs in stress comparable to the variations of quality in the phoneme, length in the chroneme and voice-pitch in the toneme. Little information as to this appears to be available as yet, but it is reasonable to suppose, for instance, that the amount of decrease of force in a diminuendo stress would be different (probably less) when the following syllable is strongly stressed from what it is when the following syllable is weakly stressed. If a diminuendo stress has thus two or more values according to circumstances, those values can be grouped together and count as being the same for practical linguistic purposes. It is likely too that a level stress would suffice to indicate crescendo stress before a following weakly stressed syllable. In this case a level stress and a crescendo stress would have to be grouped together as a single linguistic entity, in the same sort of way as tambers are grouped together into phonemes.

STRONEMES

468. The foregoing account of the nature of stress and its occurrence in language has been necessary in order to make clear how far stresses can be grouped together in a manner comparable to the grouping of sound-qualities into phonemes. It will be seen

---

[31] Tone-marks (´ and ^) might also be used to mark this distinction: thus mláda, mlâda.

[32] Presumably the same as what FRY has analysed as "crescendo-diminuendo."

[33] G. L. TRAGER, *Serbo-Croatian Accents and Quantities* in *Language*, Vol. XVI, No. 1, January, 1940.

[34] G. L. TRAGER, *Serbo-Croatian Dialect* in *Le Maître Phonétique*, January, 1940, p. 40.

that such grouping is possible in one case only, namely, where *kinds* of stress are concerned. If a particular kind of stress were termed a "strone," we should no doubt find that in such a language as Serbo-Croat two or more kinds of stress would be groupable into a single "stroneme," as suggested in the preceding paragraph. Owing, however, to the extreme difficulty of observing stress and of abstracting it from the other factors making for prominence which almost always accompany it, it is probable that the idea of the stroneme may be dismissed as of little or no value for any practical purpose.

469. Apart from Serbo-Croat and other languages, if any, which exhibit similar peculiarities, it is the *location* of strong stresses and not their type which has significance in stress languages. In this respect stress differs from all other features of speech. In a stress language every word of more than one syllable must have a strong stress somewhere,[35] and one word may be distinguished from another by the position of the strong stress. Being however a matter of location and not of kind, ordinary stresses cannot be grouped in any way into families corresponding to phonemes, chronemes and tonemes.

CHAPTER XXV

TONEMES

470. Languages in which voice-pitches are used for the purpose of distinguishing words are called "tone languages." Such languages are very numerous. They include Chinese (all types), Siamese, Burmese, etc., Bantu languages of Africa (except Swahili), numerous languages of West Africa and the Sudan, Norwegian, Swedish, Lithuanian, Serbo-Croat, Panjabi and some American Indian languages.

---

[35] Reference is here made to "word-stress" only. In the sentence, where stress is used for other purposes than word distinctions, words of more than one syllable may be entirely without strong stress. Thus, the English word *upon*, said in isolation, has a strong stress on the second syllable (ə'pɒn), but in connected speech it is often pronounced with a weak form əpən in which neither syllable has a strong stress: e.g. 'dʒʌst əpən 'gouiŋ (*just upon going*), 'miljənz əpən 'miljənz (*millions upon millions*).

The Nature of Tonemes

471. In tone languages it is commonly found that the values of the tones of particular syllables vary according to the nature of neighbouring tones in the word or sentence or sometimes according to other factors. Often too there is variation according to the situation of words in the sentence. Tones may also be affected by sentence intonation. We thus find in tones a treatment resembling that obtaining in regard to phones (tambers): the tones of tone languages can be grouped together into "tonemes" in the same sort of way as phones are grouped into phonemes, and it is tonemes and not actual tones that distinguish one word from another.

472. There is, however, a great deal of "overlapping" in tones. For example, the same actual mid pitch may stand for a high toneme in one tonal context and for a low toneme in another. Consequently the definition of a toneme cannot be exactly parallel to that of a phoneme. The following is suggested as a definition of a toneme: a family of tones in a given tone language which count for linguistic purposes as if they were one and the same, the differences being due to tonal or other context. It would seem impossible to restrict the conception of the toneme to the tones found in isolated words, since in so many of the tone languages the tonal variants are found only when words occur in conjunction with other words.

473. The various tones comprised in a toneme may be called its "members" or "allotones." Every toneme comprises one tone which can be considered as the "norm" or "principal" or most important member. It is generally the one which would be used when a word containing it is said in isolation, with the proviso, if necessary, that adjoining syllables in the word are said with specified tonemes.

Examples of the Groupings of Tones into Tonemes

474. In §§475–478 are given examples of the grouping of tones into tonemes in languages where tone is not linked with any other attribute.

475. One of the tonemes in the Cantonese language may be termed "high-falling,"[1] since its principal member is a high-falling pitch. The words ˋtɔ (much), ˋsin (previously), for instance, have this toneme and are pronounced with high-falling pitch

---

[1] The Cantonese themselves call it "level" (ˌphiŋ).

when said in isolation or when they occur at the end of a sentence. In most non-final positions, however, such words are said with a simple high pitch in which no fall is perceptible. Thus ˎtɔˎtɔ (very much), ˎsinˎsaŋ (Mr.[2]) are said with pitches which would be represented graphically thus [⁻ ＼]. A simple high tone without perceptible fall is also used whenever the syllable ends with a stop consonant, i.e. unexploded p, t or k, as in ˎŋap (say), ˎjat (one), ˎtit (little), ˎtak (possible); the tone of these words would be graphically [⁻].[3]

476.   The method of allocating tones to tonemes may be illustrated by the tonal system of the Tswana language of South Africa,[4] a polysyllabic language in which every syllable requires an appropriate tone.   The following are the chief tones found on single syllables in this language: high-level, mid-level, low-level,[5] high-falling to mid, high-falling to low, mid-falling to low. (See examples in §384.)   Of these the three falling tones only occur on syllables which are penultimate in the sentence and are long (with rare exceptions, see §479), and the low-level[5] only occurs in final position in the sentence. The fact that these four tones occur in such very special situations at once suggests that one justifiable method of tonemic classification would be to allocate these tones to the same tonemes as the much commoner high-level and mid-level tones.

---

[2] Lit. "previously born."

[3] There are many varieties of Cantonese.   The observations recorded here are taken from an analysis made by me of the pronunciation of Mr. WU KWING-TONG (ˎwuˊkwiŋˊthɔŋ) of Hongkong (see JONES and WOO, *Cantonese Phonetic Reader*).

In Mr. WU's pronunciation there exists an "extra high level tone" which he uses in final position in certain cases.   When the *Reader* was written, I regarded this tone as a variant of the high-falling tone employed solely in final positions as a kind of sentence intonation.   I have, however, subsequently learnt that it undoubtedly constitutes a separate toneme, though I have no examples from Mr. WU's speech to prove this.   Many conclusive examples have been furnished me by Mrs. ROSE FLETCHER, who is bi-lingual (English and Cantonese) and an expert phonetician, and who has examined the speech of many Cantonese.   Illustrative words are ˎkwai (home) but ⁻kwai (tortoise), ˎsaːn (three) but ⁻saːn (clothes).   It appears that in her type of Cantonese the distinction is even found in words ending with the stops.

[4] Rolong dialect.

[5] This tone may have a slight fall.

477. This system works out as follows. All the tones in ordinary sentences are either high-level or mid-level with the exception of the two final ones.[6] In the two final syllables seven combinations are possible, viz. (1) high-fall low [\ .], (2) high-fall mid [ˋ ·], (3) low-fall low [ˎ .], (4) low-fall mid [ˎ ·], (5) high-fall low-fall [\ ˎ], (6) low-fall low-fall [ˎˎ], (7) high-level high-fall [¯ \ ]. The last three of these are of very uncommon occurrence. Leaving these three out of consideration for the moment, we see that the high-fall may be regarded as a member of the same toneme as the high-level, the low-fall as a member of the same toneme as the mid-level, the low-level also as a member of the same toneme as the mid-level, while a terminal mid tone can probably be assigned to the same toneme as the high-level. In other words

penultimate [\ ] and [ˋ] "stand for" [˙]

terminal [·] "stands for" [˙]

penultimate [ˎ] and terminal [.] "stand for" [·].

478. Thus the following words said in isolation might be written phonetically as follows with narrow tone-marking[7]: pùːla̰ (rain), phɔ̀ːkɔ̀ (ram), na̰ːma̰ (meat), kxǫːmɷ (cow). With broad tone-marking they might be written phonetically thus: pūla, phɔ̄kɔ̄, nama, kxomō.

479. The three rare terminal tone-sequences [\ˎ], [ˎˎ] and [¯ \ ] show that there probably also exist two independent falling tonemes, a high-falling and a low-falling, the tones of which are not assignable to any level toneme. They completely overlap the other falling tones, but in view of the particular conditions under which they are used it seems necessary to regard them as independent tonemes. They are used almost exclusively on monosyllables, such as ɸa̰ (here), mǫ (here), è (this[8]). These would have to be marked with ˋ and ˎ both in narrow and in broad writing. Examples are, with narrow tone-marking, kɩ a ɟà: ɸa̰ (I am eating here), kɪ̄ː ĕò (here he is[9]), or, with broad tone-marking, kɩ a ɟā ɸa̰, kɪ̄ ĕò.

---

[6] Subject to the modification described in §480.

[7] The tone-marks used are as follows: ˋhigh-fall, ˎlow-fall, ‗low-level, ¯high-level; absence of mark denotes mid-level.

[8] Referring e.g. to pōlɛlɔ (story).

[9] Lit. "it is this one" (referring to ŋkwɛ̄, tiger·).

The only cases I have come across of the use of the falling tone in the second syllable of a disyllabic word are the words ka̱:na̱ (so big, so many) and ɟāa̱:na̱ (thus); they would be written with broad tone-marking kana̱, ɟāana̱. But there are presumably others.

480. In addition to the tonal system above described there exists in Tswana a peculiar tonal phenomenon, which, though it has semantic function can hardly be classed as a toneme. It is that at various points in sentences a high tone has to be made slightly lower (roughly a semi-tone lower) than the last preceding high tone, and that all subsequent high tones in the sentence have to be on this lower level—unless and until another point comes where a similar lowering has to take place. Any mid tones[10] following such a point are lowered to match. The points of lowering sometimes occur between words and sometimes in the middle of a word. Long sentences often contain quite a number of these lowerings. The points at which the lowerings take place appear to be prescribed solely by syntactical considerations. Thus the verb with a prefixed pronoun is always lowered in comparison with the subject preceding it, and the direct object is often [11] lowered as compared with the verb preceding it. The following are examples. (The points after which lowering takes place are shown by | ; the words are written with broad tone-marking.)

taū | ī bɔ̄nā | phɔ̄lɔɸɔ̄lɔ[12]	(the lion sees the animal, lit. lion he sees animal; present tense of bɔ̄na)
taū | ī bātla | phɔ̄lɔɸɔ̄lɔ[12]	(the lion is searching for the animal; present tense of batlā)
ŋ kā batla phɔ̄lɔɸɔ̄lɔ[12]	(I can search for the animal)
ɷ tʃwala kxɔrɔ̄ kā sɩkɔpɛlɔ[13]	(you shut the door with the key, present tense of tʃwalā)

---

[10] I.e. tones belonging to the "low" Tswana toneme. These are not very low except in final position. They are usually from a minor third to a major third lower than the high tones; consequently, in ordinary sentences, there is ample scope for the further lowerings described in this paragraph.

[11] Not always. Whether lowering of the direct object takes place depends upon the tense of the verb.

[12] Narrow tone-marking of last word (if final) would be phɔ̄lɔɸɔ̄:lɔ̱.

ōˉ tʃwāla kxɔ|rɔ̄ kā sɪkɔpɛlɔ[13]   (he shuts the door with the key; present tense of tʃwalā. This also means "while you shut the door with the key," a tense of the participial mood of tʃwalā in the tonal form used when direct object follows)

but ōˉ tʃwā|lā kā sɪkɔpɛlɔ[13]   (while you shut with the key, a tense of the participial mood of tʃwalā in the tonal form used when the following word is not the direct object)

mɷñna wā bāthōˉ[14]   (a man of the people, i.e. a poor man)

but mɷñ|nā | ōˉ mōˉlɪmɔ[15]   (the man is good, lit. man he good)

sɪsānā sɪxōˉlɷ[16]   (a big stump (of tree))

but sɪsānā sɪ|xōˉlɷ[17]   (the stump is big)

481. Lowerings of the type described above are not used to distinguish one isolated word from another, but they may distinguish words in connected sentences. Thus the 2nd person singular of a tense of the participial mood of tʃhōˉla (receive) is ōˉ tʃhōˉlā when a direct object follows, but the same part of the verb tʃholā (dish up) is ōˉ tʃhōˉ|lā when a direct object follows.

482. The only way in which such a tonal usage could be brought into a tonemic classification would be to distinguish two kinds of

---

[13] Narrow tone-marking of last word (if final) would be sɪkɔpɛːlɔ.

[14] Narrow tone-marking would be mɷñna wā bàːthɷ (if final). If another word were to follow, the tonal form would be mɷñna wā bā|thōˉ, or in some cases mɷñna wā bāthɷ (depending upon the grammatical nature of the following word).

[15] Narrow tone-marking of last word (if final) would be mōˉlɪ̀ːmɔ.

[16] Narrow tone-marking would be sɪsānā sɪxɷ̀ːlɷ (if final).

[17] Narrow tone-marking would be sɪsānā sɪ|xɷ̀ːlɷ (if final).

high tone. These would be identical in actual tonal value, but one would involve a lowering of a subsequent high tone, whereas the other would have no effect on succeeding tones. Representing these two kinds of high tone by the signs ˀ and ˉ respectively, the examples in the last paragraph could be indicated by the notation ō tʃhōla and ō tʃhōlā.[18]

483.   The existence of such a tonal system as that above described shows that it may be inconvenient and perhaps not always possible to group all the essential tonal phenomena of a tone language into tonemes.   This does not, however, mean that the grouping of tones into tonemes is not a valuable procedure whenever it may be feasible.

484.   It is possible that there exist languages which have significant tones but no tonemes.   In the course of a limited amount of work I was once able to do on the Shan language (which belongs to the Thai group) it seemed to me that the five tones of that language always preserve approximately the same relative values [\ . ˅ ˙ ⁄]. I did not discover any cases of a variant tone being used according to the tonal environment.   It may be that in this language the only perceptible variations of tone that exist are the result of superimposing a sentence intonation on the words.   Variations caused in this way do not come within the scope of the present enquiry.

485.   Tones groupable into tonemes appear to occur in the Somali language.   It is instructive to examine from this point of view the tone-marked texts in L. E. ARMSTRONG'S *The Phonetic Structure of Somali*.[19]   It will be seen there that the values of the Somali tones vary according to tonal context.   We find for instance that the pitch of the first syllable of **damɛːr** (donkey, m.) may be

---

[18] A. N. TUCKER, who has an unrivalled knowledge of Tswana, Sotho and allied languages, has recently completed a very detailed investigation of the tonal structure of these languages, supplementing and in some respects correcting the accounts given by previous workers in this field. He has worked out a new tonemic classification which is probably a considerable improvement on that suggested here, and he has evolved from it a simple system of tone marking well suited for purposes of orthography. For details readers are referred to his article *Sotho-Nguni Orthography* in the *Bulletin of the School of Oriental and African Studies*, Jan., 1949.

[19] See footnote 50 to §580.

either lower than or on a level with the beginning of the second syllable, i.e. [·\ ] or [.\ ] or [' \ ]. The pitch used would appear to depend upon the tones of preceding words. We see also that tiḑi (she said), which normally has the intonation [· .] takes or may take the intonation [. .] after a preceding falling tone.[20] Again, a low tone following a high-falling tone sometimes rises when a high tone follows, i.e. [\ ⁄] occurs as a variant of [\ .]. Further research is needed before we can describe precisely these tonemes and the variant tones which are comprised in them. The facts set out above seem to me, however, sufficient to demonstrate that the toneme principle will be found to apply in Somali, and is likely to elucidate certain features of that language which have hitherto been obscure. (Some of the tones may be associated with special types of stress. For this, see §§580 ff.)

486. The principle of the toneme appears to be applicable in Serbo-Croat. The tones of the two length-tone complexes of that language (§§466, 583) are not always constant, but they vary to some extent with the phonetic context. Thus when the word written in the Fry-Kostić system ˌmlaˑda (young) is said in isolation it is pronounced with the tone-sequence [⁄ ·], but when the word is immediately followed by a high-pitched syllable, its tone is of the type [- ·].

Linking of Tones with Other Attributes

487. It has already been mentioned (§446) that significant differences between words are often effected by combinations of attributes. This subject is dealt with fully in Chapter XXVI. Here we may confine ourselves to remarking that tone may be linked to tamber or to duration or to stress. Examples of the first are found in Pekingese (§§112, 242, 257, 543), of the second also in Pekingese (§557) and of the third in ordinary "stress languages" such as English, German, Italian, Russian and Greek (§§570–574), and in tonal systems such as those found in Norwegian and Swedish (§§575–578).

---

[20] It is possible that this word is weakly stressed in the cases where it occurs in Armstrong's text No. 2, and that the tone [. .] is a concomitant of the weak stress.

CHAPTER XXVI

DISTINCTIONS BY COMPLEXES OF ATTRIBUTES

488. Minimal distinctions[1] between possible sound-sequences of a given language are sometimes effected by a change in a single attribute, such as the substitution of one tamber for another or the substitution of a long sound for a short one. The English syllables si:n (*seen*) and sein (*sane*), for instance, are distinguished solely by their vowels; there are no differences perceptible to the ear in the s's or n's. Likewise the Japanese words taiko (drum) and taiko: (opposition)[2] are distinguished solely by the length of the vowel.

489. Such cases are, however, comparatively rare. Minimal distinctions much more commonly involve changes in two or more attributes simultaneously, e.g. two changes of tamber, the addition of a sound together with a change in some other sound, a change of length accompanied by a change of tamber, a change of stress in combination with a change of voice-pitch. Thus the English syllables ki:n (*keen*) and kein (*cane*) are distinguished not only by their vowels but also by the use of perceptibly different varieties of k. In Southern English pronunciation 'geili (*gaily*) differs from geil (*gale*) not only by the addition of i but also by the use of a different variety of l (§71).[3] The Sinhalese words si:tə (cold) and sitə (mind), quoted in §102, are distinguished by the length of the first vowel combined with the slight quality difference indicated in Figure 4 (p. 29). The English noun 'impo:t (*import*) is distinguished from the verb im'po:t by a difference of stress which is ordinarily accompanied by a difference of intonation (see §§457–459).

490. It is the very fact that most minimal distinctions require differences in two or more attributes simultaneously that gives rise to the phoneme theory. If minimal distinctions were always effected by changes in a single attribute, there would be no phonemes.

491. When, as is usually the case, a minimal distinction is effected by simultaneous changes in two or more attributes, it

[1] See Chapter VI.

[2] See §378.

[3] The addition or subtraction of a sound is to be regarded as a particular case of change of sound—the replacement of a sound by zero or vice versa.

generally happens that the change in one attribute greatly predominates over the change(s) in the other(s). The change in one attribute is in fact the "essential" or "primary" one, while the change(s) in the other(s) may be considered as "incidental to" or "conditioned by" the primary change. It is evident, for instance, that such English syllables as ki:n, kein and ko:n (*corn*) are distinguished essentially by their vowels, and that the accompanying differences between the k's is merely incidental to the vowel distinction. Similarly the Sinhalese words si:tə and sitə are differentiated essentially by the length of the first vowel; the slight difference of tamber accompanying this is incidental and comparatively unimportant.

492. The examples of phonemes given in the preceding chapters have for the most part illustrated cases where there is no doubt as to which change of attribute is the primary one. Cases exist, however, where the change in one attribute does not predominate in such a way as to leave no doubt that it is the primary means of differentiation. Cases indeed occur in which the differentiation is distributed between two or even among three attributes in such a manner as to render it difficult to say which takes the greater share in effecting the distinction.

493. It is easy to understand why this may be so, since what is essential in language is that the total acoustic difference between one word and another should be adequate. It does not matter by what means a sufficient acoustic distinction is arrived at. It may be produced by merely substituting one sound for another or one degree of length for another, as mentioned in §488. Or it may be produced by a considerable change in one attribute accompanied by relatively small changes in others, as mentioned in §489. But equally effective acoustic distinctions can be made by means of slighter differences in two or three attributes—differences of such a nature that no one of them would be of itself adequate to distinguish clearly one word from another.

494. Thus if there is only a moderate duration difference between two words of a language, clear differentiation between them necessitates coupling with it a difference in some other attribute, usually tamber. The smaller the duration difference the greater must be the difference in tamber or other attribute. And a point can be reached at which the relative differentiation value of the differences

of duration and tamber are approximately equal—where, in fact, it is impossible to regard the one as primary and the other incidental.

495.   The principle is well illustrated by comparing the usage in Sinhalese with that in Southern English.   In Sinhalese, as already mentioned in §§102, 489, 491, the differences of vowel duration are considerable and the accompanying differences of tamber are slight.   In Southern English, on the other hand, the differences of vowel duration are less well marked so that the requirements of distinctness necessitate wider tamber differences (see §§511 ff., also §§402 ff.).

496.   When a minimal distinction is effected by a primary change in one attribute accompanied by incidental changes in another attribute, the only feasible phonemic grouping is that made on the basis of the primary attribute and without reference to the secondary attribute.   Thus as the differences between the k's in the English words kiːn, kein, koːn are evidently incidental to the differences between the vowels, these different k's must be held to belong to the same phoneme.   In the unusual cases where the differences in two attributes are of about equal value, it is possible to make an adequate phonemic grouping in more than one way (see for instance §§514–516).

497.   The subject of minimal distinctions by complexes of attributes has been touched upon in various places in preceding chapters.   It is now necessary to discuss this matter in greater detail.

498.   The following combinations of two attributes are capable of being used for minimal significant distinctions.   There are doubtless others:

(1)   a tamber combined with another tamber in an adjacent or a neighbouring position,

(2)   tamber combined with length of the sound in question,

(3)   tamber combined with length of an adjoining sound,

(4)   tamber combined with a degree of stress,

(5)   tamber combined with a particular kind of stress,

(6)   tamber combined with voice-pitch,

(7)   the duration of a sound combined with the duration of an adjacent sound,

(8) duration combined with a degree of stress,

(9) duration combined with a particular kind of stress,

(10) duration combined with voice-pitch,

(11) a degree of stress combined with a degree of stress on an adjacent syllable,

(12) degrees of stress combined with voice-pitch (intonation),

(13) particular kinds of stress combined with voice-pitch,

(14) voice-pitch combined with voice-pitch on a neighbouring syllable or syllables,

(15) voice-pitch combined with voice-quality.

499. In the following pages examples are given of each of these cases in the above order.

(1) DISTINCTIONS BY TWO ADJACENT OR NEIGHBOURING TAMBERS

500. As has already been pointed out, many minimal distinctions are effected by a major change of tamber accompanied by a minor change of an adjacent tamber, and English syllables like kiːn, kein and koːn (corn) have been adduced as instances of this. Further instances are seen in the French words mjɛ̃ (mien) and tjɛ̃ (tien); the essential difference between them lies in the initial consonants, but there are also differences between the two j's, the j of mjɛ̃ being fully voiced and that of tjɛ̃ being partially breathed. And so on.

501. Sometimes, however, the substitution of one tamber for another is accompanied by a change in an adjacent sound which cannot be regarded as a "minor" one. When a sequence is such that an alteration for a minimal distinction involves major changes in two neighbouring sounds, it may be termed a "linked sequence." There is, of course, no hard and fast line to be drawn between major and minor changes. In the following paragraphs, however, we give some instances where it is reasonable to regard both elements of a change as being major alterations.

502. [nt] and [ŋk] are linked sequences in Spanish; the distinction t/k is evidently the principal one, but the concurrent change n/ŋ is also considerable. As already shown in §92, [an] and [ɑŋ] are linked sequences in Danish; the differences in both elements

are considerable, so much so that the difference a/ɑ is sometimes
the preponderating one to the ear, though the phonemic distinction
is undoubtedly n/ŋ (§§181, 182).

503. The following are instances of linked sequences occurring
in Pekingese. That language contains pairs of "finals" which may
be transcribed narrowly as -ʌŋ, -ən and -ɑŋ, -an. -ʌŋ and
-ən occur, for instance, in [ˉfʌŋ] (wind) and [ˉfən] (separate),
and there are no such syllables as [ˉfʌn] or [ˉfəŋ]. Notable as
these vowel differences are, we find that the difference n/ŋ must
always be considered the primary one. For in Pekingese there
is always a definite line of demarcation between the sounds n and
ŋ, whereas there is no definite line of demarcation between each
pair of vowels.[4] Besides which in the case of the third analogous
pair of finals -iŋ, -in the difference of vowel quality is insignificant.
Broad transcriptions of the above finals would therefore be
-en, -eŋ, -an, -aŋ.

504. Russian syllables such as [bji] and [bɨ] are also linked
sequences, since the opposite sequences [bi] (i.e. "hard" b followed
by i) and [bjɨ] (i.e. "soft" b followed by ɨ) do not occur in the
language.   The distinction between the existing syllables is effected
by a change of consonant (bj/b) with a concurrent change of vowel
(i/ɨ).

505. Attention has already been called to this case in §97, and
reasons why sounds like bj and b must constitute separate phonemes
were given in §95. We may add here that to determine which
change is the primary one, in comparing two linked sequences,
it is sometimes needful to examine what happens in other sequences.
A foreign observer hearing the Russian syllables [bji] and [bɨ]
for the first time would, I think, be fairly certain to take the striking
difference of vowel to be the primary means of distinction.   And if
he were to see the Russian orthographic forms (би, бы), he would
regard them as lending support to this view.   An investigation
of all the circumstances leads, however, to the conclusion that the
consonants should be regarded as the primary distinguishing
elements, and that the differences of vowel, wide though they may
often be, are secondary.   We can see this from the treatment of

---

[4] Their qualities vary to some extent with the tones.   Thus, the ə of ən
is more ʌ-like when the syllable has the third tone than when it has other
tones.

analogous sequences with other vowels [bje] and [bɛ], [bja] and
[bɑ], etc.   In the case of these other vowels numerous shades
are to be found in different connexions, shades which merge into
one another by imperceptible degrees.   There are no sharp lines
of demarcation which would render it possible to divide each set
of vowels into two phonemes.   Each set of vowels, i.e. e, ɛ and
intermediates, a⊥, a, ɑ and intermediates, etc., must therefore constitute a single phoneme, and the above-mentioned distinctions
must be attributed primarily to the consonants bj and b.   bj and
b must in fact be considered as separate phonemes, and any vowel
distinctions which may accompany them must be regarded as
secondary.   If this applies to [bje], [bɛ] and to [bja] and [bɑ],
we cannot do otherwise than apply it also to [bji] and [bɨ] in spite
of the particularly wide difference of vowel sound found in this case.
The Russian sounds i and ɨ must thus be held to be members of a
single phoneme.   This fact was known to BAUDOUIN DE COURTENAY
(the discoverer of the phoneme theory) long before 1900.   It was
stated again much later by TRUBETZKOY (*Grundzüge der Phonologie,*
p. 48, in CANTINEAU's translation, p. 54), by BLOOMFIELD, and by
BOYANUS in his paper *The i - ɨ Phoneme.*

506.   The best broad transcription of the syllables [bji] and [bɨ]
is thus bji, bi.   The notation bi (representing bji), bɨ would also
distinguish these particular syllables adequately, but would involve
an inconsistent use of the letter b.

507.   Languages exhibiting the phenomenon known as "vowel
harmony" also illustrate the principle with which we are concerned
here.   In that type of language the change of a vowel in one syllable
involves a simultaneous change of vowel in an adjoining syllable.

508.   Vowel harmony is found, for instance, in Telugu.   It
may be illustrated by such sequences as [atti], [attɑ], [ɔttu].   The
sounds a and ɔ are dependent upon phonetic context, and their
use is confined to situations like those just mentioned—a when
the following syllable contains i, and ɔ when the following syllable
contains u.   There are no sequences [attɑ], [attu], [ɔtti], [ɔttɑ],
nor do ɔ or a front a occur in monosyllabic words.   i, ɑ and u, on the
other hand, are independent sounds of the language, and occur in
monosyllabic words.   It is therefore clear that they may be said
to "constitute" phonemes and are the primary sounds in the above
linked sequences.   a and ɔ cannot be otherwise than subsidiary

sounds, and must evidently be assigned to the ɑ-phoneme (which would normally be written a).

509.   Interesting instances of vowel harmony involving sequences of an unusual kind are found in the Igbo language of Nigeria. This language presents the peculiarity that certain pairs of vowels are difficult to distinguish in isolation, but their recognition is facilitated in a great many cases by the nature of the vowels used in adjoining syllables.[5]   The vowels of Igbo fall in fact into two classes and as a rule only vowels belonging to the same class occur in a given word. The first class comprises the sounds i, ɛ, o and u, while the second class comprises e, a, ɔ and ọ.[6]   i and e are rather near to each other in sound (the i being a not particularly close one), as also are u and ọ.   But in words of more than one syllable the distinctions are helped out by the fact that if i or u occurs in a word, the other syllables of that word can only contain i, ɛ, o or u; and if e or ọ occurs in a word, the other syllables generally contain e, a, ɔ or ọ. For example, there are words izu [˙ ˙] (stealing), izo [˙ ˙] (hiding) and ezọ [˙ ˙] (buying),[7] but combinations such as izọ, ezu do not occur.   The verbal root zọ [˙] (buy) is intermediate in sound between the verbal roots zo [˙] (hide) and zu [˙] (steal) and is liable to get confused with them if said in isolation; but when the verbal noun prefix (which is i- or e- according to the root vowel of the verb) is added, it becomes quite clear in each case which verb is meant.

(2) DISTINCTIONS BY TAMBER COMBINED WITH DURATION

(a) *Vowels*

510.   Distinctions by a complex of tamber and duration of vowels are very common.   Examples were given in §§104–106. Here we will examine the question at greater length.

511.   In ordinary Southern English we find, as has already been pointed out, several cases where vowels of different quality are connected by a length relationship.   Thus, in the type of English I use, the sounds written in broad transcription i: and i differ both in duration and quality.   These attributes are subject to the relationship that the longer sound always has the "closer" quality

---

[5] This was first discovered by Professor IDA WARD.   I am indebted to her for the particulars given here.

[6] ọ denotes a sound intermediate between o and u.

[7] WARD, *Introduction to the Ibo Language*, p. 3.

in a given phonetic context.   So that if the stress and intonation conditions are constant,

the closer vowel in *deed* is longer than the opener vowel in *did*,
the closer vowel in *seen* is longer than the opener vowel in *sin*,
the closer vowel in *sheep* is longer than .the opener vowel in *ship*,
the closer vowel in the first syllable of *aesthetic* (iːsˈθetik) is longer
     than the opener vowel in the first syllable of *estate* (isˈteit).

512.   The pairs of vowels in *caught* and *cot, pool* and *pull* are in the same case.   The vowels have quite distinct qualities, but in my type of English these qualities are connected by the relation that one is always longer than the other in similar phonetic contexts. The first vowel in *naughty* is, for instance, longer than that in *knotty*, and the vowel in *boot* is longer than that in *foot*.

513.   A similar length relationship between the vowels in *psalm* and *Sam, halve* and *have*, etc., is also to be found in Southern English speech.[8]

514.   It is not always easy to decide what is the best manner of making the phonemic classification in cases such as the above. There are, as was indicated in §§492–494, border-line cases where the distinction between sound-sequences appears to be about equally divided between the length and the tamber.

515.   The above-mentioned distinctions found in my type of Southern English are near to this border-line.   They are, however, cases where in my view the length difference may be considered to preponderate, as already mentioned in §104.   This is the traditional way of regarding the sounds in question: the vowel in *deed* is generally considered to be the "long" of the vowel in *did*, and the vowels in *caught, pool, psalm* are usually thought of as being the "longs" of the vowels in *cot, pull, Sam*.   In other words, the traditional, and to my mind the most practical, method of grouping these vowels phonemically is to assign the qualities

---

[8] With many speakers (including myself) the relationship referred to in this paragraph does not hold good.   This is because we often lengthen the traditionally short *a* in a number of words, e.g. *man, bad, bag, grand*.   With these speakers the two vowel qualities belong to separate phonemes, and must be written in broad transcription with separate letters (ɑ and a, or a and ɛ or æ).   Length need not be marked except in recording the speech of those— and there are apparently some—who make chronemic use of length on the front a (æ).   (See *Outline of English Phonetics*, §§874, 875.)

of these corresponding longs and shorts to single phonemes. On this basis the sounds would be written broadly with single letters with and without length-marks: iː, i, oː, o (or ɔː, ɔ), uː, u, aː, a.

516. Being border-line cases, it would equally be possible to regard the tambers as constituting the primary differences, and the differences of length as incidental. Looked at thus, the tambers would all be assigned to separate phonemes, and would be represented in broad transcription by separate letters. The lengths being then incidental would not be marked in broad transcription: we should write the sounds by some such system as i, ι, o, ɔ, u, ɷ, a, ɑ (or æ, a for the last two).

517. In border-line cases analogy with the treatment of another sound may be suggestive. Thus the treatment of the Southern English long vowel in *bird* may be taken into consideration in coming to a conclusion as to the best phonemic grouping of the other English vowels just mentioned. It has been pointed out (§§197–202) that the vowel of *bird* is best assigned to the same phoneme as short ə, since its quality is practically identical with one of the varieties of short ə.[9] The fact that əː and ə are best treated as here described is not necessarily a reason for treating other pairs of vowels on similar lines. If, however, the other pairs are susceptible of phonemic grouping in more than one way, it is clearly advantageous to select the system which gives consistency of treatment to all the pairs, namely, the grouping suggested in §515.

518. Symbol economy in transcription is also a principle to which consideration may be given in border-line cases. It points in favour of the grouping of the above vowels as corresponding longs and shorts, as indicated in §515.

519. The above-mentioned relationships between the duration and tamber of various vowels are found not only in normal Southern English, but also in the English of Northern England.[10] It must be observed, however, that there are other varieties of English in which this traditional relationship does not hold good. Notable

---

[9] *Outline of English Phonetics*, §356.

[10] Except that words like *psalm* and *Sam* are not distinguished in the speech of many Northerners. They use an intermediate short a in both words.

among these is one type of Southern speech, in which the traditionally short vowels are in some phonetic contexts lengthened and made as long as the traditionally long vowels.[11] Those who speak in this way will pronounce such words as *six*, *lock*, *good* in isolation with long vowels, and there is no perceptible difference in length between these and their vowels in *cease*, *walk*, *food*. The distinctions are by tamber only. These vowel-qualities must in this type of speech be all assigned to separate phonemes, and must be written in broad transcription with separate letters without length-marks, e.g. by a system such as that suggested in §516: the above words would be written sɪks, lɔk, gɤd, sis, wok, fud, with the convention that all the vowels are or may be long.

520. The relationship between the traditionally long and short vowels likewise does not hold good in Scottish English, though for different reasons. Scottish speakers generally shorten the traditionally long vowels when a consonant follows. They pronounce *week* with a short close i and distinguish this word from *wick* by tamber only. *Pool* and *pull* are not distinguished at all, but both are pronounced with a short close u.[12] Similarly *caught* and *cot* are not generally distinguished in Scotland, but are both pronounced with a short vowel (about Cardinal Vowel No. 6).[13] These words would be written broadly wik, wɪk, puɫ, kɔt, with the convention that the vowels are all short.

521. In American English too there appear to be as a rule no consistent relationships between the lengths and qualities of vowels. It is therefore necessary to regard the qualities corresponding to the

---

[11] This type of Southern English is, I believe, a modern development, since it is heard chiefly from younger people. There is a possibility that it may some day supersede what may be called, for want of a better term, the "normal" Southern English manner of pronouncing, though I am disposed to think that the influence of Northern and other forms of English will prevent it from doing so—unless, as is possible, American speech, which shows similar characteristics, comes to have a preponderating influence.

[12] Generally a rather forward variety (ü).

[13] It would appear, however, from some books dealing with the phonetics of Scottish speech that some Scotsmen make a quality difference between the vowels of such words as *cot* and *caught*. The letter ǫ has been used to denote the vowel in *caught* by those who differentiate this word from *cot*. See GRANT and ROBSON, *Phonetics for Scottish Students* and the *Phonetic Reader* for infants, which was published by the Bon Accord Press, Aberdeen, in 1918.

traditionally long and short vowels as belonging to separate phonemes, and to write them with separate letters in broad transcription, thus i, ι; e, ε; o, ɔ; u, ɷ, etc.[14]

522. In a common variety of Scottish pronunciation[15] (referred to in my *Pronunciation of English*, 4th edition, Cambridge, 1958, §§180, 181) there exists a pair of diphthongs exemplifying a complex of duration and quality. These two sounds are represented phonetically in *The Pronunciation of English* by the symbols ʌi and ae. ae is always longer than ʌi, as well as having very distinct qualities; their features, both of length and of quality are illustrated in Fig. 18 on p. 58 of that book. What is particularly remarkable about these diphthongs is that they constitute separate phonemes in this Scottish pronunciation, while they both belong to the ai-diaphone of English as a whole. All the Southern English ai's are rendered in Scottish by one or other of these diphthongs. This is illustrated for instance by the fact that the words *tide* and *tied* are distinguished as tʌid and taed in the Scottish pronunciation, while in Southern English both words are pronounced taid.

523. Combinations of length differences with wide differences of quality are found in Dutch and in Hungarian. Dutch contains, for instance, close e and o which are always relatively long and open ε and ɔ which are always relatively short, a front a which is always relatively long and a very back ɑ which is always relatively short. Hungarian has also several pairs similarly distinguished, e.g. there is a front a which is always long and a very back ɑ which is always short.[16]

524. It is convenient, for purposes of symbol economy if not for any other reason, to consider the length as the primary distinction in these pairs and the tamber differences as incidental. This

---

[14] Or, indicating the slightly diphthongal character of the sounds derived from the traditionally long closer vowels: ij, i; ej (or ei); ow (or ou), o; uw, u. This manner of using j and w is recommended by BLOOMFIELD, who however uses ɔ for what is here written o, and o for ʌ.

[15] The main particulars of this type of Scottish pronunciation were first brought to my notice by J. BRAIDWOOD (a Scot) who is Lecturer in the Department of English, University of Belfast. I am indebted for other details to DAVID ABERCROMBIE, Head of the Department of Phonetics in the University of Edinburgh.

[16] The Hungarian back ɑ is almost identical with the Southern English short o-sound in *hot*.

indeed is the traditional way of regarding the sounds, and it is reflected in the common orthography. In broad transcriptions we therefore mark the length and we write Dutch ε with e and ɔ with o, and the Dutch and Hungarian back ɑ-sounds with a. Examples are Dutch beːn (*been*, leg), ben[17] (*ben*, am), roːs (*roos*, rose), ros[18] (*ros*, horse), taːk (*taak*, task), tak[19] (*tak*, bough); Hungarian ˈaːlom (*álom*, dream), ˈhalom[20] (*halom*, heap), vaːd (*vád*, accusation), vad[21] (*vad*, wild animal).

525. Several pairs of German[22] vowels are likewise distinguished by complexes of length and tamber, though except for the e and o sounds the tamber differences are less than those of English, Dutch or Hungarian. The length-differences are as a rule greater than the corresponding differences in English. This is as one would expect (see §§492–496). There are six such pairs, and I see no adequate reason for departing from the traditional view that the sounds should be considered as pairs of corresponding longs and shorts. Classifying them thus the sounds can be written in broad transcription by six letters with and without a length-mark. Examples are ʃtiːl (*Stiel*), ʃtil (*still*), ˈbiːtet (*bietet*), ˈbitet[23] (*bittet*), ˈiːnen (*ihnen*), ˈinen[24] (*innen*), ˈhaːken (*Haken*), ˈhaken (*hacken*), ˈoːfen (*Ofen*), ˈofen (*offen*),[25] muːs (*Muss*), mus[26] (*muss*), ˈfyːlen (*fühlen*), ˈfylen[27] (*füllen*), ˈhøːle (*Höhle*), ˈhøle[28] (*Hölle*).

526. It would be possible to treat the tambers as the primary means of differentiation in such pairs of German words, as also in similar pairs of Dutch and Hungarian words, and to treat the length differences as incidental. Classifying on this principle the

---

[17] Narrower transcription bɛn.
[18] Narrower transcription rɔs.
[19] Narrower transcription tak.
[20] Narrower transcription ˈhalɔm.
[21] Narrower transcription vad.
[22] Stage pronunciation, as described by VIËTOR (*Die Aussprache des Schriftdeutschen*, etc.).
[23] Narrower transcription ˈbɪtət.
[24] Narrower transcription ˈʔɪnən.
[25] Narrower transcription ˈʔɔfən.
[26] Narrower transcription mʊs.
[27] Narrower transcription ˈfʏlən.
[28] Narrower transcription ˈhœlə.

above twelve German tambers would all be counted as separate phonemes. Twelve letters would be required to write them in broad transcription, and the length-mark would be superfluous. From the point of view of writing and printing as well as on linguistic grounds, such a system would, in my view, be less satisfactory than the other.

527. Differentiations of vowels by complexes of duration and quality are found to a limited extent in "monosyllabic" languages of the Far East. Thus in Cantonese, in Thai (Siamese), and in Shan we find a vowel resembling the English aː which is always long and a vowel resembling the English ʌ which is always short. In most of these cases it seems convenient to treat the duration as the primary distinguishing element and the difference in tamber as secondary. In broad transcription we should therefore write the ʌ as a. Examples are: Cantonese ˋsaːm (three), ˋsam[29] (heart); Thai ´saːn (to weave), ´san[30] (sharp edge), ˍaːp (to bath), ˍap[31] (stuffy); Shan ˉmaːn (pregnant), ˉman[32] (his), ˍmaːn (glass, be correct), ˍman[33] (hold tight).

528. In Vietnamese, however, where a similar distinction is found, it seems better to mark the differences by using separate symbols, treating the length as incidental. For this, see the notes on the phonetics of Vietnamese by E. HENDERSON in Le Maître Phonétique, January, 1943, pp. 7, 8.

529. There are many other languages besides those above referred to in which vowels are differentiated by complexes of duration and tamber. In fact where essential differences of length exist, these differences would appear to be more often than not accompanied by quality differences. Even in the languages which are reputed to distinguish words by duration alone we very frequently find some accompanying differences of quality. Sinhalese is a case in point, as we have already seen (§§102, 103). Another is Estonian. This latter language contains nine vowels, all of which can be long or short. Close observation shows that in six of these (i, e, o, u, y and ə) slight differences of quality accompany the differences

---

[29] Narrower transcription ˋsʌm.
[30] Narrower transcription ´sʌn.
[31] Narrower transcription ˍʌp.
[32] Narrower transcription ˉmʌn.
[33] Narrower transcription ˍmʌn.

of duration; in only three cases (ɛ, a and ø) are the qualities of short and long vowels indistinguishable.[34] There even appears to be a slight difference of quality between the French long and short ɛ in the pronunciation of many French people.

(b) Consonants

530. Differentiations by complexes of tamber and duration in consonants are comparatively rare. They form, however, a conspicuous feature of Tamil. In that language long voiceless plosives occur in intervocalic positions, but the corresponding short sounds in similar positions are in the case of p and t fricative and voiced (β, ð), in the case of ʈ a voiced flap (ɖ or ɽ), and in the case of k a fricative (a variety of x, sometimes also voiced, ɣ). Thus there are words which would be written in narrow transcription **teppam** (raft), **keβi** (cave), **katti** (knife), **kaði** (heavenly state), **kaːʈʈu** (show), **kaːɖu** (jungle), and, as already mentioned in §86, **pakkam** (side), **maxan** or **maɣan** (son), **aɹuçi** (decaying). β, ð, x are never lengthened. Nor are medial p, t, ʈ, k ever quite short; they are at times shorter than completely doubled consonants, but are never shortened to such an extent as to render it impossible to regard them as on the whole long.

531. As with other complexes, one may either take the length or the tamber to be the primary distinguishing feature. It is convenient on practical grounds to regard the length as primary and the tambers as subsidiary in this language, since this plan effects an economy of several letters in writing. In broad transcription **keβi**, **kaði**, **kaːɖu**, **maxan**, **aɹuçi** would thus be written **kepi**, **kati**, **kaːʈu**, **makan**, **aɹuki**.[35]

(3) Distinctions by Tamber Combined with Length of an Adjoining Sound

532. Differentiation of sequences by two rather similar sounds together with a difference in length of an adjoining sound was exemplified in §§187–191. It was shown there that in common types of English the somewhat similar pairs of sounds t and ɖ,

---

[34] See L. Krass, *The Phonetics of Estonian.*

[35] Most of these particulars and examples are taken from J. R. Firth's *Short Outline of Tamil Pronunciation* to which readers are referred for further information.

s and ʒ, etc., are used for differentiating words, but that when they are in terminal position the distinction is strengthened by a difference in the length of the preceding sound. When the final sound is ḍ, ĝ, ʒ, etc., a preceding vowel is much longer than when the final sound is t, k, s, etc. Pairs of words such as siːḍ (*seed*) and siːt (*seat*), rouḍ (*road*) and rout (*wrote*), are thus distinguished by a complex of two attributes: the tamber of the final consonant and the length of the preceding vowel.

533. Cases like lenḍ and lent, painḍ (*pined*) and paint (*pint*), penʒ (*pens*) and pens (*pence*) are similar, except that the length is spread over the vowel and the penultimate consonant; it generally affects the consonant more than the vowel (§191).

534. In all these cases it is necessary, as already indicated in §§190–191, to regard the tamber as the primary distinguishing element and the length as secondary, since there are cases where differentiations are made by these sounds without the aid of length.

(4) Distinctions by Tamber combined with a Degree of Stress

535. Often differences of stress are not accompanied by any perceptible quality differences. Thus there are no appreciable differences between the qualities of the vowels of the strong and weak syllables of such English words as ˈabstrakt (*abstract*, adj.), ˈhʌmbʌg (*humbug*) or between the vowel in sekt (*sect*) and the weakly stressed vowel in ˈinsekt (*insect*).

536. There is, however, at least one important language, namely Russian, in which differences of stress regularly involve differences of tamber. There are, for instance, varieties of ι occurring exclusively under weak or medium stress, while the use of close i-sounds is confined to strongly stressed positions (see §§332, 333). Again, the sound which we may call the "normal" Russian a, as in da (да, yes) when said in isolation, is used only in strongly stressed positions. Its place is taken in medium and weakly stressed positions by sounds of the ʌ and ə types. In particular, ʌ is used to the exclusion of a and ə (1) in pre-tonic positions,[36] (2) in pre-pre-

---

[36] I.e. in syllables immediately preceding the strongly stressed syllable of a word of more than one syllable.

tonic positions[37] when initial in the word, and (3) in certain pre-pre-tonic sequences of vowels.[37a] ə on the other hand is employed to the exclusion of ʌ and a in all post-tonic positions, and in pre-pre-tonic positions other than those appropriate for ʌ (3 above). The cases are illustrated by the following examples: [vʌ'da] (вода, water), [dʌ'vatj] (давать, give), [kʌr'man] (карман, pocket); [apjilj'sjin] (амельсин, orange); [nʌu'tʃatj] (научать, to teach); [kʌʌpji'ratsijə] (кооперация, co-operation); [xərʌ'ʃo] (хорошо, well); [bləgədʌ'rjitj] (благодарить, thank); ['komnətə] (комната room); ['jabləkə] (яблоко, apple); ['gorət] (город).

537. Similar considerations apply to the other Russian vowels. Thus an obscure variety of u [ɷ] occurs to the exclusion of normal u in syllables that do not bear strong stress: for instance, the medium stressed u in bu'maga [bɷ'magə] (бумага, paper) differs in quality from the strongly stressed u in 'dumatj ['dumətj] (думать, think).

538. Although in Russian differences of stress are accompanied by differences of tamber, it is clear that the stress must always be regarded as the primary means of differentiation and that the differences of tamber are incidental. The reason is that the tamber differences are numerous and some of the shades differ but slightly from each other; the qualities of the weakly stressed vowels do not in fact fall into sufficiently definite families to make it practicable to take them as a primary means of differentiating sound sequences.

539. It is clear therefore that the Russian sounds a, ʌ and ə belong to a single phoneme. This being so, appropriate broad transcriptions of the examples in §536 are va'da, da'vatj, kar'man; apjilj'sjin; nau'tʃatj, kaapji'ratsija; xəra'ʃo, blagada'rjitj, 'komnətə, 'jablaka, 'gorət. Similarly with other Russian vowels.

---

[37] I.e. in syllables prior to the pre-tonic (at any distance).
[37a] These are listed by D. WARD in his *Russian Pronunciation*, pp. 20, 21.

13

540. The same manner of distinguishing sequences is exemplified to a limited extent in Italian and Spanish. It is noteworthy for instance in Italian that a final weakly stressed o always has an "opener" value than o in other situations (see §210). The two o's in ˈdopo, for instance, have distinctly different qualities. And in both Italian and in Spanish weakly stressed a in final position has a somewhat more obscure (ə-like) quality than the strongly stressed a's.

541. It is appropriate to add a word here on the subject of the use of ə in English, supplementing what was said in §337. Although this sound only occurs in weak syllables, its use does not illustrate the principle with which this section is concerned; for, in my opinion, it does not occur in weak syllables to the exclusion of other vowels. We find ə, it is true, "representing" various other vowels in ˈfoutəgraf, fəˈtogrəfi, ˌfoutəˈgrafik, ˈmeməri, məˈmoːrïəl,[38] ˈaksidənt ˌaksiˈdentl, ˈregjulə, ˌregjuˈlariti, etc. But with these must be compared such cases as ˈdeskant (cp. ˈdistənt), ˈkontrast (cp. ˈbrekfəst), ˈpiːkok (cp. ˈhadək), and the examples in §535, in which, in my view, e, a, o and ʌ have weak stress, and which therefore show that ə constitutes a phoneme separate from a, o, ʌ, e, etc. (see also §148). (For another view, see §204.)

(5) Distinctions by Tamber combined with Type of Stress

542. Distinctions by this combination are very uncommon. They have, however, been observed by G. L. Trager in a Croatian dialect, where it appears that certain vowel qualities (e.g. a somewhat diphthongal eːᶠ) are associated with diminuendo stress and certain other vowel qualities (e.g. pure eː) are associated with crescendo stress. (See the article by him on the Serbo-Croatian dialect of Svirće in *Le Maître Phonétique*, January, 1940, pp. 14, 15.)

(6) Distinctions by Tamber combined with Voice-Pitch

543. Distinctions of this nature have been already noted as existing in Pekingese, and they are doubtless to be found in other types of Chinese. Examples have been given in §§112, 113 and 257. Another is that in Pekingese the triphthong which may be written

---

[38] Also miˈmoːrïəl.

iau varies with the four tones. In particular, when said with the third (low-rising) tone it has a very open value, which might be written narrowly eɑo or even ɛɑɔ. (A difference of duration is also involved. See §557.)

544. Differentiation by tamber combined with voice-pitch is, however, not an essential characteristic of all monosyllabic tone languages by any means. It does not appear to be found, for instance, in Cantonese, Siamese, Shan or Burmese.

545. When distinctions are effected by tamber plus voice-pitch (tone), it seems clear that the tone is always the predominating element and the tamber subsidiary. That this must be the case in Pekingese is shown by the fact that in the case of many of the syllables of that language there is little or no variation of tamber accompanying changes of tone. Thus the syllables ˉi, ´i, ∕i and ˅i show practically no differences of tamber. Furthermore, in cases where there are differences of quality I think it is correct to say that as long as the words are pronounced with proper tones they remain intelligible even though the appropriate variations of tamber are not observed; whereas they would not be intelligible if pronounced with exact vowel tambers and incorrect tones.

546. Differences of tamber such as those mentioned in §543 would therefore not be shown by differences of symbol in broad transcriptions of Pekingese. (See, however, footnote 15 to §257.)

547. Slight differences of tamber accompany differences of tone in Serbo-Croat. (See Fry and Kostić, *Serbo-Croat Phonetic Reader*, pp. 7 and 8, and the diagram on p. 9 of that book. Here again the differences of tamber are evidently entirely subsidiary to the differences of tone.)

(7) Distinctions by Duration of a Sound combined with Duration of an Adjoining Sound

548. In Chapter XXII (§376, etc.) mention was made of the well-known fact that sequences are often distinguished from one another solely by the duration of a single sound. We must now call attention to another not uncommon use of duration, namely, the distinction of sequences by the relative lengths of two or more adjacent sounds.

549. This manner of using length is found to a limited extent in French. The pair of words bɛt (*bette*) and bɛːt (*bête*) differs chiefly in the length of the vowel, but this difference is accompanied by a compensatory difference in the length of the final consonants. The t of bɛt is noticeably longer than that of bɛːt. (See §371.)

550. A more extensive use of the same principle forms a characteristic feature of Italian. The usage in that language is that when a strongly stressed vowel[39] is long the following consonant is short, and that when a strongly stressed vowel is short the following consonant is long ("double"). This is exemplified in such pairs of words as ˈkaro[40] (*caro*, dear), ˈkarro (*carro*, waggon), ˈvano[40] (vain), ˈvanno (they go), ˈseta (silk), ˈsetta (sect), ˈbɛlo[40] (*belo*, bleating), ˈbɛllo (*bello*, beautiful), ˈnɔte[40] (notes), ˈnɔtte (night).

551. The principle extends to groups formed of a vowel + two consonants. If the vowel is long the consonant group is short and vice versa. When the consonant-group is long, the length either affects one of the consonants only, or is spread over the two, according to circumstances. Thus the group dr in ˈpadre is short, while in kwattro, tanto, molto, the consonant groups are long. In these three latter words it is the t that takes the length. This has to be shown by doubling the t in the phonetic transcription of ˈkwattro, since writing ˈkwatro would indicate a lengthening of the a (-aːtro being a possible Italian combination). It is, however, not necessary to write tantto, moltto, since -aːnto, -oːlto are not possible Italian combinations.

552. The same principle is followed in Swedish and doubtless in many other chrone languages. Illustrations from Swedish are kɑːl[41] (*kal*, bald), kall (*kall*, cold), tɑːk[41] (*tak*, roof), takk (*tack*, thank you), ˇkɑːla[41] (*kala*, plural of *kal*), ˇkalla (*kalla*, plural of *kall*), ɑːt[41] (*art*, sort), svatt (*svart*, black), heːt[41] (*het*, hot, masc.

---

[39] The conditions apply only in the case of strongly stressed vowels. Weakly stressed vowels are always short in Italian, but they may be followed by long or by short consonants. Compare koˈnoʃʃere (*conoscere*), konˈnettere (*connettere*), kaˈmino (*camino*, chimney), kamˈmino (*cammino*, I walk).

[40] In narrower transcription the stressed vowel would be marked with the sign of length: ˈkaːro, ˈvaːno, etc.

and fem.), hɛtt (*hett*, hot, neut.), ˈɛːra[41] (*ära*, to honour), ˈhɛrrə (*herre*, master).

553. In languages exhibiting this peculiarity of pronunciation on a considerable scale it is probably best to consider the chronemes as being applicable to the consonants only, the differences of vowel length being regarded as incidental to the consonant lengths. This is in fact the principle followed in the common orthography of Italian and (with some exceptions) in Swedish. The alternative plan of applying the chroneme to the vowels would not be practicable, at any rate for Italian, on account of the fact that in that language the lengthening of consonants in pretonic positions is not linked to any marked extent with shortness of the preceding vowel.

(8) DISTINCTIONS BY DURATION COMBINED WITH DEGREE OF STRESS

554. It sometimes happens in stress languages that strong stress is accompanied by longer duration than weak stress. Examples of this have already been given in §§393, 394. In some of the cases observable in English the difference of duration between strong and weak syllables is only slight; there is, for instance, little if any difference of length between the corresponding vowels of the words ˈbilou (*billow*) and biˈlou (*below*), or those of ˈinkriːs and inˈkriːs. Where, however, the long vowel is in a weakly stressed syllable immediately preceding a strong stress, the difference in length is greater; it may be noticed, for instance, in comparing ˈtoːment (*torment*, n.) with toːˈment (v.) or in the examples in §393.

555. Italian, on the other hand, furnishes very clear examples of the association of length with stress. In that language the strongly stressed syllables are normally much longer, either in vowel or in consonant (§§550, 551), than the weakly stressed syllables: thus the second syllable of paˈtata (potato) has a vowel considerably longer than either of the others, while the second

---

[41] It is not certain whether the vowel length-mark can be dispensed with in broad transcription of Swedish, or whether ɑ can be written a without giving rise to ambiguity. A decision on these points can only be come to after an investigation of the lengths and qualities of vowels in weakly stressed syllables.

syllable of **saranno** (they will be) is a good deal longer than the first and third by reason of the long **n**.[42]

(9) DISTINCTIONS BY DURATION IN COMBINATION WITH A TYPE OF STRESS

556. It is probable that differentiations by this combination are only found in conjunction with differences of tone. The instances quoted from Serbo-Croat in §§560, 583 appear to involve differences in types of stress. They are cases in which it is difficult to say whether any one of the attributes predominates over the others. I am disposed to consider the length and stress as subsidiary to the tone. It is, however, worthy of note that FRY and KOSTIĆ have evolved an adequate phonetic notation for Serbo-Croat on the basis of duration and stress. (See §466.)

(10) DISTINCTIONS BY DURATION COMBINED WITH VOICE-PITCH

557. Differentiations by this combination are found in Pekingese and doubtless also in other monosyllabic tone languages of the Far East. Words having the third Pekingese tone (the low-rising) are said with longer syllabic elements than words of similar sound but other tones. Thus, for instance, ⟋mo (smudge) has a noticeably longer vowel than ⁻mo (touch) or ⟋mo (ghost) or ⟍mo (ink), and the **a** of ⟋ma (horse) is longer than the **a**'s of ⁻ma (nurse), ⟋ma (hemp) and ⟍ma (abuse). This length is clearly subsidiary to the

---

[42] Weakly stressed syllables in which the vowel is followed by a long consonant or by one of certain consonant groups are naturally longer than other weakly stressed syllables. Such are the first syllables of **kam'mino** (I walk), **ver'ranno** (they will come), **al'tsare** (to raise).

It is possible that the first syllables of such words as **setti'mana** (week), **suppli'mento** (addition), **lunga'mente** (for a long time) might be found by mechanical measurements to be nearly or even quite as long as the first syllable of **'sɛtte** (seven), **'tsuppa** (soup), **'lungo** (long), but it must be observed that they are long not only on account of the consonants following the vowel but also because they bear a fairly strong degree of stress ("secondary stress").

Even final syllables with strong stress may be considered to be long in Italian, despite the fact that the vowels of such syllables are actually short. That they are felt as long is shown by the fact that when a word beginning with a consonant follows, that consonant is lengthened: thus the second syllable of **fa'ra** (he will do) is potentially long; it is actually long in **fa'ra b'bɛne** (he will do well).

tone, and does not need to be marked in broad transcription. (Under some conditions the third tone is also accompanied by special tambers. See §§112, 113, 242, 257.)

558. Serbo-Croat is another language in which words are differentiated by a combination of duration and voice-pitch. (Type of stress is, however, also involved, as already mentioned in §556.) The nature of the lengths, stresses and tones of this language have been concisely set out by D. B. FRY and Đ. KOSTIĆ in the introduction to their *Serbo-Croat Phonetic Reader*, and the following particulars are taken from that work and from other information given me by Professor FRY.

559. The Serbo-Croat language contains short, fairly long and very long syllabic sounds (i.e. vowels and syllabic r). The fairly long and the very long syllabic sounds are distinguished from the short syllabic sounds, and from each other, not only by their duration but also by special tones. The fairly long sounds have a rising tone (here represented by ´), while the very long sounds are usually[43] said with a rising-falling tone (here represented by ^). The short syllabic sounds have no definite tones, but syllables containing them may have significant strong stress[44] or significant medium stress,[45] or of course they may have stress which is weak by comparison with that of neighbouring syllables. Syllables bearing the strong stress generally, though not necessarily, have a prominent voice-pitch (e.g. a high pitch if the neighbouring syllables are low); syllables bearing the medium stress have much the same pitch as neighbouring weakly stressed syllables.

560. The usage is illustrated by the following Serbo-Croat words:

(a) very long syllabic sound with rising-falling tone contrasted with strongly stressed short sound:

ˈdruga (next, f.), drûːga (friend),

---

[43] When words containing very long syllabic sounds occur in unimportant positions, they are often said without their characteristic rising-falling tone: they become "toneless." When this happens, the distinction between the long sound and a similar short sound with medium stress (§461) would appear to be one of duration only.

[44] The strong stress is of the diminuendo type.

[45] The medium stress appears to be of the level or slightly crescendo type.

'kɲiga (book, nom. sing.), kɲîːga (book, gen. pl.),
'leta (summer, gen.), lêːta (flight),
'toj (this, f. dat.), tôːj (this, loc. sing.);

(b) very long syllabic sound with rising-falling tone contrasted
with medium-stressed short sound:
ˌpuna (full, m. gen. sing.), pûːna (full, f. nom. sing.),
ˌprimorju (coast, dat.), prîːmorju (coast, loc.),
ˌzrna (grain, gen. sing.), zr̂ːna (grain, acc. pl.),
ˌɲix (they, f. dat.), ɲîːx (they, m. gen.);

(c) very long syllabic sound with rising-falling tone contrasted
with fairly long sound with rising tone:
móˑra (seas, gen.), môːra (must);

(d) fairly long syllabic sound with rising tone contrasted with
medium-stressed short syllabic sound:
sam (to be), sáˑm (himself).

561.   Differentiations by combinations of duration and voice-
pitch are also characteristic of Rhineland German.   In that type
of German there are two types of long vowel and diphthong: the
moderately long ("unterlang" in the terminology of Professor
MENZERATH) and the fully long ("lang" in MENZERATH's terminology).   These are accompanied by special intonations which may
be termed "high" and "low" respectively.[46]

---

[46] Special combinations of duration and voice-pitch are doubtless to be found
in some other types of German, and I have in fact been told that something
of the kind occurs in the German of Munich.   The late Professor PAUL
MENZERATH of Bonn appeared to hold the view that these or analogous distinctions are made in most parts of Germany.   I am not in a position to
judge of the extent of the areas over which this type of pronunciation is found.
But I find it difficult to believe that it is as widespread as MENZERATH
suggested.   The experienced phoneticians VIËTOR, SIEBS and E. A. MEYER
have made no mention of it, and they have not indicated it in their transcripts.
(See VIËTOR, Deutsches Aussprachewörterbuch; TH. SIEBS, Deutsche Hochsprache; ERNST A. MEYER, Deutsche Gespräche.)   The distinctions appear to
have been unknown also to H. KLINGHARDT, the authority on intonation,
and there is no indication or reference to them in his Übungen in deutschem
Tonfall.   The distinctions also found no place in the sections dealing with
vowel-length in SIEVERS' Grundzüge der Phonetik, though he spoke of "long"
and "over-long" vowels in other connexions (§696 of the fifth edition) and
stated that the true difference between long and short vowels is that the
long ones are "prolongable" ("dehnbar") while the short ones are not.

562. These terms have specialized meanings here, as the values of the tones vary with the sentence intonation. The two chief forms of each are as follows:

"high" denotes high-falling [＼] when the word as a whole is said with falling intonation; it denotes mid or low rising to high, [⁄] or [／], when the sentence requires that the word as a whole should be said with rising intonation;

"low" denotes mid descending to low [＼] when the word as a whole is said with a falling intonation; it denotes mid or low level with or without a slight rise, i.e. intonations of the types [_] and [⁄], when the sentence requires that the word as a whole should be said with rising intonation.

563. In the following paragraphs the vowels of moderate length are marked with ·, and those of full length with ꞉. Diphthongs with the moderate length are written without mark, and those with full length are written with ꞉ after the first letter.

564. The principles involved may be illustrated by the words me·r (*mehr*, more), me꞉r (*Meer*, sea), 'ʃnaider (*Schneider*, instrument for cutting), 'ʃna꞉ider (*Schneider*, tailor). The common intonations of me·r and me꞉r are: (1) with falling intonation [＼] and [＼] respectively, (2) with rising intonation [／] and [⁄] respectively. The intonations of the words *Schneider* are illustrated by the following sentences:

'hi·r ist dɛr 'ʃnaider (instrument) [＼ ·· ＼ .]

'hi·r ist dɛr 'ʃna꞉ider (tailor) [＼ ··＼ .]

He made no mention of "unprolongable" long vowels. Curiously enough, however, he gives in the section on *consonant*-length (*Grundzüge*, p. 260) one example of a pair of words distinguished by the length of a diphthong: he indicated *braut* (brews) as having a longer u than *Braut* (bride), but it is not clear whether he is there referring to dialect speech.

I have made enquiry of several Germans from parts other than the Rhineland, who have informed me that they have never heard of any such distinctions.

It may be added that, according to MENZERATH, the fully long vowels and diphthongs are capable of prolongation beyond their normal length. They are, in his terminology, "dehnbar." The vowels and diphthongs of moderate length cannot receive extra prolongation; they are not "dehnbar."

He has stated that "prolongability" ("dehnbarkeit") is an infallible criterion for determining which type of length a vowel or diphthong has (see his article on the subject in *Le Maître Phonétique*, July, 1934, pp. 69, 70).

dɛr ˈʃnaider ist ˈdaʴ [·╱ ̈ ̈ ＼]
dɛr ˈʃnaːider ist ˈdaʴ [·- ̈ ̈ ＼]

565.   Other examples of words which in Rhineland German exhibit the above combinations of length and voice-pitch are:

moderate length with "high" tone	full length with "low" tone
fiˑl (*fiel*)	fiːl (*viel*)
rain (*Rhein*)	raːin (*rein*)
vaˑr (*wahr*)	vaːr (*war*)
ˈbauer (*Bauer*, cage, one who builds)	ˈbaːuer (*Bauer*, peasant)
ˈtsaˑlen (*Zahlen*, plur. of *Zahl*)	ˈtsaːlen (*zahlen*, v.)
ˈʃøˑner (*schöner*, adj. masc., after *ein* for instance)	ˈʃøːner (*schöner*, comparative)
hiˑr (*hier*)	heːr (*her*)
iˑn (*ihn*)	tsiːl (*Ziel*)
ˈʃtyˑle (*Stühle*)	ˈyːber (*über*)
ʃtuˑl (*Stuhl*)	beˈfeːl (*Befehl*)

(11) DISTINCTIONS BY A DEGREE OF STRESS COMBINED WITH A DEGREE OF STRESS ON AN ADJACENT SYLLABLE

566.   Differentiations merely by a degree of stress on a single syllable are very uncommon. They occur, however, in Serbo-Croat, as already mentioned (§461). Occasional examples are also to be found in English, where a word with two strong stresses may be semantically distinct from another word having the same sounds but only one strong stress. I have not yet found any convincing examples of this in ordinary Southern English, though I think it likely that a few exist. Instances may, however, be observed in the speech of those who pronounce the weakly stressed prefix *re-* as riː-; with them *remark* (observe) and *re-mark* (mark again) are distinguished as riːˈmaːk and ˈriːˈmaːk. (There is probably a certain difference of duration accompanying this distinction by stress.)

567.   On the other hand differentiations by relative stress on two neighbouring syllables are fairly frequent. This is the common case usually known as differentiation "by the position of the stress," as in the pairs of English words ˈbilou (*billow*), biˈlou (*below*),

'inkri:s (*increase*, n.), in'kri:s (*increase*, v.), 'impo:t (*import*, n.), im'po:t (*import*, v.). (See §§453 ff.)

568. The essential difference between such pairs is not merely that a particular syllable is "stressed" (to use the convenient but inexact way of saying "pronounced with strong stress"), but that the neighbouring syllable(s) should be at the same time "unstressed" (the common term for "pronounced with weak stress"). Stress as commonly understood is thus in reality a combination of two attributes: a strong stress on one syllable and a weak stress on a neighbouring one. When therefore we say that in a stress language two words are distinguished "by the position of the stress," we really mean that they are distinguished by the relative strengths of the stresses on two syllables.

569. The subject of distinctions by strong and weak stress on neighbouring syllables has already been discussed at length in the chapter on stress (Chap. XXIV).

(12) Differentiations by Degrees of Stress combined with Voice-Pitch

570. It was pointed out in §§455, 456 that when words are differentiated by stress alone, the distinctions are by no means clear. In order that distinctions by degrees of stress should be clearly perceived by the hearer it is almost essential that the stresses should be accompanied by differences in some other attribute. Accordingly it is nearly always found in stress languages that strong stresses are accompanied by prominent intonations.

571. Thus, as already indicated in §457, if English words such as 'bilou (*billow*) and bi'lou (*below*) or 'impo:t (n.) and im'po:t (v.) are said in isolation with a falling intonation, they have tonal forms which may be represented graphically thus:

'bilou ⎱
'impo:t ⎰ [＼_]   bi'lou ⎱
                         im'po:t ⎰ [· ＼]

And if they are said in isolation with a rising intonation, their tonal forms are of the following types:

'bilou ⎱
'impo:t ⎰ [· ╱]   bi'lou ⎱
                          im'po:t ⎰ [· ╱]

In fact, in nearly every case, such differentiations in English are effected by stress coupled with intonation. (See further, §§457–460.)

572. Intonations such as those shown in §571 cannot be regarded as "significant word tones" in the generally accepted sense of the term. They are special cases of *sentence intonation* or portions of sentence intonations, and such words can be and are said with a variety of other sentence intonations. Some of these do not help to render the stressed syllables prominent (see §436).

573. Hence, we find ourselves obliged to regard the stress as constituting the essential difference between pairs of English words like the above, in spite of the fact that the stresses are generally linked with special intonations and that when they are not so linked the distinctions are difficult to perceive.

574. Similar considerations apply to other stress languages, such as German, Italian, Spanish, Russian and Greek. The relations between stress and intonation in English, German and Russian have been investigated in considerable detail,[47] and the researches have made it clear that in these languages the stress is from the point of view of word-meanings the essential attribute and that intonation is subsidiary to it.[48] Similar conditions no doubt also prevail in the other stress languages.

575. In a few languages, of which Norwegian and Swedish are the best known, use is made of significant tones which are linked to degrees of stress. The tones in these languages take the form of tone patterns which may be spread over two or more syllables. The salient points or "nuclei" of the tones are always strongly stressed, but it seems clear that the stress is subsidiary to the tone. If Norwegian or Swedish sentences were said with correct intonation but with equal stress on all the syllables, it would I think be found that native hearers would perceive the general effect to be substantially correct. But correct stressings with marked alterations in the intonation would, I believe, sound incorrect and might in some cases suggest wrong word-meanings. In exemplification of this type of tonal usage we give in the following paragraphs a

---

[47] See R. KINGDON, *The Groundwork of English Intonation*; D. JONES, *Outline of English Phonetics*; ARMSTRONG and WARD, *Handbook of English Intonation*; H. KLINGHARDT, *Übungen in deutschem Tonfall*; M. L. BARKER, *Handbook of German Intonation*; S. BOYANUS and N. B. JOPSON, *Spoken Russian*.

[48] We are leaving out of account here the important functions of intonation as a modifier of sentence meanings.

description of the main features of one of the Norwegian tone systems, namely, a common South-Western pronunciation.

576. This form of Norwegian contains two tonal patterns; they have been called the "simple tone" and the "compound tone" by some writers. The simple tone is used, for instance, in the Norwegian words ˈbœnnər (peasants) and the compound tone in ˈbœnnər (beans, prayers). The nucleus of the Norwegian "simple" tone consists of a low or low-falling pitch (graphically [ˍ] or [ˎ]) combined with a strong stress. The nucleus of the Norwegian "compound" tone consists of a high-falling pitch (graphically [ˋ]) combined with a strong stress. These tones, besides having the salient features just mentioned, require that preceding and following weakly stressed syllables should have certain pitches relative to them. A weakly stressed syllable preceding a strongly stressed syllable with "simple" tone has a higher pitch than that tone, while a weakly stressed syllable preceding a strongly stressed syllable with "compound" tone has a lower pitch than the beginning of that tone. The treatment of weakly stressed syllables following a strongly stressed syllable depends upon whether they terminate a statement or not. If they terminate a statement, they are all said on low level pitch; if they do not, they are said on an ascending sequence.[49]

577. Statements consisting of two clauses therefore present tonal patterns like the following:

(a) "simple" tone in both clauses [· · · ˈ ˋ . .]

(b) "simple" tone in 1st clause and "compound" tone in 2nd clause [· ˎ · · ˋ . .]

(c) "compound" tone in both clauses [· ˋ · · ˋ . .]

(d) "compound" tone in 1st clause and "simple" tone in 2nd clause [· ˋ · · ˎ . .]

578. Each of the tonemes in the type of Norwegian here referred to comprises therefore two very markedly different tones, namely,

---

[49] It would appear, however, that in the pronunciation of many Norwegians no difference is made between the tones of unstressed final syllables and unstressed non-final syllables; the pitch rises in both cases. In this pronunciation all clauses, whether final or not, have tones of the types [· ˍ · ·] ("simple") or [· ˋ · ·] ("compound").

the tone used finally in a statement and that used in other situations. Each of these in turn comprises sub-varieties depending upon the pitch of the syllables preceding and following in the sentence. In particular, when several weakly stressed syllables precede a compound tone, the salient part of that tone tends to begin higher than when only a single weakly stressed syllable precedes it.

579. Special sentence intonations can of course be superimposed upon what may be called the normal intonation of Norwegian sentences. These give rise to still other variants of the tones. It is, however, not possible to count such further variants as members of the tonemes described above. It appears necessary to consider emphatic speech, or any special kind of speech requiring a deviation from the "normal" intonation, as another form of the language having its own tonemes.

(13) DIFFERENTIATIONS BY PARTICULAR KINDS OF STRESS COMBINED WITH VOICE-PITCH

580. The researches of Miss L. E. ARMSTRONG into the phonetics of Somali show that that language is one in which differentiations are made by complexes of voice-pitch and types of stress.[50] There

---

[50] See L. E. ARMSTRONG, *The Phonetic Structure of Somali* (in *Mitteilungen des Seminars für Orientalische Sprachen zu Berlin*, XXXVII, Part 3, 1934).

Prior to Miss ARMSTRONG'S work it was thought that Somali was an ordinary stress language, i.e. one in which words were distinguished by the location of strong stresses.   Previous observers had perhaps not been on the lookout for tones.   MEINHOF, for instance, used stress-marks in his transcripts of Somali words, but he made no mention of word-tones beyond expressing the opinion that there were not likely to be any (see *Die Sprache der Hamiten*, pp. 168, 169).   Even Dr. M. VON TILING, who has an excellent ear, made no mention of tones in her remarkable works *Die Sprache der Jabárti mit besonderer Berücksichtigung der Verwandtschaft von Jabárti und Somali* (in *Zeitschrift für Eingeborenen Sprachen*, XII, 1, 1922), and *Somali-Texte*, though I once gathered from a conversation with her that certain of her observations had made her suspect the existence of tones.

When Miss ARMSTRONG started work on Somali in 1931, she discovered that many words were distinguished from each other by what appeared to be tone only.   I heard these tones from one of her native collaborators, and can testify to the accuracy of her observations in this matter.   It subsequently proved that, at any rate in some cases, words were differentiated not by tones only but by tones combined with types of stress.   I heard examples of this too from the same native speaker.

are in Somali, as far as is at present known,[51] two types of strong stress, an even or slightly crescendo type and a diminuendo type. The first of these is accompanied by a level or slightly rising tone, while the second is accompanied by a high-falling tone. The even stress is sometimes of high pitch (marked with ´ in the ARMSTRONG notation). The falling tone is denoted by ` in the ARMSTRONG notation.

581. It would seem that every syllable containing a long vowel has one of these stresses with its appropriate tone. The stresses (with appropriate tones) may also apparently be spread over two or more syllables containing short vowels. Whether they may be spread over sequences containing both long and short vowels or more than one long vowel has not yet been ascertained.

582. The following are examples of the two types of stress in Somali. The tones shown are those used when the words are said in isolation.

(1) Level or slightly rising tone with even or crescendo stress:
   (a) on single syllables: geːs [-] (side), suːn [-] (road), diːn [-] (religion), œːg [-] (beacon), qaːn [-] (debt)[52];
   (b) spread over two syllables with short vowels: inan [··] (daughter), bahal [··] (thing), galab [··] (evening), soddoh [··] (mother-in-law);
   (c) spread over three syllables: arbaʕa [···] (Wednesday);
   (d) in words of more than one syllable containing one long vowel, the pitch of that vowel being high: ʕáːwa [¯.] (to-night), ħéːɖo [¯.] (wooden dish), qáːlin [¯.] (young he-camel), kúːʃa [¯.] (the necklace), láːbta [¯.] (the chest), géːsta [¯.] (sides);
   (e) in words of more than one syllable containing one long vowel, the pitch of that vowel being mid: qaːlin [-·] (young she-camel), kuːlo [-·] (necklaces), gaːɖi [-:] (carriage), feːɖo [-·] (ribs), sagaːl [·-] (nine), qaɖoːn [·-] (bark of tree), xamiːs [·-] (Thursday), ʃabɛːl [·-] (female leopard);

[51] I say, "as far as is at present known," since some of the differences may prove on further investigation to be differences of tone only.
[52] These words are often pronounced géːs [´], súːn [´], etc., with high and slightly rising tone, when another word follows in the sentence.

(f) in words containing two long vowels, see (3).

(2) Falling tone with diminuendo stress:

(a) on single syllables: gèːs [\ ] (horn), sùːn [\ ] (strap), dìːn [\ ] (tortoise), dœ̀ːg [\ ] (green grass)[53];

(b) spread over two syllables with short vowels: inan [˙.] (son), bàhal [˙.] (wild beast), bàdag [˙.] (goose), tiḍi [˙.] (she said), wàddo [˙.] (path), sànka [˙.] (the nose);

(c) in words of more than one syllable containing one long vowel: dœ̀ːgga [\ .] (the green grass), tiːħa [\ .] (the shower), gèːska [\ .] (the horn), itàːl [˙ \ ] (strength), habèːn [˙ \ ] (night), xamìːs [˙ \ ] (long shirt), ʃabˌɛ̀ːl [˙ \ ] (male leopard);

(d) in words containing two long vowels, see (3).

(3) The case of words containing two long vowels:

(a) When both tones are level and of mid pitch, the stresses appear to have about equal force; if there is any difference it is that the second has slightly stronger stress than the first.

Example: ʕɛːsaːn [- -] (female kid).

(b) When both tones are level and one is of high pitch, the high-pitched one appears to have the stronger stress.

Example: náːgtaː [⁻ _] (that woman).

(c) When one tone is falling and the other level, the falling tone appears to have the stronger stress.

Examples: ʕɛːsàːn [- \ ] (male kid), gèːskaː [\ _] (that horn).[54]

---

[53] Words of this type are apparently always said with approximately the same high-falling tone when other words follow in the sentence.

[54] Further investigation of the stress and tone system of Somali is needed. It would not surprise me if it were eventually found that the language is not a stress language in the ordinary sense of the term, but that it is essentially a tone language—one in which special stresses or stress effects are incidental to the tones.   The effects which have hitherto been regarded as strong stresses may prove to be not strong stresses at all but *prominences* (§§434 ff.), occasioned by particular sequences of tone coupled in some cases with length.

It is at least clear from examples such as those quoted in §582, (1) (a) and (2) (a), that the mid-level tone and the falling tone distinguish words.

583. Differentiation by complexes of voice-pitch and types of stress is also found in Serbo-Croat, but in that language the distinctions are helped out by a certain difference in the duration of the vowel. The examples mó·ra (of the seas) and mô:ra (must) quoted in §560 (c) illustrate this. The first syllable of mó·ra is believed to have crescendo stress; it also has a rising tone. The second syllable of mó·ra, when said in isolation has a mid pitch. The first syllable of mô:ra has crescendo-diminuendo stress coupled with a rising-falling tone, and the second syllable of the word pronounced normally in isolation has low pitch. (Length is also involved, the o of mô:ra being longer than that of mó·ra, as explained in §559.)

(14) Differentiation by Voice-Pitch on one Syllable combined with Voice-Pitch on a neighbouring Syllable or Syllables

584. This is the same as the case of "tones spread over more than one syllable" (§575). It will be observed, for instance, that in Norwegian the terminal pitch-sequence [↘ .] by itself is ambiguous if the fall on the penultimate is a moderate one. It may stand for either the "simple tone" or the "compound tone." When, however, another syllable precedes, there is no longer any ambiguity. If the pitch of the preceding syllable is higher than that of the penultimate, i.e. if the pitch-sequence is one that would be represented graphically by [· ↘ .], the tone is the "simple" one. If, on the other hand, the pitch of the preceding syllable is

---

And the examples in (1) (d) and (2) (c) make it practically certain that the high-level tone and the falling tone have significant function. I have heard words of these types pronounced by a native; the difference of tone is striking to anyone who is on the look-out for it; it is always consistently made. The difference in tone between such words as gé:sta and gè:ska was one of Miss Armstrong's most remarkable discoveries.

Questions which remain to be solved are (1) whether the distinction between the high-level tone and mid-level tones illustrated in (1) (d) and (1) (e) are used for effecting significant distinctions, (2) whether falling tones as well as high-level tones are used on syllables which are long on account of the presence of a closing consonant, such as the first syllables of sànka (the nose), wàddo (path), and (3) whether such tonal forms as [¯ .], [↘ .], [_ ·], [· ˙ .] are to be regarded as sequences of tones or as single tones spread over more than one syllable.

14

lower than that of the beginning of the penultimate, i.e. if the pitch-sequence is of the type [. ⌐ .], then the tone is the "compound" one.

(15) DIFFERENTIATIONS BY VOICE-PITCH COMBINED WITH VOICE-QUALITY

585. There exist tone languages in which certain tones are accompanied by a special kind of voice-quality, i.e. "breathy" voice or "creaky" voice. Such are Burmese and Vietnamese.

586. Vowels bearing the low-level or falling tones in Burmese are always said with breathy voice-quality, while vowels with the high-level tone are said with harsh or "creaky" voice-quality. Examples of words said with breathy voice are ˍhle (boat), `pjɔ (to speak); an example of a syllable requiring creaky voice is ˉpja (to show). The usage is explained, with further examples, in the *Burmese Phonetic Reader* by ARMSTRONG and PE MAUNG TIN, pp. 21–25.

587. The tones of Vietnamese have been examined from the point of view of accompanying voice-quality by Miss E. HENDERSON, and a short account of them was given by her in *Le Maître Phonétique*, January, 1943, p. 7. She finds that among other tones there are two which may be described as "rising-breathy" and "rising-creaky," and that these differ somewhat in pitch as well as in voice-quality, though the difference in voice-quality is the predominating one. In her words: "The pitch-pattern of the 'rising-breathy' tone is a short fall from middle to low pitch, a pause on low pitch followed by a sharp rise to high pitch. . . . This tone is fairly long and is usually accompanied by 'breathy' voice. The 'rising-creaky' tone, which is always pronounced with strong 'creak,' consists of the low-creaky tone followed by a quick rise or jump to a fairly high pitch." There are also differences in pitch between the "low-breathy" and "low-creaky" tones of the same language, the "low-breathy" being accompanied by a slight fall. Miss HENDERSON has suggested representing these combinations of tone and voice-quality by the following signs: ᵛ rising-breathy, ᵛ rising-creaky, ˎ low-breathy, ˍ low-creaky. She has furnished me with a number of Vietnamese words exemplifying them; among them are ᵛzai (belt), ᵛzai (dribble), ˎzai (long), ˍzai (stupid), ᵛlaɲ (clear, bell-like sound), ᵛlaɲ (satin), ˎlaɲ (good), ˍlaɲ (frozen).

CHAPTER XXVII

DIAPHONES

INDIVIDUAL DIFFERENCES OF SPEECH

588. When one compares the speech of one person with that of another speaker of the same language, differences of pronunciation are generally to be found. The differences are of various kinds.

589. In the first place everyone has his own particular quality of voice. This sometimes differs considerably from that of others and sometimes hardly at all.

590. Differences of voice-quality are as a rule ignored in phonetic work. We regard "speech-sounds" as being so to speak superimposed on the speaker's voice-quality. Although voice-quality forms an integral part of every voiced sound uttered in speech, we can in imagination subtract that part of the sound-quality which is personal to the speaker and examine the remainder of the quality as if it had a separate existence. We ignore personal voice-quality in the same sort of way as we ignore the scraping sound made by the reproducing needle of a gramophone. When therefore we judge a certain sound uttered by one speaker to be "the same" as one uttered by another speaker, we really mean "as nearly alike as their different voice-qualities allow."

591. A second type of difference between the speech of one person and that of another consists in different distributions of phonemes in particular words or sentences. Thus in the South of England some people pronounce *again* as əˈgein, while others sound it əˈgen. Likewise there are two current pronunciations of *yesterday* (ˈjestədi and ˈjestədei), *accomplish* (əˈkompliʃ and əˈkʌmpliʃ), *direct* (diˈrekt and daiˈrekt), *girl* (gəːl and geəl) and many other words.

592. Speakers may differ too in the lengths of sounds they use, and the differences of length may or may not be accompanied by differences of quality. With some English people, for instance, the vowel sounds in *jam*, *bad* and *grand* are short; others use the

same quality but lengthen the vowel.[1] Similarly in Parisian French one hears both **bag** and **ba:g** (for *bague*), **tabl** and **ta:bl** (for *table*). In these cases there are differences of length without differences of quality.

593. Again in the South of England we find most people pronouncing *off* and *lost* as **of, lost**, but some pronouncing **o:f, lo:st**. Here the difference is one of length combined with difference of quality. A similar case is that of *room* which is pronounced **rum** by some and **ru:m** by others.

594. In stress languages individual speakers sometimes show variations in the manner of stressing words. Thus in Southern English one hears *exquisite* pronounced as **'ekskwizit** and **eks'kwizit**, *formidable* as **'fo:midəbl** and **fo:'midəbl**, *dirigible* as **'diridʒəbl** and **di'ridʒəbl**, *contents* (n.) as **'kontents** and **kən'tents**, *adult* as **'adʌlt** and **ə'dʌlt**. In the North we find *magazine* pronounced **'magəzi:n**, *criticize* pronounced **kriti'saiz**, *yesterday* pronounced **jestə'dei**, where the South has **magə'zi:n, 'kritisaiz, 'jestədi** or **'jestədei**.

595. Differences in intonation are also common. People's pitch limits vary, for instance. Moreover different speakers often use different forms of sentence-intonation, some of which may be individual or local varieties of well-known intonation patterns. They may differ too to some extent in the choice of intonation pattern used in particular contexts.[2] There are also special intonation patterns characteristic of the speech of different parts

---

[1] Lengthening of this vowel is very common in London English (see §130 and footnote 8 to §513). Those who lengthen it have one phoneme more than those who always keep it short, since their **a**-sound in these words cannot be regarded as the short of the **a**-sound they use in *calm, large*, etc. A broad transcription of their pronunciation requires the introduction of an additional letter. Either the letter **ɑ** must be used in *calm, large*, etc. (thus **kɑ:m, lɑ:dʒ**, etc.), or a special letter (**ε** or **æ**) must be used in *jam, grand, back*, etc. (thus **dʒεːm, grεːnd**, etc., or **dʒæːm, græːnd**, etc.). Those who have in addition to the above two long sounds another long **a:**, distinct from these, replacing the more normal **aiə** (see §606, also footnote 11 to §249, and my *Outline of English Phonetics*, §414) have two phonemes more than those with the pronunciation I have been recording throughout this book. To represent their pronunciation broadly necessitates the use of two letters besides **a**, viz. **ε** (or **æ**) and **ɑ**. *Had* (strongly stressed), *hired* and *hard* would need a transcription such as **hεːd** (or **hæːd**), **ha:d, hɑːd**.

[2] Notice, for instance, how different B.B.C. news readers say "*That is the end of the news*".

of the country—patterns which it would be difficult to explain as variants of any of the well-known Southern English typical patterns.

596. Lastly, the actual sounds used by one person are often found to differ from the corresponding sounds used by other speakers of the same language. Thus if one asks a number of Englishmen to say the word *get*, one usually finds quite a number of different kinds of **e** among them. Such differences are often said to constitute "free variations." They must be carefully distinguished from "allophones" (members of phonemes).

597. It is with such "free variations" that the present chapter is concerned.

THE NATURE OF DIAPHONES

598. It is convenient to have a name for a family of sounds consisting of the sound used by one speaker in a particular set of words (said in isolation) together with corresponding though different sounds used in them by other speakers of the same language. Such a family may be termed a "diaphone."

599. The following are some examples of diaphones containing several sounds.

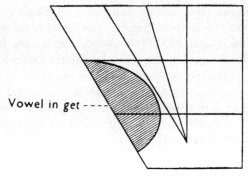

FIG. 10. Diaphonic Area of the English Vowel in *get*.

600. A typical instance is that of English "short e" referred to in §596. The various shades of **e** which may be heard from different English speakers in such words as *get, fetch, egg* are roughly as shown in the annexed diagram (Fig. 10). It is probable that any sound included in the shaded area of this diagram will be found to be some English person's "short **e**."

601. Another instance, which is noteworthy on account of the unusually large number of sounds included in the diaphone, is the case of the vowel sounds used by different English speakers in such words as *home, go*. These include a monophthongal o: (Scotland and Northern England), a diphthong of the ou-type beginning with a sound near to cardinal o (Northern, Western), and (in the South) several other kinds of diphthong beginning with opener kinds of o and with lesser degrees of lip-rounding, extending as far as ɔu. In the South too there are yet other types of diphthong in common use in these words. Some of them start with spread or nearly spread lips, and they include sounds of the types əu,[3] ʌu, au (London), öü ("clerical" accent). All the above sounds can be grouped together as "free variants" or members of a single diaphone.

602. An example of a consonantal diaphone is seen in the English ʃ. Its quality varies noticeably from speaker to speaker, the variations depending partly upon the position taken up by the tongue, partly upon the point at which the articulation is made and partly upon the position of the lips (which with some are protruded after the manner shown in Figure 101 of my *Outline of English Phonetics* and with others are spread).

603. Examples from foreign languages of diaphones of fairly wide extent are the German long a:, the Spanish sound of *ll* and the Hindustani sound əι.[4] The German a: varies from about cardinal 5 (Hamburg, Lübeck, etc.) to about cardinal 4 (Berlin). The Spanish diaphone written *ll* comprises three very distinct members, ʎ, j and (especially in South America) ʒ. The sound of Hindustani əι varies from a well marked diphthong which could be represented narrowly by ʌι (Lucknow) to a monophthongal or almost monophthongal ɛ: (Lahore).

604. Diaphones may comprise subsidiary members of phonemes without the corresponding principal members. For instance, the kind of t I use in position of weakest stress, as in ˈbetə (*better*), ˈgetiŋ (*getting*), is a weakly articulated sound without much aspiration—nearly ḍ in fact. But there are other speakers who use ʔ in this position and pronounce ˈbeʔə, ˈgeʔin, though their

---

[3] My ou is rather like this.

[4] Formerly written *ai* in romanic systems.

t's in other positions are similar to mine: the diaphonic variants are thus confined to subsidiary members of the t-phoneme.[5]

605. Style of pronunciation has to be considered in connexion with the idea of the diaphone. As is well known, most people use more than one style of pronunciation. (Mention has been made of this in §28.) The style depends upon the circumstances under which they are speaking. There is what we may call the "ordinary" or "slow conversational" style,[6] there are very rapid familiar styles, and there is formal style used for instance in reciting or reading aloud to a large audience, and there are styles intermediate between these. With some speakers there is little difference between the styles beyond the use of a certain number of abbreviations and assimilations in rapid familiar style which would not be made in slower styles. But with others the differences are considerable and may involve the use in formal and in very rapid styles of sounds not occurring at all in the "ordinary" style. When such additional sounds are introduced, they generally constitute special phonemes. They are also included in diaphones with the sounds which would replace them in "ordinary" style.

606. The case is exemplified by pronunciations of words like *fire, tired*. There are English people who in deliberate speech say such words with a disyllabic vowel sequence of the type aiə, but who in rapid conversational speech substitute a single diphthongal sound aə or a particular variety of monophthongal aː—sounds which are non-existent in their deliberate style. These sounds constitute separate phonemes, though they belong to the same diaphone as the aiə of their deliberate style of speech.[7]

607. Another example of the use of special sounds in particular styles of speech may be observed in the treatment of the English words which have weak forms containing ə as well as strong forms with other vowels. Thus one occasionally hears such words as

---

[5] I am assuming that the ʔ of these speakers *is* a member of their t-phoneme. That it is so is probable, though this has not yet been proved to my knowledge.

[6] What P. Passy called "prononciation familière ralentie."

[7] With those who reduce aiə to aː this sound is a phoneme separate from the common long aː (of *far, tarred*, etc.), and the two sounds have to be distinguished in broad transcription of the rapid style. This is best done by using the symbol ɑ to denote the common long a (thus fɑː, tɑːd) and transcribing *fire, tired*, etc., with aː (faː, taːd). See also footnote 1 to §592.

and, have pronounced in formal speech with a vowel intermediate between the ordinary short **a** and **ə**; this happens in situations where conversational speech would have **ən(d)** or **n(d)** and **(h)əv**. This intermediate sound is an "obscured" **a**, which may be written phonetically **ä**. It is probably not to be regarded as a separate phoneme, since the style of speech in which it occurs is almost certainly erratic and therefore not reducible to phonemes (see Chap. XXVIII). The sound would, however, belong to the same diaphone as the ordinary short **a**.

608. Variphones (§628) are presumably to be treated as particular cases of diaphones.

609. Varieties of sound heard in erratic pronunciation (Chap. XXVIII) are sometimes groupable into diaphones. Those whose pronunciation is erratic generally speak with a mixture of dialect and if they sometimes use the sound of one manner of speech, and sometimes the corresponding sound of another manner of speech, the two sounds can be grouped together into a diaphone just as they would if the two manners of speaking were used consistently by two different speakers. (Groups of this nature may perhaps sometimes be considered as particular types of variphone. See §648.)

OVERLAPPING OF DIAPHONES

610. Overlapping of diaphones is of common occurrence, i.e. a particular sound may be the one used in one set of words by one speaker but in another set of words by another speaker. This is especially liable to happen, when a sound lies near the limit of a diaphonic "area." For instance, the English **e** and **a** diaphones overlap after the manner shown in Figure 11. This means that a high variety of **a** ([a⊥] or [æ]) may be the sound used by one speaker in words like *bad, back, jam*, but the same sound may be a diaphonic variant of **e** and may be heard from some speakers (chiefly Northern) in *bed, beck, gem*.

611. The English **ou** and **au** diaphones likewise overlap. In Scottish English words like *mouth, about* are pronounced with ʌu, while, as we have already seen (§601), ʌu is one of the variants in the **ou**-diaphone. If a Londoner were to hear someone say **ə'bəut**, without knowing anything of the other sounds used by the speaker, he would naturally interpret it as *a boat*. But if a Scotsman heard the same utterance, he would take it to mean *about.*

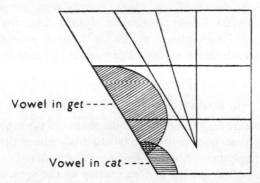

Vowel in *get* ----

Vowel in *cat* ----

FIG. 11.   Overlapping of the English short **e** and **a** Diaphones.

612.   Similarly the sounds [hæi] and [bæit] mean *high* and *bite* to some but *hay* and *bait* to others.   Some people's way of pronouncing pə'ziʃn (*position*) is barely distinguishable from other people's pronunciation of pə'zeʃn (*possession*).   The American way of saying *possible* is much the same as the Southern English pronunciation of *passable*.   And so on.

613.   It will be seen then that sounds lying near to the limits of diaphonic "areas" are recognized as belonging to one diaphone or another not so much by their inherent quality as by their relationships to the speaker's other sounds, and by the contexts in which the words are used.   If, as is to be assumed, the speaker's sentences are intelligible, the correspondences of the sounds he uses with those used by others are inferred from the general effect of his speech.   Single words said by him in isolation may be ambiguous to people who use diaphonic variants remote from his, but they become intelligible as soon as they are said in sequence with other words.

614.   The following is an actual case which was once brought to my notice.   A child was evacuated from London in 1940 and sent to live with a family in the country who use a pronunciation similar to mine.   When asked his name by the children of the family, he gave it as "dʒaimz."   The children took this to be a name they had never heard of before—a name that they would naturally have spelt *Jimes* if they had been asked to write it.   It had to be explained to them that what the boy said was the London way of pronouncing *James*. But when this London boy carried on a connected conversation, he was understood without any difficulty. No doubt all his other vowels were proportionately different from those who pronounce dʒeimz, and the necessary allowances are instinctively made by hearers in such a case. Context evidently plays a very large part in ensuring intelligibility between people who use widely differing members of diaphones.[8]

Sounds belonging to Two Diaphones

615. A sound may belong to two diaphones of the same language. One case is that just mentioned (§§610–614) where there is over-lapping of diaphones. Another is when a single sound of the speech of one person corresponds to two sounds of the speech of others.

616. The pronunciations of *or* in English afford an illustration of the latter case. Without entering into details of all the variant pronunciations heard in words written with *or*, which are rather involved, we may exemplify the point under consideration by the pronunciation of those who use an open oː [ɔː] in all such words as *form, order, port, force, board* and of those who divide such words into two categories, viz. (1) words such as *form, order, north* in which they use the open oː [ɔː] and (2) words such as *port, force, board, course* in which they use a diphthong oə beginning with a close o.[9] There is, in the words of the first category, a diaphone

---

[8] The extent to which the employment of unusual sounds can be carried without interfering with intelligibility is illustrated by a case of a peculiar type which once came under my observation. The speaker was a man whose vowels were mostly considerably lower than those normally heard. His (so-called) iː was practically ei, his short i resembled most people's short e, his short e was a kind of ɛ, his (so-called) uː was on the o level, and so on. The relations of his vowels to each other were of the same order as those of normal speakers, but the distances between them were less than usual. His whole vowel system was in fact compressed into an area below the e-o line on the vowel diagram. Everyone noticed that his speech was peculiar. It sounded somewhat blurred, but as a rule there was no difficulty in under-standing what he said.

[9] For lists of the words in the two categories, see Ripman and Archer's *New Spelling*, Appendix VII, or my *Outline of English Phonetics*, footnote 36 to §308.

Another diphthong ɔə beginning with an open o (ɔ) is also used by many English speakers in some of these words. We are leaving this out of consider-ation in the present discussion.

consisting of a monophthongal **oː** [ɔː] with slight quality variants. In the words of the second category there is a different diaphone which includes not only the members of the diaphone just mentioned but also diphthongal sounds of the **oə**-type. The Southern English monophthongal **oː** [ɔː] thus belongs to two diaphones. It should be noted that in the speech of those who use **oə** in words of the second category the sounds **oː** [ɔː] and **oə** belong to separate phonemes; they distinguish several pairs of words, e.g. **'boːdə** (*border*), **'boədə** (*boarder*), **boːn** (*born*), **boən** (*borne*), **moːn** (*morn*), **moən** (*mourn*), **hoːs** (*horse*), **hoəs** (*hoarse*).

617. The case is further exemplified by words like *food, boot, good, foot*, except that the sounds involved are not different phonemes but are members of the same phoneme conditioned by length. Most English people distinguish two categories of *oo*-words, (1) *food, boot* and other words, which are said with long **uː**, and (2) *good, foot* and other words, which are said with a short and opener **u** [ɷ]. Scottish people, however, do not as a rule make this distinction; they use a close short **u** in all these words.[10] We find therefore two diaphones. There is firstly what we may call for convenience the long **uː** diaphone which comprises **uː** and certain variants (**uw, ɷu**, etc.), together with the Scottish **u** and its variants. Secondly, there is what we may term the short **u**-diaphone, which comprises the English short open **u** [ɷ] and also the Scottish **u** with its variants. Every variant of the Scottish **u** thus belongs to both of these diaphones.

618. Yet another example of a sound belonging to more than one diaphone is the glottal stop (ʔ) which in English belongs to three diaphones. It is used by many where more normal pronunciation has a variety of **t** (e.g. **'beʔə** for **'betə**), by some where the normal pronunciation has **k** (e.g. **'beiʔə** for **'beikə**) and by a few where the normal pronunciation has **p** (e.g. **'piːʔl** for **'piːpl**). ʔ thus belongs to the **t, k** and **p** diaphones in certain types of English.

DIAPHONES AND PHONEMES

619. It must be observed here that the users of particular diaphonic variants have their own phonemes, which differ from those of people using other diaphonic variants. Thus when we

---

[10] In Scotland the sound heard is generally of a central type [ü], but the quality varies with individuals.

say that a certain English person's short **e** is particularly close, we mean that his principal **e** (as in *get, fetch, egg*) is a rather close sound, perhaps not much opener than cardinal No. 2; he will have also subsidiary members of the phoneme, the chief of which will be a moderately open **e** used in such a word as *help* (see §88). When, on the other hand, we say that a person's short **e** is an open one, we mean that his principal **e**, as in *get*, is an open one—it may be as open as cardinal No. 3, or even opener—and that his subsidiary **e** in *help* is opener still.

620. The use of particular diaphonic variants may involve unusual phonemic distributions. Thus if we assume that the **ʔ** of those who pronounce **'beʔə, 'beiʔə, 'piːʔl** (§618) is not a separate phoneme,[11] this sound has to be assigned to the same phoneme as either **t**, **k** or **p**; **t** would presumably be the most appropriate.[12] The words *baker* and *people* are thus said by these speakers with unusual pronunciation which would appear in a broad transcription as **'beitə, 'piːtl**.

621. It is sometimes difficult to determine whether two sounds are merely diaphonic variants or whether they belong to different phonemes. The difficulty is illustrated by the **a**-sounds of Northern French, since there is considerable fluctuation in the values of the sounds and their distribution in words. The position is clear enough in the type of French recorded by PAUL PASSY. That variety of French comprises a front **a**, a back **ɑ** and some shades of sound intermediate between these. The sounds are clearly assignable to two phonemes since the front **a** and the fully back **ɑ** both occur long and short in similar phonetic contexts, as is shown by the following examples from PASSY's pronunciation: **mwa** (*moi*), **mwɑ** (*mois*), **la** (*la, là*), **lɑ** (*las*), **wat** (*ouate*), **drwɑt** (*droite*), **tirwaːr** (*tiroir*), **krwɑːr** (*croire*). In the same type of French intermediate **a**-sounds occur in certain non-final syllables. Those which are definitely **ɑ**-like are assignable to the **ɑ**-phoneme, e.g. those in

---

[11] This has not yet been proved. To demonstrate it would necessitate an exhaustive investigation of the conditions under which **ʔ** and **t**-sounds occur in weakly stressed positions in the pronunciation of the speakers who use **ʔ**. (See further footnote 3 to §712.)

[12] Although the **ʔ** belongs diaphonically to **k** and **p** as well as to **t**, it would be inadvisable to assign it phonemically to more than one of these for the reasons given in Chapter XX.

gate (*gâter*), kase (*casser*), krwarɛ (*croirais*), while the others, including "middle" a's such as those in gars5 (*garçon*), artikl (*article*) are assignable to the a-phoneme.[13]

622. I believe PASSY's speech to have, been a very usual type of Northern French, and, owing to its consistency and the definiteness of its phonemes, it is a form of French particularly well suited for practical teaching of the language. There are, however, other varieties of Northern French differing considerably from his in the matter of the a-sounds. I have known one Parisian of Parisian parentage who had no front a at all, and who always used a back ɑ. On the other hand it appears that there are some who have no back ɑ, and who use a front or middle a exclusively. Others again use more than one a-sound, but distribute the sounds in words in a manner different from that described by PASSY. For instance, it is not uncommon to hear Northern French people using back ɑ in every terminal position (e.g. in *moi* as well as in *mois*) and a front a in various other positions (in *casser*, for example). (See also §131.)

623. The existence of these variations of pronunciation has as a result that a and ɑ and intermediate sounds have to be grouped together into a single diaphone in French, but that at the same time the sounds are in the speech of many separable into two phonemes.

BEARING OF THE THEORY OF DIAPHONES ON THE THEORY OF PHONEMES

624. It has been necessary to deal at some length with the theory of diaphones in order to make clear the distinction between diaphones and the allophones (members) of phonemes, and to show why it is necessary to take as a basis of the definition of the phoneme the pronunciation of a single individual speaking in one particular and consistent style (§28).

624*a*. Some of those interested in the nature of the phoneme have attempted to find a place for diaphones (which they generally

---

[13] In a great number of instances we find, in this type of French, non-final syllables containing a front a indistinguishable from the a of final syllables. Such are the first syllables of ʃase (*chasser*), frape (*frapper*), ale (*aller*). It would seem that the commonest case of "middle a" belonging to the front a-phoneme is where r follows.

call "free variants") within the definition of the phoneme. No such attempt was made by the initiators of the phoneme theory (see my "*History and Meaning of the Term 'Phoneme'* "), nor indeed in my opinion can any such attempt possibly succeed. That this is so is evident from several of the considerations put forward above, and in particular from the fact that the circumstances under which two phones fall into one diaphone (§§598 ff.) have nothing in common with the circumstances under which two phones may be members (allophones) of a single phoneme as originally conceived.

624b. The impossibility of incorporating the conception of the diaphone into the definition of the phoneme is likewise shown by the fairly common occurrence of a phone belonging to two diaphones (§§610–618), and the comparative rarity of possibilities of assigning a sound to one of two or more phonemes. (See, for Japanese, §323 ff., for Pekingese, §195, 196; also Y. R. CHAO's *The Non-uniqueness of Phonetic Solutions of Phonetic Systems*.)

625. It is conceivable that some sort of "mentalistic" definition of a phoneme could be devised which would include diaphonic variants (see Chap. XXIX). It might, for instance, be maintained that a phoneme is an "ideal sound"[14] which is "realized" in one way by one person under a given set of conditions, and in another way by the same person under other conditions and yet in other ways by other persons. I am not at present prepared to formulate any definition of this nature. Psychologists may in due course be able to determine whether any such definition is possible. I would only say here that there appear to be difficulties in the way. It would be necessary to show, for instance, that different uttered sounds *are* realizations of the same ideal sound and not realizations of different ideal sounds. And even if it proves possible to do this for one speaker, it may prove difficult or impossible to show that an ideal sound of one speaker is identical with that of another.

626. I would conclude this chapter by remarking that the idea of the diaphone is of limited application only, and cannot like the idea of the phoneme be elaborated into a complete and universal theory applicable to all consistent types of speech. This is due mainly to the difficulty of deciding the extent to which deviations from a type are to be admitted as belonging to "the

---

[14] Presumably an abstraction of the third or fourth degree. (See my paper on *Concrete and Abstract Sounds* in the *Proceedings of the Third International Congress of Phonetic Sciences* (Ghent, 1938), pp. 4–6.)

same language" as that type, and at what points the limits must be set beyond which deviating sounds are to be regarded as belonging to separate languages or dialects and therefore not to be comprised in the diaphones of the language under consideration.[15]

CHAPTER XXVIII

ERRATIC PRONUNCIATION

627. It is presumably a fact that a person never pronounces a given word twice in precisely the same way, even in the same context.[1] He may be said to aim at the same pronunciation, and generally produces what may roughly be called "the same" sounds, but every utterance doubtless differs from every other in details which are usually too minute to detect either by ear or by apparatus. With some speakers, however, involuntary variations of sound are clearly perceptible to outside observers. Such variations are generally found in one of three cases: (1) when the language is one containing a relatively small number of phonemes and where consequently absolute precision in the pronunciation of certain sounds is not essential, (2) when a person speaks with a mixture of dialect, (3) when a person has made intentional changes in his pronunciation. In all these cases speakers are inconsistent in their pronunciation, and use variants apparently at random.

VARIPHONES

628. To denote a group of sounds coming under (1) I have suggested the term *variphone*.[2] Variphones are thus "unstable" sounds—sounds which are liable to "variation" independently of their phonetic context.

629. One of the most noteworthy cases of a variphone is "the Japanese **r**." In the pronunciation of many if not most Japanese this "sound" is very variable; they sometimes use a sound resembling

---

[15] It will be observed that in discussing diaphones the term "a language" is used in its common and rather vague sense, and not in the restricted sense attributed to it in the definition of the phoneme (§28).

[1] If there is such a thing as "the same context."

[2] Some critics have objected to this hybrid term, but as far as I know no one has yet suggested any other single word which meets the case. H. E. PALMER employed the term "free phoneme" (*Principles of Romanization*, p. 55); this, however, has the disadvantage of requiring the use of "contactual phoneme" or "bound phoneme" to denote what is here termed simply a "phoneme."

an English fricative r (ɹ), sometimes a lingual flap (ɾ), sometimes a
kind of retroflex d (ɖ), sometimes a kind of l, and sometimes sounds
intermediate between these. One and the same speaker will use
all these forms indiscriminately; he will pronounce, say *kore* (this)
as koɹe, koɾe, koɖe, kole, or with intermediate pronunciation
without being aware that his pronunciation varies. ɹ, ɾ, ɖ, l,
etc., may be called "members" of the variphone. In the absence
of special training Japanese speakers can neither hear the difference
between these members nor make any one of them at will. (One
result of this is the well-known difficulty they have in hearing or
making the difference between r and l when they speak European
languages.)

630. Variphones consisting of r-like and l-like sounds would
also appear to occur in some languages of Africa, for instance, in
Bambara and Malinke.[3] (The case must be distinguished from the
use of r-like and l-like sounds as members of the same phoneme.
See §§81–83.)

631. The following are some other examples of variphones.
ŋg and ŋ form a variphone in the speech of Midland districts of
England (Birmingham, Chester, etc.). Many English people from
these districts use the two indiscriminately, both in words such as
finger, *longest* (elsewhere ˈfiŋgə, ˈloŋgist) and in words like *singer*,
longing (elsewhere ˈsiŋə, ˈloŋiŋ). Without training they cannot
hear the difference between ŋg and ŋ, nor can they make the
difference at will.

632. In Saxon German, and apparently in some types of South
German, p, b̦ and voiced b constitute a variphone. Saxon Germans
commonly use these sounds indiscriminately; they will pronounce
Blatt indiscriminately as plat, b̦lat or blat and they will pronounce
platt likewise; so also with all the other words written with *p* or *b*.
t/ḏ/d, and s/ʐ/z, etc., likewise constitute variphones in these types
of German.[4]

633. In initial position d and ð appear to form a variphone
in Spanish, the two sounds being used indiscriminately by many
Spaniards in this situation. Thus when the word *doce* is initial

---

[3] Referring to these languages, WESTERMANN and WARD say: "l and r
are interchangeable in a great many words, dialectally and even with
individuals." (*Practical Phonetics for Students of African Languages*, p. 184.)

[4] I have heard a South German university professor pronounce *schon*
sometimes ʃoːn and sometimes ʒoːn, the presence or absence of voice being
apparently immaterial.

it is pronounced both ˈdoθe and ˈðoθe; both pronunciations may be heard from the same speaker. Similarly with b and β, g and ɣ.

634. Variphones consisting of mb and b, nd and d, etc., are found in varieties of Greek and in Kikuyu. Many, if not most, Greeks will pronounce σαράντα (forty) indiscriminately as saˈranda or saˈrada in ordinary conversation,[5] and they will pronounce δὲν ξέρω (I don't know) sometimes as ðeŋˈgzero and sometimes as ðeˈgzero. It appears that without special training these Greeks can neither hear nor make the difference between nd and d, ŋg and g, etc. When learning English without phonetic training they can neither hear nor make any difference between *band* and *bad*, but pronounce both words as band and bad indiscriminately.

635. In Kikuyu, as has already been observed, mb, nd, etc., appear to be felt by the natives to be single sounds, and in initial position simple b, d, etc., are sometimes unconsciously substituted for them.[6] (Plosive b, d, etc., do not occur as separate phonemes in the ordinary form of the language; see §79.) Thus mborī (goat), ndere (mortar) are sometimes pronounced [borī], [dere] with plosive b and d.[7]

636. Variphones have a place in the phoneme theory. For the purpose of that theory the members of a variphone count as if they were a single sound, which may itself constitute a phoneme or which may be a member of a phoneme. The Japanese r, for instance, is a variphone the members of which do not appear to be in any way conditioned by phonetic context; it is therefore a variphone which itself constitutes a phoneme.[8] On the other

---

[5] Some Greeks when trying to speak very precisely will use a spelling pronunciation saˈranta, but this would appear to be unnatural to most Greeks and in any case belongs to a different style of speech which we are not concerned with here.

[6] ARMSTRONG, *Phonetic and Tonal Structure of Kikuyu*, §90.

[7] The transcriptions [borī], [dere] here are narrow. In broad transcription of Kikuyu b, d (without preceding m, n) stand for β, ð.

[8] At least this is what seems to be the case in normal Japanese. Some observers, however, have maintained that the members *are* to some extent conditioned by phonetic context, e.g. that a more l-like sound is used before o. They maintain in fact that there is a Japanese r-phoneme having two or more of the above-mentioned sounds as members. This may be true of some types of Japanese, but there certainly appear to exist other types, where no such system is found, i.e. where the sounds mentioned in §629 constitute a true variphone and are not connected by any phonemic relation.

hand, in the pronunciation of those Spanish speakers who use d and ð indifferently in initial position, this variphone d/ð is a member of their d-phoneme; the members of this phoneme are then d (used after n), ð (used in other medial positions and finally), and the variphone d/ð (used initially).

637. It is worthy of note that sometimes if we take account of variphonic forms, we find ourselves obliged to add to the number of phonemes in a language. Thus Kikuyu, as normally recorded, may be said to contain two labial consonant-phonemes; they may be written m and b, but it has to be remembered that the principal member of the latter phoneme is β. There exists also mb, which, though a "single sound" in the conception of the native, may, according to one view (§79), be regarded as a composite of the m and b phonemes; ordinary plosive b may be taken as being the member of the b-phoneme used when m precedes. But, as has already been mentioned (§635), many Kikuyu speakers use a variphone mb/b in initial positions. An analysis of their speech must necessarily admit three labial consonant-phonemes, the variphone mb/b having to be regarded as a separate phoneme. Fortunately this need not complicate the transcription, since the variphone may without ambiguity be written mb. The same transcription is arrived at if we simply ignore the variant b for initial mb, as being unessential to the pronunciation of the language. If, however, we were to ignore the other variphonic form mb, the analysis would give three phonemes requiring three separate letters in transcription (m, β and b).

Mixture of Dialect

638. One frequently meets with people whose speech has been influenced by two or more environments, and who consequently speak with mixed dialect. Their speech often shows irregularities and inconsistencies. There are, for instance, people of Scottish origin who have lived for a long time in England and who will pronounce the vowel in such a word as *home* sometimes in the Scottish way and sometimes in an English way or an approximation to an English way; they will sometimes make a difference between the vowels in *food* and *good* and sometimes not; they will sometimes

sound an r in such a word as *burn* and sometimes not, without any apparent system.[9]

639.   The following are a few other examples.   There are English people who pronounce words like *slightly, mutton* sometimes with a glottal stop ('slaiʔli, 'mʌʔn) and sometimes with t ('slaitli, 'mʌtn). I have known one speaker of Irish origin who sometimes pronounced the English θ in the normal English way and sometimes substituted a dental t̪ for it, as is done in Irish dialects of English.   French people may be met with in Paris who speak with traces of Southern accent, e.g. who will sometimes pronounce *donner* with an o-like vowel in place of ordinary Parisian ɔ.   Swiss speakers of French who have lived for a long time in France often lose some of the characteristic features of Swiss French pronunciation but occasionally revert to them without knowing it, and so on.

640.   It would seem that erratic pronunciation due to mixture of dialect is very prevalent in the United States.   For example, there are Americans who sometimes make a distinction between *Mary* and *merry* and sometimes not, who are inconsistent in their use of ɑ, ɒ and ɔ, of æ, a and ɑ, and so on.[10]

---

[9] There is some evidence to show that excitable people who have a mixed pronunciation tend under stress of emotion to revert to the pronunciation they acquired in the first instance.   If this could be proved, it would show a sort of system in their manner of speaking; the variations might be found to accord in some way with the "context of situation."   The speaker would in fact sometimes talk in one "dialect" and sometimes in another.

[10] Examples are to be found in transcriptions of records that have been given in various issues of *American Speech*.   For instance, a speaker whose pronunciation was recorded in the issue of February, 1941, p. 40, is seen to have erratic pronunciation of "stressed *er*"; he uses three sounds (there written with the symbols ɜ, ɝ and ʌː) indiscriminately, where a consistent speaker would use only one.   Another speaker whose pronunciation was transcribed on p. 41 of the same issue uses two vowels (there written ɜ and œ) indiscriminately in similar cases.   The "stressed *er*" of another speaker, a specimen of whose pronunciation was given on p. 179 of the issue of October, 1942, is sometimes a variety of ɚ (there written ɝ) and sometimes a diphthong of the type əʊ (there written ɜɪ).   In the issue of October, 1939, a speaker was represented as pronouncing the word *hole* in four different ways: hoʊl, hoʊɔl, hoʊl and hoʊːəl.

INTENTIONAL CHANGES OF PRONUNCIATION

641. Erratic pronunciations are not unfrequently met with which originate in voluntary attempts to alter one's pronunciation. After a time such voluntary changes may become definitely fixed so that the new pronunciation comes to be used involuntarily. More often, however, the speaker's pronunciation becomes in the end erratic; he sometimes uses the new pronunciation and sometimes the old without being aware of the variation in his speech.

642. Intentional changes of pronunciation are made for a variety of reasons. The commonest is presumably where a person comes into an environment where some feature of his original pronunciation might give rise to misunderstanding or is very unusual. Thus, as the sequence **'pasəbl** means *passable* in Southern England and *possible* in America, an Englishman permanently resident in America might well make intentional adjustments in his manner of saying these words. If he did so, it is likely that at times he would unintentionally revert to his original English pronunciation.

643. People not unfrequently change or attempt to change their pronunciation purposely for other reasons. Sometimes they believe (because they have been so taught) that some other pronunciation is "better" than what they acquired naturally in childhood; sometimes they try to make their speech correspond more nearly to current spelling; sometimes they imitate the speech of others whom for some reason they consider worthy of imitation; sometimes they adopt or try to adopt the recommendations of some dictionary; sometimes they follow or try to follow some tradition. I have even known a man alter his pronunciation purposely so as to make his language more consistent for a pedagogical reason. In all such cases erratic pronunciation is liable to result; the use of the new pronunciation does not always become absolutely habitual, but the speaker reverts from time to time to his "natural" pronunciation.

644. An example not unfrequently met with in France is the case of people whose pronunciation of such words as *mêler*, *aimable* varies, people who pronounce the first syllable sometimes with an open ε and sometimes with a "middle e." Those who have this erratic pronunciation are doubtless people whose "natural" pronunciation has middle or close e but who have either been taught that ε is more "correct" or are influenced by orthography.

645. Tradition is no doubt responsible for the erratic pronunciation of r which may be observed very frequently on the French stage. Many actors when speaking in declamatory style employ lingual r and uvular ʀ indiscriminately. Presumably in their "natural" pronunciation they use uvular ʀ, but there is a tradition that lingual r is "correct" in declamatory style, and they aim at using it but often fail to do so.[11]

646. It seems probable that the use of a sound of the quality of the British English short o (ɒ) in American English is "unnatural," and is consciously acquired by those who use it; hence its lack of stability.[12] The same no doubt applies to the variety of "middle a" (between the American a (æ) and ɑ) which is said to be used by some Americans in such words as ask, path.

647. It has been necessary here to make these references to mixed dialect and intentional changes on account of their fairly frequent occurrence. It is evident, however, that erratic pronunciations other than those found in variphones have no place in the phoneme theory. The speech of those whose pronunciation is unstable cannot be reduced to phonemes at all, unless the instability is due to the existence of a variphone.

648. It may be added that there may possibly exist variphones which have originated from intentional or unintentional changes of pronunciation. Possibly, for instance, t and ? may be considered to form a variphone in the speech of some of those who use them indiscriminately in such words as slightly, fortnight as mentioned in §639, although this erratic pronunciation almost certainly arises either from mixture of dialect or from spelling-pronunciation.

---

[11] This may be observed for instance in SARAH BERNHARDT's gramophone record of a passage from Rostand's La Samaritaine (His Master's Voice record No. G.C.3H171, II), an analysis of which was given in my Intonation Curves, pp. 31–37.

[12] ɒ "cannot be considered a stable and well recognized phoneme in General American" (KENYON, American Pronunciation, tenth edition, p. 185).

CHAPTER XXIX

MENTALISTIC AND FUNCTIONAL CONCEPTIONS OF THE PHONEME

649. The conception of the phoneme put forward in this book may be described as a "physical" one, since the phoneme has been treated as "a family of sounds."[1] It is only right, however, to mention that other conceptions of the phoneme exist and, in particular, a conception which may be termed "mentalistic," and another which may be termed "functional" or "structural." Not being a psychologist, I am not in a position to expound a mentalistic view in a manner that would satisfy experts in psychology. All I can do is to give a rough idea of what appears to me to be meant by those who take a mentalistic view of the phoneme, in the hope that readers who have had psychological training may investigate its merits.

650. The idea of those who hold a mentalistic view would appear to be in essence that a phoneme is a single "abstract sound"[2] or "sound image," which the speaker is capable of bringing to mind at will, and which he (subconsciously) endeavours to manifest concretely when he speaks.[3] In some phonetic contexts he succeeds in giving accurate concrete expression to the "sound image," but in other phonetic contexts he fails to do so and,

---

[1] "Abstract" sounds of the first degree. See my paper on *Concrete and Abstract Sounds* in the *Proceedings of the Third International Congress of Phonetic Sciences* (Ghent, 1938).

[2] Presumably of the second degree.

[3] A critical examination of this statement may show that, like many other statements concerning fundamental concepts, it implies a vicious circle. I am not sure that it is possible to give any "definition" of a phoneme, other than a "physical" one, which does not contain an implicit reference to the thing to be defined. This does not mean that we should not do our best to arrive at definitions of fundamental concepts. (See my article *Some Thoughts on the Phoneme* in the *Transactions of the Philological Society*, 1944.)

utters a sound resembling though not identical with the sound aimed at.[4]

651. To give an example, it may be supposed that a particular speaker of English has a conception of an "abstract" or "ideal" t-sound. He brings this sound accurately into concrete manufestation when he says such a word as ten, but he utters various approximations to this in other phonetic contexts, e.g. in trap, eitθ, ˈletə, ˈsetl, ˈbʌtn. Similarly he may have a conception of an "ideal" short a, which appears accurately when he says kat, tap, and many other words; when he says such a word as ˈalfəbit (*alphabet*) he may be considered to aim at producing the same sound, but the vowel which actually emerges is somewhat different.[5]

652. Professor BAUDOUIN DE COURTENAY,[6] the first to formulate the phoneme theory,[7] took a "psychological" view of the phoneme. He defined phonemes as "mental images,"[8] and accordingly distinguished two kinds of phonetics which he called "physiophonetics" and "psychophonetics" respectively. He applied the term "physiophonetics" to the study of sounds actually uttered, and used the term "psychophonetics" to denote the study of the "mental images" which uttered sounds are intended to represent. He likewise distinguished two kinds of phonetic writing which he

---

[4] According to this theory the sound-image would appear to be in perpetual existence in some non-material way. For it is presumably not possible to bring to mind at will a non-existent thing.

[5] The differences between the varieties of short a are well heard if one whispers words containing this phoneme. In whispered speech the resonance pitches of the vowels become audible, and it is found for instance that the front resonance pitch of the a in ˈalfəbit is lower than that of the commoner short a of tap, etc.

[6] 1845–1929.

[7] For details as to the early work on the phoneme readers are referred to my paper *The History and Meaning of the Term "Phoneme"* (published in 1957 by the I.P.A., and obtainable from the Secretary of the Association, Dept. of Phonetics, University College, London). Here we need only mention that BAUDOUIN DE COURTENAY's ideas began to take shape about 1870. It seems that the first published formulation of the theory was in an essay by one of his pupils named KRUSZEWSKI which appeared at Kazan in 1879. BAUDOUIN DE COURTENAY, in his *Próba teorji alternacyj fonetycznych* (Essay on a theory of phonetic alternations, Cracow, 1893), ascribed the invention of the word "phoneme" to KRUSZEWSKI.

[8] See Z. M. AREND, *Baudouin de Courtenay and the Phoneme Idea*, in *Le Maître Phonétique*, January, 1934.

termed "physiophonic" transcription and "psychophonic" transcription, the first being a symbolization in writing of sounds actually uttered, and the second being a symbolization of the phonemes, i.e. his "mental images" or sounds which the speaker supposedly aims at uttering. These terms correspond in the main to the "narrow" and "broad" of the English phoneticians—terms originally invented by HENRY SWEET[9] and used by him in his *Handbook of Phonetics* (Oxford, 1877).[10]

653. Among others who have held a mentalistic view of the phoneme was the eminent linguistician E. SAPIR. His opinions were ably set out by him in an article *Sound Patterns in Language* which appeared in *Language*, Vol. I, 1925, pp. 37–51, and in an article *La Réalité Psychologique des Phonèmes* in the *Journal de Psychologie*, January–April, 1933. These articles should be closely studied by all who interest themselves in the theory of the phoneme. In *Sound Patterns in Language* he used the term "ideal sounds" apparently to mean phonemes (regarded mentalistically), and expressed the view that " 'ideal sounds,' which are constructed from one's intuitive feeling of the significant relations between the objective sounds, are more 'real' to a naive speaker than the objective sounds themselves." In the same article he said that "a complex psychology of association and pattern is implicit in the utterance of the simplest consonant or vowel." And again, "A 'place' is intuitively found for a sound (which is here thought of as a true 'point in the pattern,'[11] not a mere conditional variant[12]) in such a system because of a general feeling of its phonetic relationships to all other sounds" (p. 47). And again at the end of the article: "The whole aim and spirit of this paper has been to show that phonetic phenomena are not physical phenomena *per se*, however necessary in the preliminary stages of inductive linguistic research it may be to get at the phonetic facts by way of their physical embodiment. The present discussion is really a special

---

[9] 1845–1912.

[10] SWEET'S investigations in the field of phonetics likewise began about 1870. He did not treat the subject on psychological lines, and his researches were carried on independently of those of BAUDOUIN DE COURTENAY. It is therefore interesting to find that these two great pioneers arrived at similar practical conclusions concerning phonetic transcription.

[11] Meaning presumably a principal member of a phoneme.

[12] Meaning presumably a subsidiary member of a phoneme.

illustration of the necessity of getting behind the sense data of any type of expression in order to grasp the intuitively felt and communicated forms which alone give significance to such expression."

654. There are authorities who reject the mentalistic conception of the phoneme, but who at the same time maintain that the phoneme cannot be described in terms of the sounds by which it is manifested. They define the phoneme by reference to its function in the structure of language.

655. Foremost among these was TRUBETZKOY,[13] for whose opinions I have great respect. TRUBETZKOY appears to have regarded phonemes as the minimum segmental elements of language which are capable, by substitution, of distinguishing one word from another. He defined them as "phonological entities which from the standpoint of the language under consideration cannot be subdivided into smaller consecutive entities,"[14] and expressed the view that they are "differentiating signs,"[15] and can only be defined by reference to their function in the structure of each language.[16]

656. TRUBETZKOY also said that a phoneme is "the sum of the phonologically relevant features of a 'Lautgebilde'."[17] The meaning he attached to the term "Lautgebilde" is not clear to me. He evidently did not mean by it "sound-image" in the mentalistic sense, for he expressly stated that "the phoneme is a linguistic and not a psychological idea."[18] TRUBETZKOY was far too able a thinker to use his technical terms loosely, and I believe he was perfectly clear in his own mind as to what he meant when he used such terms as "phoneme" and "Lautgebilde." But, owing to the deficiencies of language as a medium of expression,[19] I, and perhaps

---

[13] 1890–1938.

[14] N. S. TRUBETZKOY, *Grundzüge der Phonologie*, p. 34 (now available in a French translation by J. CANTINEAU, bottom of p. 37).

[15] *Ibid.*, p. 41 (CANTINEAU, p. 46).

[16] *Ibid.*, p. 39 (CANTINEAU, p. 44).

[17] *Ibid.*, p. 35 (CANTINEAU, p. 39).

[18] *Ibid.*, p. 37. At times TRUBETZKOY employed the terms "Lautabsicht" (sound-intention) and "Lautvorstellung" (sound-image), but eventually rejected them as inadequate (*Grundzüge der Phonologie*, p. 37, CANTINEAU, p. 42).

[19] "Speech, indeed, is nothing more than a series of rough hints which the hearer must interpret in order to arrive at the meaning which the speaker wishes to convey" (L. R. PALMER, *Introduction to Modern Linguistics*, p. 82).

others, have not as yet fully understood his meaning. It is satis-factory, however, to find that TRUBETZKOY'S view leads to the same practical conclusions as other formulations of the theory, namely, that it provides the essential materials for the analysis of language structure and a sound basis for phonetic writing.

657.   BLOOMFIELD appears to have envisaged the phoneme theory up to a point in much the same way as TRUBETZKOY. He defined phonemes as "minimum units of distinctive sound-feature,"[20] and as "the smallest units which make a difference in meaning."[21] He has said too that "the phonemes of a language are not sounds, but merely features of sound which the speakers have been trained to produce and recognize in the current of actual speech-sound."[22] W. F. TWADDELL, on the other hand, has expressed the view that phonemes have no real existence either "physically" or "mentally," but are merely "abstractional fictitious units."[23] This appears to be also the view of L. HJELMSLEV and the Danish school. According to them it would seem to be immaterial whether languages are pronounced accurately or not, or indeed, whether any pronunciation is given to the phonemes at all. It is not necessary here to enter upon any discussion of the validity of such opinions, since such discussion would inevitably resolve itself into a discussion of the reality or unreality of things in general and of "ideas" in particular. It is sufficient for the present purpose to remark that these views though neither physical nor mentalistic would seem to lead to the same practical conclusions as the other views referred to.

658.   It may be added that I find all the attempted definitions of the phoneme to be unsatisfactory on account of the apparent impossibility of knowing precisely what is meant by "a language."

---

[20] L. BLOOMFIELD, *Language*, p. 79.

[21] *Ibid.*, p. 136.

[22] On the other hand BLOOMFIELD, very unfortunately in my opinion, introduced the term "secondary phoneme" to denote any sound-attribute (suprasegmental feature) which serves to make a minimal distinction between one word and another. His numerous followers in America have ceased to use his qualifying word "secondary," and the result has been that the term "phoneme" has acquired in America a meaning quite different from that intended by the European pioneers. See my paper *The History and Meaning of the Term "Phoneme,"* §§41, 42.

[23] W. F. TWADDELL, *On defining the Phoneme* (Language Monographs, published by the Linguistic Society of America, No. XVI, 1935).

The term "a language" is a vague one with psychological or super-physical connotations. It may presumably be said to mean the total material upon which a person can draw when he speaks. But where is that material? It surely "exists" only in some mentalistic or non-material sense. In fact it looks as if it were one of the numerous primary notions which cannot be defined, but upon which we nevertheless erect sciences.

659. It should be pointed out too that phonemes can hardly be said to "exist" if sounds can be "assigned" to them in the manner suggested in various places in this book. If a phoneme has any sort of superphysical "existence," it presumably follows that all concrete manifestations of it are predetermined, so that there can never be any doubt as to the phoneme to which any particular sound in a given setting belongs. A possible alternative view is that most phonemes have a superphysical "existence," but that there are exceptional cases of phonemes of an indefinite or transitional nature. The difficulties of reconciling any synchronic theory of phonemes with many of the diachronic phenomena observable in the history of languages lend some support to this possibility. (See Chap. XXXII.)

660. However that may be, I submit that it is incumbent on us to keep an open mind on all these matters, and to give special attention to the possibility that the phoneme may after all prove to have an "existence" of some kind, which may become evident in a remote future, if, as is thought by some, evolution brings with it a further development of men's faculties, giving them a clearer perception than most of us at present possess of a fourth dimension of space or a second dimension of time.[24]

CHAPTER XXX

THE PRACTICAL USE OF THE THEORY OF PHONEMES

661. I take it as axiomatic that every man is endowed with certain abilities which he can use for the general good. People with ability for applied phonetics have in a particularly high degree the capacity for doing "useful" work—by which term I mean

---

[24] See *Concrete and Abstract Sounds*, especially p. 6.

218 THE PHONEME: ITS NATURE AND USE

work "conducive to the ultimate well-being of humanity." In contrast with workers in some other scientific fields, they can keep in view throughout their investigations a definite humanistic object towards which they can direct their attention, namely, the improvement of the means of oral and written communication between man and man. The findings of phonetic science give people skill in communicating effectively with each other.[1]

662. It is because phonemes are the basic elements of communication by language that an investigation of their nature and their potentialities is "useful" in the above sense.

663. Phonemes are the basic elements in that they cannot help constituting indivisible semantic units of which languages are composed. They are the elements which, when put into sequences (and in some languages supplemented by other significant features), make larger semantic entities, namely, morphemes,[2] words and sentences. The main uses of the theory of these elements are outlined in the following paragraphs.

664. Firstly, it must be observed that the phoneme, as described in this book, is a conception of a phonetic nature, and the formulation of the phonemic structure of a language is one of the aids to acquiring a good pronunciation by the learner of that language. By means of phonetics he learns to utter foreign sounds. By memorizing, or with the aid of phonetic transcription (see §§669 ff.), he learns how "to use the right sound in the right place"—which he can do, if desired, before concerning himself with meanings. From formulations of phonemic structure he learns how "sounds are modified according to context" in the language he is learning, and how the principles of such "modification" differ from those followed in his native language.

665. Secondly, it is the phonemic idea that forms the basis for the non-phonetic branches of linguistic science, i.e. semantics, morphology, grammar, etc. These branches are concerned with the order in which phonemes are placed in constructing the larger semantic

---

[1] HENRY SWEET pointed out years ago that phonetics is an art as well as a science (*Practical Study of Languages*, p. 4).

[2] The units of form, such as stems, prefixes, suffixes. See TRUBETZKOY, *Grundzüge der Phonologie*, p. 225 (CANTINEAU's translation, p. 270).

entities, with the additions, subtractions and substitutions of phonemes made for different purposes, and with the incidence of the other semantic elements (if any). Phonemes in fact lie at the root of everything that is required for enabling language learners to use the right words, to put the words into their various forms, and to use the forms appropriately. In fact, all practical linguistic attainments may be said to depend ultimately on the theory of phonemes.

666. Thirdly, the phoneme theory has a particularly important use in connexion with the construction of systems of writing. The analysis of a language into its constituent phonemes furnishes us with the means of writing it in the simplest manner that is consistent with avoiding ambiguity. That the phoneme theory can render this service has already been demonstrated in preceding chapters, but it will be well to give in a separate chapter (Chap. XXXI) a summary account of the principles involved together with a few examples in illustration.

CHAPTER XXXI

FURTHER REMARKS ON PHONETIC WRITING

667. The assignment of one letter[1] to each phoneme of a language, together with suitable marking of any other significant sound-attributes, is both necessary and sufficient for representing every "word" of the language unambiguously in writing. The use of as many letters as there are phonemes is *necessary* because the use of fewer letters would cause words of different pronunciation to be written alike. It is *sufficient*, since to employ a greater number of letters would mean either writing a sound in more than one way or exhibiting distinctions of pronunciation which the native speaker is as a rule unaware of, and which are of no importance from his point of view. In either case the superfluous letters would not serve to distinguish words from each other or help to specify what words were meant.[2]

---

[1] "Letter" is to be taken in these paragraphs to include digraphs when they are appropriate.

[2] Except when it may be advisable to introduce unpronounced letters into an orthography with a view to making written distinctions between words of identical pronunciation (homophones). (See §§704, 705.)

668. Two kinds of simple writing can be established with the aid of the phoneme theory, namely, *phonetic transcription* and *orthography*.

PHONETIC TRANSCRIPTION

669. *Phonetic transcription* is a style of writing in which the principle of representing each phoneme by a particular letter (or sometimes more than one letter if the transcript is "narrow") is strictly adhered to not only for isolated words but also for connected sentences. Its chief objects are (1) to put on record the phonemic make-up of languages, and (2) to facilitate the acquisition of a good pronunciation of foreign languages, by showing the learner which of the sounds of the language are the appropriate ones to use in any given word or sentence. The simplest form of transcription adequate for this purpose is that which records the language by means of one letter for each phoneme, i.e. what is called an "allophonic" or "linguistically broad transcription." When the student of the language has learnt to utter correctly the various members of each phoneme and knows the conventions governing the use of the members, the broad transcription is an infallible guide for indicating to him which sounds are to be used in any particular case. The transcription must be supplemented by marking any other significant attributes (e.g. lengths, stresses or voice-pitches) that may occur in the language. Such a form of transcription shows in writing the structure of the language to be learnt.

670. It is sometimes convenient in the practical teaching of languages to use transcriptions which are to some extent "narrowed," by the addition of letters or marks representing special members of phonemes. They are called "allophonic" or "linguistically narrow" transcriptions. The idea of using such forms of transcription is to help the student of a foreign language to learn the rules governing the use of particular members of phonemes, rules which he must learn sooner or later if he wishes to pronounce well. In my experience such aid is generally unnecessary, and it has the disadvantage of making the transcription needlessly complex. When the rules governing the use of particular members of phonemes are simple, as is usually the case, they should be formulated by the teacher and learnt by the pupil. Thus it is in my experience just as easy for the learner of English to put into practice the instruction "You must give I the dark sound whenever it is final or followed by a consonant" as to learn that "in transcribing English the letter I is never written finally and before consonants; its place is taken by ł." Likewise it is just as easy for the English student of French to learn when the letter y stands for the consonantal value in broad transcription as to learn when he should write y̆ (or the special letter ɥ) in narrow transcription.

671. When, however, the rules governing the use of special members of phonemes are involved and difficult to remember, the use of narrowed transcriptions can be justified as a help to learning these rules, though I do not think the use of such transcripts is indispensable. If, for instance, I were called upon to teach the pronunciation of a type of German in which x and ç belonged to a single phoneme,[3] I should feel disposed to narrow the transcription by using the two symbols [x] and [ç]. I should do this on the ground that [ç] is very unlike [x] in sound and that the principles governing the use of the two sounds are rather involved.[4] I believe, however, that good results could also be obtained by using the letter x only, provided that hyphens are inserted where necessary to show whether a sound begins or ends a syllable.

672. For a similar reason there is something to be said in favour of representing the short weakly stressed German e-sounds, by ə in phonetic texts intended for learners of that language, and of using y̆ or ɥ to denote the consonantal y in teaching French.

673. In a more complicated case, such as the use of the numerous variants of a in Arabic, the representation of the main variants by special symbols is certainly justifiable. GAIRDNER indicated three and sometimes four members of the a-phoneme in his books,[5] this being one way of helping students of spoken Arabic with the difficult task of learning when to use the variants. But the end is achieved at the cost of legibility of the texts. If this method is used, I consider it desirable to pass on to broadly transcribed, and therefore more easily legible, texts as soon as the learner has

---

[3] I.e. a type in which *Wacholder* and similar words are pronounced with h following the x as mentioned on p. 69, footnote 37.

[4] See §230.

[5] W. H. T. GAIRDNER, *The Phonetics of Arabic* and *Egyptian Colloquial Arabic.* Also ELDER, *Egyptian Arabic Phonetic Reader.*

a fairly clear idea of the situations in which the variant **a**'s are used.[6]

674.   Similarly a phonetic notation distinguishing perhaps three members of the **e**-phoneme of Pekingese might be found useful to some learners of that language in early stages, on account of the difficulty of remembering the circumstances under which each is used. (The sound is conditioned, not only by tone, as mentioned in §112, but also by the sounds preceding and following. It is, for instance, **e**-like when preceded by **i**, but **ʌ**-like when preceded by various consonants, such as **f, k**. And the **ʌ**-like quality varies according as the sound is final or followed by **ŋ** or **n** (§503).) And if CATFORD's description of the phonemic structure of the Kabardian language of the Caucasus is correct,[7] it would be most difficult to learn the principles governing the use of the vowel variants without some help in the shape of a narrow transcription of the vowels in connected texts.

675.   It is probable that a certain narrowing of transcription would be useful in teaching English learners to make proper use of vowel **harmony** in Somali. (See ARMSTRONG, *Phonetic Structure of Somali*, p. 149.)

676.   When narrow transcriptions are used for helping learners to remember the conditions under which various members of phonemes are employed, it is desirable from time to time to test their understanding of the principles by prescribing as an exercise the rewriting in broad transcription of a passage written narrowly. Later the learners may with benefit reverse the process and practise converting broad transcriptions into narrower ones.

677.   It should be noted that narrowings of transcriptions for learners of any particular language may differ according to the nationality of the learner.

678.   It is sometimes helpful to introduce narrowings into phonetic transcriptions intended for use in comparative work, and particularly in the comparison of different forms of a language. For instance, when teaching the history of English pronunciation,

---

[6] It is now thought by some that there are two **a** phonemes in Cairene Arabic. This possibility furnishes an additional reason for narrowing the transcription.

[7] J. C. CATFORD, *Specimen of Kabardian with Notes on the Pronunciation*, in *Le Maître Phonétique*, July–December, 1942.

I find it convenient to narrow the transcription of present-day English by making use of the letters ε and ɔ. The reason is that older forms of English (Chaucerian, for example) are believed to have contained long ε: and ɔ: as well as long e: and o:. Consequently in transcribing such older forms the short vowels corresponding to ε: and ɔ: must necessarily be written with the letters ε and ɔ. And as these short sounds were no doubt much the same as those used to-day in the same words, it is convenient to use these letters in modern English texts transcribed for purposes of comparison. (But in a description of modern Southern English—and particularly in transcriptions designed for teaching Southern English to foreign learners—the more familiar letters e and o can well be used in place of ε and ɔ.)

679. For a similar reason I feel that GAIRDNER did well to use two signs for the glottal stop (ʔ and ʡ) in his transcriptions of the colloquial Arabic of Cairo, since it seems hardly possible for any learner of colloquial Arabic to ignore completely the classical (in which the ʡ is pronounced as q).

680. The following is an example of a different kind. In writing the Sotho language broadly the letter l serves to represent the d used in that language whenever i or u follows, since the sound l never occurs in that position: the two sounds d and l belong to a single phoneme. In the allied language Pedi there is no d, but there is the peculiar d-like l (referred to in §§81, 127) and an ordinary l, both of which occur before i and u; the sounds occur therefore as separate phonemes, and a special letter (ɹ or d) must be assigned to the d-like l. It may therefore well happen that a writer comparing the Sotho and Pedi languages would find it convenient to denote the d-sound by d instead of l in Sotho words. This is in fact what A. N. TUCKER has done in his *Comparative Study of the Suto-Chuana Group of Bantu Languages*; see particularly p. 49 of that book (first edition).

681. Forms of transcription containing special letters to show that particular sounds of a language differ from analogous sounds of some other language are called "comparative" or "typographically narrow" transcriptions. It is customary, and perhaps necessary, to use both linguistically and typographically narrow transcriptions in works dealing with the comparison of existing dialects, and particularly in dialect atlases. In transcribing connected dialect

texts, however, it is possible and in my view advisable in the interests of legibility and clear exposition to broaden the transcription and to make it unambiguous by prefixing to the transcribed texts of each dialect a summary of the conventions to be observed in reading them.

682.   Some teachers have advocated the use of "typographically narrow" transcriptions in texts designed for language learners. It has been proposed, for instance, that the English vowel in *red* should be represented by a symbol other than e or ɛ on the ground that it is intermediate in quality between the two French sounds generally transcribed with e and ɛ, that the English vowel in *hot* should be represented by some letter other than o or ɔ since these are used to denote other shades of vowel sound in French, that a special symbol should be used to denote the English r-sound since this English consonant differs from the Italian r. Long teaching experience has led me to the conclusion that it is as a rule inadvisable to introduce letters for such reasons in transcripts for language learners. The additional letters complicate the texts, and do not in my experience facilitate the task of the pupil except in very unusual cases. (See further my article *Types of Phonetic Transcription*, in Appendix A to the 8th edition, 1956, of my *Outline of English Phonetics*.)

683.   There is no end to the number of symbols that might be introduced on these grounds. For instance, if special letters were adopted for the above-mentioned English sounds, an equally good case could be made out for representing the English consonant t by a specially designed letter to show that it differs from the t of Spanish or Hindustani, for using different letters for the ð-sounds of English and Danish because the sounds are not quite the same, or for representing the Japanese u by ɯ on the ground that it has less lip-rounding than the European u-sounds, or for denoting it by some specially designed letter in order to remind readers that it is not a completely unrounded u.

684.   The right solution of the problem of international phonetic transcription for language learners is, I believe, that the number of letters should be as small as practicable, and that each letter should have an elastic value. Among the values which each letter can represent is naturally a "cardinal" one. But it should, in my opinion, be a recognized principle that when a letter is not needed to denote a "cardinal" sound, it may be used for representing other

sounds having reasonably near relationships to that cardinal sound. And cases may occur where it is convenient to assign to a given letter other values than the cardinal whether or not the cardinal sound occurs as a member of a phoneme of the language to be transcribed.

685. Stated in other terms the principle amounts to this: a particular letter cannot have precisely the same value in all the languages in which it is used; the learner of any particular language must familiarize himself with the value (or values when the phoneme has more than one member) assigned to it in that language.

686. But whether use is made of "comparative" symbols or not, the fundamental basis of transcription for language learners is and must be a representation of phonemes.

687. Here may be mentioned the fact, well known to linguisticians, that when one is making a phonetic investigation of a language not previously analysed, it is necessary to start by noting down all the sounds one hears, using therefore an "impressionistic" transcription which may ultimately prove to be very narrow. In the initial stages of such work the observer should give no thought to possible groupings into phonemes, and above all he should endeavour as far as possible to rid himself of his natural tendency to think of any of the sounds as groupable into phonemes in the same manner as similar sounds of his own language. It is often only after writing out numerous texts in very narrow transcription that the proper phonemic groupings emerge, and that the investigator can in consequence devise the simplest way of writing the language phonetically. Good examples of the method of procedure are given in SAPIR's article *La réalité psychologique des phonemes* mentioned in §653.

688. I have emphasized in §34 and elsewhere[8] that phonemic analysis can, in my opinion, only be based on "words" and not on connected speech. In order to ascertain the phonetic structure of a language the investigator must therefore know what sound-sequences are to be considered to be "words." He must be familiar not only with ordinary word-division, but also with the divisions of compound words and possibly even to word-like prefixes and suffixes. If he is concerning himself with a language which has not yet been reduced to words, it is necessary for him to settle for himself what the "words" are.

---

[8] E.g. *Some Thoughts on the Phoneme*, pp. 127–132.

689. Broad (phonemic) transcripts should, in my view, show word divisions and (by hyphens) the elements of compound words and any word-like prefixes and suffixes, except when the divisions are self-evident. For without these indications transcripts might be ambiguous. This applies even to a language like French where a syllable often begins with the final consonant of a word which is closely linked to the initial vowel of a following word. See my article *The Hyphen as a Phonetic Sign* (*Zeitschrift für Phonetik*, IX, 2, 1956).

690. One further general observation on transcription is needed here. Though broad transcription of a language is unambiguous in the sense that it records every word of the language in such a way that all words of different pronunciation are kept distinct in writing—so that all words are readily recognizable and the reader can attach the dictionary meanings to them—it gives no indication of the numberless other shades of meanings which in oral inter-course are continually superimposed on these meanings by sentence intonation, special voice qualities, special lengths and stresses, gestures and so on. Rough hints of some of such superimposed meanings may be suggested in writing by punctuation marks, italic print, underlining, etc.; but such devices are at best of very limited application, and they very often do not show at all adequately to the foreign learner how he should utter the words so as to suggest the desired meanings. A good deal of the necessary information may be given to him partly by rules and partly by special markings of length, stress and intonation incorporated in or placed next to the transcription. They cannot be regarded as a "narrowing" of it, since they apply to the sentence only and are not concerned with the differentiation of meanings of individual words.

ORTHOGRAPHY

691. The second kind of writing, *orthography*, is what is needed for ordinary current intercourse in writing. This too, if it is alphabetic, should have the principle "one letter per phoneme" as its basis, but it generally has to differ in several ways from a transcription for language learners. The chief points of difference are set out in the following paragraphs.

692. A transcription for those wishing to learn to speak a foreign language. must record the pronunciation to be actually used in each sentence transcribed. It must take account of the fact that in sentences words often have pronunciations different

from those they have in isolation. Words may, for instance, have
"weak forms" as well as "strong forms"[9]; they may have special
pronunciations in the sentence due to assimilations[10] or elisions[11]
or coalescences[12]; or again, there may be special phenomena such
as liaison in French[13] or doubling of initial consonants in Italian.[14]

693. In an orthography, on the other hand, it is not as a rule
advisable to show variant pronunciations of such types. What
is needful in an orthography is that every "word" should have a
definite and easily recognizable visual form. Subject to rare
exceptions, each word should be written in one way only, and
its orthographic form should in most cases be based on the
pronunciation it has when said in isolation.[15] To alter the spelling

---

[9] Such as the two pronunciations of *at* in 'wot ə juː 'lukiŋ at? (*What are
you looking at?*) and 'steiiŋ ət 'houm (*staying at home*). (See the sections
on weak forms ("gradation") in books on the phonetics of English, e.g. my
Outline of English Phonetics, Chapter XVI.)

[10] Such as the substitution of faif for faiv (*five*) in the compound 'faifpəns
(*fivepence*), or in French the common substitution of bɛg for bɛk (*bec*) in
bɛg də gaːz (*bec de gaz*), or in Italian the substitution of m for n in such an
expression as um pɔko (*un poco*, a little).

[11] Such as the elision of the t of nekst (*next*) in neks taim (*next time*),
or in French the elision of the ə of də (*de*) in such an expression as pɑ d dãʒe
(*pas de danger*), or in Kikuyu the elision of the final a of araata in araata
ɛɛga (good friends) which is pronounced araːt ɛːga [·⁻_.].

[12] Such as the use of ɛ in place of final a + initial e in Kikuyu, e.g.
njerɛːnɔ [·-˙] (this road), which stands for njera enɔ [····]. (See
ARMSTRONG, *Phonetic and Tonal Structure of Kikuyu*, Chapter III.)

[13] As shown, for instance, in le vil (*les villes*) but lez ɔm (*les hommes*).
(See PASSY, *Les Sons du Français*, §§244–249; ARMSTRONG, *Phonetics of French*,
Chapter XIX; STÉPHAN and JONES, *Colloquial French for the English*, Chapter
LII; and other books on the phonetics of French.)

[14] As shown, for instance, in da kki (*da chi*, from whom) as compared
with di ki (*di chi*, of whom). (See A. CAMILLI, *Pronuncia e grafia dell' italiano*,
§§89–95. Also A. CAMILLI, *I rafforzamenti inizziali in italiano*, in *Le Maître
Phonétique*, July, 1909 and May, 1911.)

[15] Words susceptible to liaison in French would be exceptions. The liaison
forms are, in most words, the only convenient pronunciations to take as a
basis for orthography. Such words as *les, beaux, haut, hautes, aller, allez,
allais, allait, allaient*, would appear in an international orthography as *lez,
boz, hot, hotəz, aler, alez, alɛz, alɛt, alɛt*, with the convention that the final
consonant is silent in speech except when liaison is used. To write non-
liaison forms in an orthography would lead to much confusion on account
of the variability in the use of liaison in speech. It would also add considerably to the number of homographs.

in order to conform to changes of pronunciation in connected speech would merely render the written words less easy to recognize. Spellings representing special pronunciations heard only in connected speech might often necessitate a mental translation into the sounds of the spoken language before the reader could recognize what words they were intended to represent; often too they would look like other words. Reading would in fact be hampered by the use of such variant spellings.

694. The point may be illustrated by an extreme case. A man may say **tem mins sem** in the course of conversation, and his hearers will understand his meaning just as well as if he pronounced the expression in a precise manner. But if such a form as *tem mins sem* were used in current writing, it would merely constitute a puzzle which the reader might or might not decipher easily.[16]

695. An orthography differs also from a phonetic transcription for language learners in that it generally has to serve for a wide range of speakers with varying accents. The results are twofold. Firstly, some of the letters or combinations of letters have different significations with different speakers. Thus, if *ei* were chosen for writing the vowel element of such words as *day*, *plate*, its phonetic meaning would be various types of **ei** with some speakers, a pure long **eː** with many in Scotland and the North, varieties of **ɛi** and **ai** in London, and so forth. Secondly, where local or other variants are a matter not of sound formation but of sound distribution, some pronunciations have to be ignored, and orthographic forms adopted which are phonetic for some speakers though not for others.

696. The following are examples of the latter case. In a reformed spelling of English, *mark* and *farm* would have to be written as they are now, since this spelling accords with the pronunciation of a majority of those whose mother tongue is English. It is not phonetic for me and for many others in the South of England, who pronounce **maːk**, **faːm** with precisely the same sound as **laːf** (*laugh*), **kaːm** (*calm*), etc. We could not, however, expect

---

[16] The appropriate writing in an international phonetic orthography would be *ten minits tu seven*. The spellings of the last two words would be invariable and would take no account of the fact that writers might pronounce **tu** or **tə** or **t**, **ˈsevən** or **ˈsevn** or **ˈsebm** or **sem**.

the majority of the English-speaking world to accept spellings like *maak, faam,* which would be unphonetic to them. On the other hand, the distinction between the vowels of *boot* and *book, food* and *good, pool* and *pull* which is made throughout large areas of the English-speaking world would doubtless have to be shown in a reformed spelling, in spite of the fact that no such distinction is made in Scotland.

697. So also terminations like *-est, -less, -ness* would have to be distinguished from *-ist, -is,* etc., in a reformed spelling of English. The former are pronounced -ist, -lis, -nis by many, including myself, but -əst, -ləs, -nəs by others. I think, therefore, that the Simplified Spelling Society has been well advised to distinguish between the short i's that have common variants with ə and those which do not normally have such variants: they write *puerist* (for present spelling *purist*),[17] *tenis, ofis,* etc., but *puerest* (for present spelling *purest*),[17] *goodnes,*[17] *hoeples,*[17] etc.

698. It might likewise prove advisable to make allowance for the widespread distinction of vowel between words like *port, forth, course, hoarse,* etc., and *short, north, horse,* etc., despite the fact that many do not observe the distinction in their speech. Such words could be written in an international orthography *port, forθ, kors, hors,* and *ʃɔrt, nɔrθ, hɔrs,* etc.

699. Striking compromise spellings would have to be adopted in a phonetic orthography for French. All possible *"e mutes"* would have to be written, although numbers of them are not sounded in Northern French. The distinction between a and ɑ, so commonly made in the North of France, would probably have to be ignored; possibly also the distinction between ø and œ. Distinctions in the length of ε would probably have to be shown, though many French speakers do not observe them. And last, but by no means least, numerous unpronounced letters would have to be introduced, as indeed they are in present-day spelling, on account of the phenomenon known as "liaison" (see footnote 15 to §693).

700. In a phonetic orthography for German, *p* and *b* would both have to be used, despite the fact that many Germans do not

---

[17] International phonetic orthography of these words would be *pyurist, pyurest, gudnes, houples.*

differentiate the sounds. A phonetic orthography for Hindustani would have to include the letters *q, f, z, x* and *ɣ*, although a great many speakers of that language do not use the sounds which these letters denote; they substitute k, ph, ɟ, kh and g for them.[18] And so on.

701. When two pronunciations of a word enjoy wide currency and appear to have equal claims to representation in orthography, it may be found advisable to admit two spellings. Thus it seems reasonable in a phonetic orthography for English to admit two spellings of words like *grass* and *path*, viz. *graas, paaθ* and *gras, paθ*, since both pronunciations are in wide use. The admission of these spellings would obviate the need for English-speaking children to memorize lists of words spelt in a way that is unphonetic for them. The same applies to various isolated words, e.g. *aiðer* and *iiðer, akompliʃ* and *akɔmpliʃ*,[19] *garraaʒ* and *garrej, agein* and *agen*. Similarly in a phonetic orthography for French the present *août* might appear as *au* or *aut* or *u* or *ut*, and the present *but, obus* might be spelt *byt, obys*, or *by, oby*;[20] *mauvais* might be written either *mɔvɛz* or *movɛz*,[21] *mœurs* might have two forms *mœrs* and *mœr*, and *alcoolique* the two forms *alkɔɔlikə* and *alkɔlikə; donc* might be written *dɔŋk* or *dɔŋ*[22] according to the pronunciation of the writer, and so on. In a phonetic spelling of Italian *cosa* might be written *kɔsa* and *kɔza*, since both pronunciations are common.

702. Other departures from phonetic consistency are often desirable in an orthography to avoid cumbrous spellings or on other grounds of practical convenience. Thus it would probably be found advisable in a reformed spelling of English on international lines to write *ju* (or *yu*) to represent the ju: of such words as *new, hue*, in place of the cumbrous though more accurate *juu* (or *yuu*). This simplification would be advisable in spite of the fact that the

---

[18] See *The Problem of a National Script for India*, pp. 8, 9.

[19] The sound ʌ is adequately represented by *ə* in an orthography.

[20] Or *byt, obys*, etc., if the system were one employing *y* and *j* with English values.

[21] See footnote 15 to §693.

[22] With preference for *dɔŋk* which would differentiate it from the word *dɔŋ* (gift). (Note that in a phonetic orthography for French it is convenient to use *ŋ* as the sign of nasalization.)

short *ju* of 'monjumənt, etc., is phonemically distinct from it. (The case is one where there is a phonemic distinction which does not happen to be used for differentiating any words; there is not to my knowledge any pair of words distinguished by ju: and ju in English.) In an international phonetic orthography for German it would no doubt be found advisable to denote most, if not all, strongly stressed long vowels by doubled letters, e.g. to write not only *Boot* and *Moos* as now, but also *vool* (for *wohl*), *hoox* (for *hoch*), *groos* (for *gross*), etc. But there are cases where it would be unnecessarily cumbersome to write *oo*. Notable are pretonic syllables, where a simplification to single *o* could be made provided that the few words containing the ordinary short o (ɔ) in pretonic open syllables were listed as exceptions. Thus one could without inconvenience write *Lokomotiive*, *kloroform*, *Honoraar*, in place of the cumbrous though more accurate *Lookoomootiive*, etc., possibly also *vomit* instead of *voomit* (for the present *womit*), etc.; but it would be necessary to specify the few exceptional words in which the *o* would have the ordinary short sound, e.g. *folɛnden* (for *vollenden*), *Koleek* (for *Kolleg*), *Korɛktuur* (for *Korrektur*).[23]

703. It is sometimes possible to depart from the strictly phonetic principle in orthography in order to distinguish homophones, i.e. words of identical pronunciation but different meanings. This is justifiable when there are suitable grounds for the spellings chosen, and when the spellings of both words are unambiguous. It might, for instance, be considered advisable in a phonetic orthography for German to write final *b*, *d* and *g* in place of *p*, *t* and *k* in those words where derivative forms have the sounds b, d and g. Such spellings would not be ambiguous, since the sounds b, d and g never occur finally. Thus there would be a certain advantage in continuing to distinguish the words at present written *Rat* and *Rad* (which are both pronounced ra:t) by using the forms *Raat* and *Raad*; these spellings would show the relationships with the plurals, which would presumably be written in

---

[23] It would also be possible to effect an economy of letters in connected texts by representing strongly stressed long vowels by single letters before *v* and *z* since short vowels do not occur before these consonants in German. Thus there would be no ambiguity if *leezen* and *Løøve* were simplified to *lezen* and *Løve*. A further economy might be effected by writing final long vowels, other than *e*, with single letters, e.g. *ja*, *vi*, *vo*, *Zoofa* (but *Zee*, *Alee*).

phonetic orthography *Reete* and *Reeder*.   Another example is found in the Hindustani words pronounced *ke*.   J. R. FIRTH has suggested that it would be advantageous in a phonetic spelling for Hindustani to distinguish the post-position from the conjunction by writing the latter as *ky*.[24]   So also, if a phonetic orthography were ever adopted for French, it might be found desirable to distinguish the words for "steal" and "fly" which are homophones with most French speakers,[25] by writing them *vɔler* and *voler* in accordance with a distinction of pronunciation heard in French-speaking Switzerland.

704.   It may even at times be found advisable to introduce unpronounced letters into orthography in order to show relationships between words or to distinguish homophones.   Thus, though strict phonetic orthography of such French words as the plurals *hauts*, *prêts* would be *hoz*, *prɛz*, it would no doubt be preferable in a reformed spelling on international basis to insert *t* and write *hotz*, *prɛtz*, to show the relationship of these words to the singulars *hot*, *prɛt* and the feminines *hotə*, *hotəz*, *prɛetə*, *prɛetəz*.   Incidentally *prɛtz* would thus be distinguished visually from the homophone *prɛz* (present spelling *près*).

705.   So also it might be found advisable to introduce a few historical spellings into a reformed orthography for English in order to distinguish homophones.   One might, for instance, distinguish the two *sən*'s as *sən* and *sənn* (present spelling *son*, *sun*) and the two *eit*'s as *eit* and *eiht* (present spelling *ate*, *eight*).[26]

706.   The examples given in the foregoing paragraphs (§§691–705) suffice to show how different an orthography must needs be from a transcription designed for teaching pronunciation.   Nevertheless it

---

[24] As FIRTH has pointed out, *y* is the appropriate letter for representing the Hindustani so-called "short i" in a romanic phonetic orthography. Since the normal short i-sound never occurs finally in that language, no ambiguity can arise from the occasional use of *y* to denote *e* in final position. A *y* in this position could not mean anything else but e to a Hindustani speaker.

[25] Both pronounced vɔle in Paris, and both pronounced vole in various other parts of France.

[26] Another course would be to write *ate* as *et* in accordance with the common pronunciation, and ignore the variant *eit*.   The idea of writing *h* in a reformed spelling of *eight* was suggested to me by Mr. WILLIAM BARKLEY.   (See his book, *The Two Englishes*, p. 37.)

is clear that if an orthography is to do its work with the maximum
of efficiency, and be easy to learn, it should have the principle
"one letter per phoneme" as its basis. It should in fact come as
near to a phonetic transcription as the special requirements of
orthography allow.[27]

CHAPTER XXXII

THE PHONEME IN THE HISTORY OF LANGUAGES

707. The study of the history of a language involves among
many other things a study of what happens to its phonemes in the
course of time. It is found that changes in phonemic structure
frequently take place as languages develop, and that the changes
are of many different types.[1] In the following paragraphs examples
are given of twenty-nine types of phonemic development. There
are doubtless others.

708. (1) *Phonemes remaining unchanged.*—Often phonemes
appear to have remained stationary for long periods, that is to say,
as far as we can tell, both principal and subsidiary members (if
any) have retained the same values during those periods. Such
are in all probability the p, m and w phonemes of English from

---

[27] The reasons why a phonetic orthography has to differ from a phonetic
transcription are further elaborated in my paper *Dhe Fonetik Aspekt ov
Speling Reform* (published for the Simplified Spelling Society by Sir Isaac
Pitman and Sons), and in my paper on *Differences between Spoken and Written
Language* published by the Association Phonétique Internationale.

[1] When we speak of the sounds and phonemes of a language at some past
date, we mean the sounds and phonemes which we think are likely to have
been used by typical speakers of a particular region at that period. We
cannot establish the pronunciation of bygone days with the precision attainable
by direct observation of the speech of to-day, though we have reason to think
that it is often possible to reconstruct old pronunciations with a very fair
degree of accuracy. (See, for instance, the evidence quoted in my article
on the pronunciation of Shakespeare's day on pp. 38–41 of *English Pronunciation through the Centuries*, published by the Linguaphone Institute.) It must
be remembered too that there doubtless existed at all previous periods in
the history of a language just as many different ways of pronouncing as
there are now, if not more.

Old English times to the present day and the French i-phoneme during a similar period.

709.   (2) *Change affecting an entire phoneme.*—Sometimes all the members of a phoneme have changed in value and still remained together as a phoneme.   An example is the change of the Vulgar Latin u (derived from Classical Latin long u:[2]) into y in French. The principal member of this phoneme was doubtless a close u identical with that of Modern Italian.   Its representative in Modern French is a close y; example, Latin 'mu:ro (< Classical 'mu:rum) > French my:r.   We cannot tell if there were any subsidiary members of the Vulgar Latin u differing appreciably from the principal u, but if there were, they have all been replaced by varieties of y in Modern French; thus the somewhat open y commonly used in French in non-final positions, as, for instance, in fyme (*fumer*), may well have come from a somewhat open u in the Vulgar Latin fu'ma:re (< Classical fu:'ma:re).

710.   This type of change must be distinguished from the case where one phoneme is substituted for another in the course of the development of a language.   The latter is exemplified by the substitution of œ for a former ɔ in the Parisian French pronunciation of *joli* and *absolu* (ʒɔli > ʒœli, apsɔly > apsœly, footnote 3 to §306) and by the substitution of i: for e: in Early Modern English in the words which had had ɛ: in Middle English, as in *meat* (me:t > mi:t), *sea* (se: > si:).   (See §716, where it is shown that in Early Modern English e: emerged as a phoneme without any short vowel attached to it as a subsidiary member.)

711.   (3) *Change in principal member, a subsidiary member being unchanged but remaining attached to the new principal member.*— An example of this is seen in the development of the Latin b in Spanish.   It is believed that, at one time, the Latin phoneme represented by the letter *b* had ordinary voiced b-sounds as its principal and subsidiary members similar to those found in the Modern French b-phoneme.   This developed in Spanish into a phoneme having the fricative sound β as its principal member and plosive b as a subsidiary member, the latter being used when

---

[2] It cannot be doubted that in late Vulgar Latin the Classical Latin *short* u acquired o-quality as in Modern Italian, and joined the phoneme containing the long close o.

m precedes. Example: Latin 'bibere > Spanish [βe'βer], but
Latin im'bibere > Spanish [embe'βer].

712. (4) *Change in a subsidiary member of a phoneme with
continued attachment to an unaltered principal member.*—This case
is one which may be expected to arise fairly frequently, but it is
difficult to find examples of which we can be certain on account of
lack of evidence as to the values of subsidiary members in times
past. A possible illustration is the development which has led to
the use of ʔ in place of a previous t following a strongly stressed
vowel in many types of modern English. Instances are seen in raiʔ,
'liʔl, 'mʌʔn which are common modern pronunciations of *right, little,
mutton.* It is commonly supposed that the use of ʔ in such words
is a modern innovation, and that formerly the words were always
said with t.[3]

713. Possibly the use by some English speakers of əi as a variant
of ai in unstressed syllables is another case in point.[4] It is so if
a sound of the ai-type was at one time used in all positions and
subsequently the weakly stressed ai's were altered to əi. It appears,
however, impossible to prove that this happened.[5]

714. (5) *Change in a principal member together with development
of a new subsidiary member.*—The apparently recent development

---

[3] The example is not one of which we can be very certain for two reasons.
Firstly, it has not yet been definitely established that t and ʔ belong to the
same phoneme in the speech of any of those who pronounce in this way.
The problem is complicated by the fact that many of those who use ʔ in
these words are erratic in their speech; also by the fact that ʔ is also used
by some where the older pronunciation is supposed to have had k or p (e.g.
'beiʔə for *baker*, 'piːʔl for *people*). (See §620.)

Secondly, it is not impossible that this use of ʔ is of some antiquity. It
is difficult otherwise to explain its wide distribution in different parts of Great
Britain and in America. The fact that words of the above types have been
regularly written with *t* from the earliest times does not tell us much. For
if the sound ʔ had been in use in (say) Old English, it could hardly have
been denoted otherwise than by *t* (or perhaps *k*) when people first attempted
to write English with the Latin alphabet.

[4] This is the pronunciation represented in SWEET'S *Primer of Spoken
English*, where he wrote, for instance, ai in *ties* and *besides*, but əi in
sympathize and *idea*.

[5] Another possible development is that all the Middle English iː's changed
to a sound of the əi-type as explained in §718, and that then the stressed ones
developed still further into varieties of ai.

of the phoneme of London dialect corresponding to "average" English long u: may be an example of this. The principal member of this dialectal phoneme is əü; it is heard in such words as [tˢəü] (*two*), [məün] (*moon*). There is a subsidiary member of the ǫ-type used before "dark" l, as in [skǫːl] (*school*), [rǫːl] (*rule*), etc.

715.   That this is an example of the case under consideration rests on the assumption that these London dialect sounds are derived from a single sound identical with, or at least not unlike the "average" English u:. It is difficult to prove this definitely to be a fact, but it is perhaps not too much to assume that "average" English is on the whole more conservative than particular local dialects, and that for that reason the assumption has some justification.

716.   (6) *Change in a principal member resulting in its becoming attached to another phoneme.*—Instances of this have been frequent in English on account of the fact that several short vowels have, in all probability, undergone little or no alteration for hundreds of years, while the long vowels have all changed greatly since the Middle English period. The history of the vowels in such words as (1) *rest, yet,* (2) *meat, sea,* (3) *make, face* provides two illustrations. It is believed that the vowel of such words as *rest, yet,* has been (on an average)⁶ a variety of ɛ for the last thousand years. As to the other vowels there is evidence to show that in Middle English the first was a long ɛː and the second a very front long aː, and that both these gradually changed to "closer" sounds, reaching, by the sixteenth century, values in the neighbourhood of cardinal eː and ɛː respectively. At a certain point during this development the sound representing Middle English long ɛː must have become detached from the phoneme containing short ɛ, while the new long ɛː emerging from the earlier aː must have become attached to it instead. This transference may be presumed to have taken place at the time when the quality of the new ɛː had nearly reached that of the short ɛ, and when the previous ɛː would have progressed

---

⁶ Several varieties of vowel are heard in such words at the present day, the varieties being both individual and local. Doubtless such varieties have always existed. In fact their existence in early times is attested by variant spellings. We can only concern ourselves with what may be considered to have been an average pronunciation, namely, a sound not far from cardinal ɛ.

some distance in the direction of close eː. This would presumably
have been in the late fifteenth or early sixteenth century.

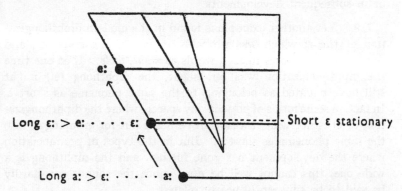

FIG. 12. Diagram showing the Development of Middle English ɛː and aː.

717. (7) *Change in a principal member of a phoneme resulting
in the appearance of a new phoneme unattached to any member of
previously existing phonemes.*—The development of Middle English
ɛː referred to in the last paragraph furnishes an example of this.
When this sound was replaced by closer ones (i.e. varieties of eː)
and became detached from the phoneme containing short ɛ, it
evidently did not attach itself to any other short vowel of the
language. (The only other short vowel near to it in quality was i,
and in the sixteenth century this sound would naturally have
been in the same phoneme with the long iː of such words as *see,
meet,* which by that time had replaced the Middle English eː.)

718. Another example found at the same period was no doubt
the diphthong əi,[7] which developed from Middle English iː, and
must have become detached from the phoneme containing short i,
to which its Middle English predecessor (iː) had belonged, without
becoming associated into the same phoneme as any other sound
existing at the time. Thus, in Middle English, the vowels in
ˈmiːlə (*mile*) and milk would have been grouped together in the
same phoneme. But when iː had developed sufficiently in the

---

[7] A diphthongal sound intermediate between iː and ai which was probably
in use in the sixteenth and seventeenth centuries. See my article on *Shakespeare in the Original Pronunciation,* in *English Pronunciation through the
Centuries,* pp. 36–45.

direction of əi, it must have become separated from the short i and have constituted a separate phoneme, as it has continued to be in subsequent developments.

719.   Yet another example is found in the modern diphthongization of the ɛː which was probably in use in the sixteenth and seventeenth centuries in such words as *make, table*. If at one time the diphthongization was but slight, the diphthong (ei) might still have counted as belonging to the same phoneme as short ɛ. In fact, in some forms of present-day speech, where the diphthongization of ei is not wide, a case can be made out for grouping it into the same phoneme as short e. But in the types of pronunciation where the development has gone further, and the diphthong is a wide one, this cannot well be done, since the sounds can hardly be said to be sufficiently nearly related.

720.   (8) *Change in a subsidiary member resulting in its becoming attached to another phoneme.*—Developments of this type are fairly common. The i and u phonemes of Classical Latin provide an example. The Classical Latin i-phóneme evidently comprised two members, a closer vowel when long and an opener one when short. The opener one must have been at one time sufficiently near in quality to the close one to justify using the same letter *i* to represent both. We may consider the quality used when the vowel was long as being the principal member of this phoneme. The subsequent history of the words containing these sounds shows us that in Vulgar Latin (a language which no doubt had considerable resemblance to Modern Italian) the previous short i opened further and became similar in quality to the previous long eː, while length ceased to have significant function, and the Italian system of lengthening strongly stressed vowels in open syllables came into being. Thus arose developments like Classical Latin 'nivem > Vulgar Latin 'neːve, Classical Latin 'ubi > Vulgar Latin 'oːve. The Classical Latin short i and u thus developed in such a way that they left the i and u phonemes and entered the e and o phonemes.[8]

721.   Incidentally, it is possible that in Classical Latin the short e-sound, which doubtless was pronounced as a variety of ɛ,

---

[8] It is noteworthy in this connexion that Classical Latin long uː became y in French (nuːda > ny, etc.), while Classical Latin short u generally remained u in French (ursum > urs, gustum > gu, etc.).

would have belonged to the same phoneme as the long eː.[9] But when the usage in regard to length changed, as mentioned in the preceding paragraph, the short ɛ became long in many words (e.g. Vulgar Latin and Italian ˈpjɛːtra, from Classical Latin ˈpɛtra) and must therefore have separated itself from the phoneme used in the words which contained eː in Classical Latin.

722. Another example is found in the Latin a-phoneme which is represented in French by a and ɛ and ə according to circumstances: Vulgar Latin ˈparte, sal, ɔrnaˈmento > French paːr (part), sɛl (sel), ɔrnəmã (ornement). There clearly must have been a time when the Latin a-phoneme had a member tending towards ɛ, which eventually joined the French ɛ-phoneme derived from other sources. (For a > ə, see §725.)

723. A further example is offered by the Old English ɛ-phoneme, which no doubt at one time had as a member a very open variety of ɛ used before ɹ, which eventually joined the a-phoneme. Example: hɛɹt(ə) (written in Old English heorte), which subsequently became haɹt and in modern times haːt.

724. Again, the first part of the development by which Latin intervocalic t eventually disappeared in French was no doubt a stage in which it was replaced by d. ˙Thus ˈviːta would in all probability have first become ˈviːda, a change from one phoneme to another, before becoming ˈviːðə (and eventually ˈviːə and vi).

725. (9) *Change in a subsidiary member resulting in its becoming a new separate phoneme.*—This case is illustrated by the emergence of French ə from Latin a. No doubt in early Vulgar Latin weakly stressed a had much the same value as strongly stressed a, as in Modern Italian. But there must have been a time when this phoneme as used in Gaul developed an obscured a as a member employed in weakly stressed positions. Eventually the French sound ə emerged from this. Thus Vulgar Latin ɔrnaˈmento became in French ɔrnəmã. The appearance of ə as a separate phoneme would appear to date from the time when the vowel in such words began to be written with *e*, which coincides with

---

[9] This is on the assumption that Classical Latin *ae* was pronounced ae. It is possible, however, that Classical Latin *ae* was pronounced ɛː from earliest times, as it doubtless was in Vulgar Latin. If this were the case, the short ɛ would naturally have belonged to the same phoneme as the ɛː.

the period when other unstressed Latin vowels became obscure, i.e. about the tenth or eleventh century.[10]

726. (10) *Appearance of a new phoneme by coalescence of two sounds.*—In some forms of English sequences of vowel + ɹ have coalesced into single sounds, namely, "ɹ-coloured" vowels. Such a sound is aɹ (ɹ-coloured a) which may be heard from many South-Western dialect speakers in words like haɹːt, ˈgaɹːdn (*heart, garden*).[11]

727. (11) *Change in a subsidiary member, with the result that it coalesced with an adjacent sound to form a new phoneme.*—This is exemplified in the change l > u in Old French. It is clear that at an early period the l-phoneme had as a subsidiary member a "dark" l (ł) used before consonants. Statements to this effect were made by Latin grammarians, and Early French spellings with l (such as *altre, chevals, chevels*) indicate that a l-like sound was probably still used before consonants. The ł must ultimately have been replaced by the acoustically similar sound u, and, as there is no reason to think that the syllables consisting of vowel + ł ever became disyllabic, this u must have been non-syllabic and must immediately have combined with the preceding vowel to form a diphthong—a new phoneme. Thus altrə (written *altre*), which came from Vulgar Latin ˈaltero, would very easily have become aŭtrə (written *autre*)ᵢ This in turn eventually developed into the present-day oːtr(ə), after no doubt passing through some such intermediate stage as ˈɔŏtrə. The change from ł to ŭ in such words appears to have begun not later than the tenth century and to have been complete by the twelfth century.

728. (12) *Change in the conditions under which a sound is used involving separation from the phoneme to which it formerly belonged.*—Such separation may take place as the result of the elision of a "determining" sound.[12] It may also take place as the result of lengthening sounds previously short or shortening sounds previously

---

[10] See NYROP, *Grammaire Historique de la Langue Française*, Vol. I, §§162, 253, 257 and elsewhere.

[11] For the occurrence of such sounds in American English, see L. SPRAGUE DE CAMP on *American Retroflexed Vowels*, in *Le Maître Phonétique*, July, 1942, p. 22. I am disposed to think that the American syllabic ɹ (which = əɹ) should be regarded as a member of the r-phoneme, differing from the American consonantal r mainly by its length (see §750).

[12] A sound which determines what member of a neighbouring phoneme in a sequence is to be used.

long, and doubtless also in other circumstances. The following are examples of the first of these cases. An example of the second is given in §734.

729. In Early French the nasalized vowels were evidently members of the ordinary vowel phonemes, viz. the members used when nasal consonants followed. Thus, since the French b5 (*bon*) is derived from the Latin ˈbɔnum, which gave rise to ˈbɔːno in one type of Vulgar Latin, it is clear that the nasality of the vowel must have been brought about by the influence of the following n. The complete development was no doubt of the type ˈbɔnum > ˈbɔːno > ˈb5ːno > b5n > b5. Similarly with m, as in ˈlampa > ˈlãmpə > lãːp (*lampe*). It was during the last stage of these developments that the nasalized vowels must have changed their phonetic status. As long as the nasal consonant was present these vowels would naturally have belonged to the ordinary vowel phonemes, but as soon as the nasal consonants disappeared, they must have become separate phonemes as they are to-day in Northern French. It is probable that this was a comparatively recent occurrence.

730. The Old English f-phoneme furnishes another example of the conversion of a subsidiary member into a separate phoneme through elision of a determining sound. The principal member of this phoneme was f,[13] but there was evidently a subsidiary member v used between voiced sounds. Thus *feorr* (now *far*) and *hlaf* (now *loaf*) were no doubt pronounced fɛɹ, ɬɑːf, but it is clear that *drifan* (now *drive*) must have been pronounced ˈdriːvan or ˈdriːvən. When the final ə of words like *drive, mile* ceased to be sounded—an elision which apparently began to take place in the fourteenth century[14]—v must have become a phoneme separate from f, since the elision brought v into final position in many words: Middle English ˈdriːvə became driːv,[15] and so on.

731. The Modern English ŋ-phoneme probably originated in a similar manner. There is reason to think that in Old English ŋ was a member of the n-phoneme and was used to the exclusion of n before k and g. The analogy of mb and nd makes it probable

---

[13] North of the Thames. South of the Thames there was as a rule no f-sound; v was probably used in all positions, except when immediately preceding breathed consonants.

[14] In Southern England; much earlier in the North.

[15] Later drəiv and draiv.

that the written *ng* of Old English was pronounced ŋg, as it still is in the speech of many in the Midlands, and that the g of final -ŋg was dropped at the same period as the b of final -mb. Spellings indicate that this disappearance of b began in the fourteenth century. It would doubtless therefore have been about this date that ŋ became a phoneme separate from n.

732. An interesting example of the appearance of a new vowel-phoneme consequent upon the elision of a determining sound is afforded by a form developed from the earlier English sequence riu in the speech of some Americans.[16] In most types of English the i of this sequence has been elided and the modern pronunciation is simply ru(:). If, as is likely, the older sequence had a forward u [ü] as is the case with many modern speakers in such words as *new*, *music* (§89), this [ü] has generally reverted to the principal member of the phoneme; I believe most people pronounce *brew*, *rule*, etc., with the same shade of vowel as *too*, *school*. In some forms of American English, however, the forward u has been retained after the disappearance of the preceding i or j. This type of English consequently has a phoneme ü separate from the u-phoneme. *Brewed* and *brood* are with them distinguished as brüd, brud.

733. The following example from Russian is of a similar nature. Some Russians use pronunciations like aü, əü in place of the normal sequence aju [aju, əju]. They pronounce, for instance, znaüt, ˈsluʃəü, in place of the normal ˈznajut, ˈsluʃaju [ˈznajüt, ˈsluʃəjü] (знают, they know; слушаю, I am listening). In this pronunciation ü constitutes a phoneme separate from u, since the sequence əu also exists in Russian. Therefore if, as may be supposed, the pronunciations aü, əü are developments of older pronunciations aju, əju, these reductions exemplify the appearance of a new phoneme through the elision of j.[17]

---

[16] That the sequence riu was in use in the seventeenth century was indicated by JOHN WALLIS, who in his *Grammatica Linguæ Anglicanæ* quoted the word *brew* as an example of iu (p. 12 of the first edition, 1653).

[17] Those who favour a mentalistic view of the phoneme will probably not agree with the proposition that ü is a separate phoneme from u in the pronunciation of these speakers. They would, I believe, regard aü and əü as "realizations of the phonemic sequence aju." TRUBETZKOY, whose view was stated to be not "psychological" (see §§655 656), used a similar expression when mentioning this case (*Grundzüge der Phonologie*, p. 56, CANTINEAU'S translation, p. 65).

734. Examples of lengthening causing separation of sounds from phonemes to which they are believed to have been formerly attached are seen in the form of modern Southern English in which the traditionally short vowels are lengthened. As has been pointed out in §519 and elsewhere, there are now many Southern English speakers who pronounce words like *this, box* and *book* with long vowels (ðɪːs, bɒːks, bʊːk). The length relationship between these vowel qualities and those of such words as piːs (*piece*), tɔːks (*talks*) and buːt (*boot*) is no longer maintained, so that the sounds ɪ, ɒ and ʊ have in the speech of those who pronounce in this way become phonemes separate from the closer i, o and u of these latter words.

735. (13) *Appearance of a new phoneme through the influence of words borrowed from a foreign language.*—There are two cases of this: (a) when a foreign sound is imported into the language, and (b) when the introduction of foreign words causes two members of a phoneme to become separate phonemes.

736. Examples of (a) are the English diphthong oi (imported from French), the sound h in Norman French (imported from Germanic), the Hindustani q, f, z, x, ɣ (imported from Persian and Arabic).

737. An example which can be seen in progress at the present day is the importation of a b-phoneme into Kikuyu. When the English word *book* is used in Kikuyu, it is said in the most natural speech with the Kikuyu phoneme mb, thus mbuːku [- ·]. It seems, however, that many Kikuyu speakers give it an English pronunciation buːku with a sound b differing both from the Kikuyu mb and from the normal Kikuyu initial b (which = β).

738. An example of (b) is said to be observable in the pronunciation of some Japanese who employ ɸ before vowels other than u in borrowed European words. They use, for instance, ɸirumu as the equivalent of the English film, when the more natural Japanese pronunciation would be hwirumu [ɸuirumu].[18] In ordinary Japanese ɸ belongs to the h-phoneme, as shown in §77, but in the pronunciation of these speakers ɸ constitutes a phoneme separate from h.

739. The emergence of v as a separate phoneme in English, though primarily the result of elision of a determining sound, as

---

[18] PALMER, *Principles of Romanization*, pp. 87, 88.

explained in §730, may have been aided by the influx of French words beginning with v, such as *voice*, *veal*, which many people would doubtless have endeavoured to pronounce in the French way.

740. (14) *Appearance of a new phoneme through contraction.*— Examples are the French j and w phonemes, which had their origin in syllabic i (or e) and u (or o). Thus the j of lj5 (*lion*) comes from a syllabic e (Latin le'oːne(m)[19]), and the w of wi (*oui*) from a syllabic o (Old French *o + il*). Prior to these contractions it would seem that there was no j or w in French, the Latin j and w having both become fricative, the j changing towards ʒ and z, and the w changing to v.

741. (15) *Disappearance of a phoneme.*—Sometimes a phoneme disappears completely from a language. One of three things happens in this case: either (*a*) the sounds of the phoneme, or some of them, are replaced by other sounds already existing in the language, or (*b*) the sounds disappear leaving no trace, or (*c*) the disappearance of the sounds is compensated for by length or some other attribute.

742. (*a*) is illustrated by the treatment of the sixteenth-century English eː subsequent to its development from Middle English ɛː referred to in §716. In the fifteenth or sixteenth century the sound appears to have become a phoneme separate from short ɛ, as we have already seen; but shortly afterwards, probably in the course of the seventeenth and the beginning of the eighteenth century, people ceased using it altogether and substituted the long member of the i-phoneme of that period for every eː.[20] (We cannot assign any reason for this substitution. It would seem to have been detrimental to the language, since several pairs of words previously differentiated came to be pronounced alike: *sea* and *meat* came to be pronounced like *see* and *meet*.)[21]

---

[19] Which appeared in Old French as *leun* (presumably pronounced le'õn).

[20] According to Bishop WILKINS (*Essay towards a Real Character and a Philosophical Language*, 1668, p. 363) the eː was still in use in his day. He considered the sound to be the long of the vowel in *bet*, thereby (in our terminology) still attaching it to the same phoneme as the short ɛ.

[21] There is no question of the eː becoming gradually closer and eventually reaching iː. The change from a fairly close eː to iː must have been a sudden one, since as there already was an iː in the language, it would not have been possible for an eː of more than a certain degree of closeness to exist simultaneously with it.

743. Other illustrations of (*a*) are the substitution of l for the
Old English ɫ, as in ɫɑːf > Middle English lɔːf > Modern English
louf (*loaf*); the substitution of j for ʎ in Modern French; the substitution of a for Portuguese non-nasal ɐ in Brazilian[22]; the
substitution of the b-phoneme for the Latin w (or v) phoneme
in Spanish.[23]

744. An example of (*b*) is the disappearance of the Early English
x-phoneme which may have comprised two or more clearly distinguishable members. In many words this consonant ceased to be
sounded, and left no trace: such are Old English heːx (written
heah) which became in Middle English simply hiː (written *hy*, etc.)
and in later English həi and hai (*high*), and Old English ˈɑːxte
(*ahte*) which became in Middle English ˈɔːxtə (or perhaps ˈɔuxtə)
and eventually ɔːt (*ought*).

745. Case (*c*) is dealt with in §§750 ff.

746. (16) *Disappearance of a subsidiary member of a phoneme.*—
Sometimes, while a phoneme continues to exist, one of its members
disappears. The Early French d-phoneme affords an example of
this. That this phoneme had d as principal member is evidenced
by the fact that Latin initial d appears also as d in Modern French,
as in ˈduːrum > ˈduːro > dyːr (*dur*). It is, however, fairly certain
that the phoneme had a subsidiary member of the ð-type in intervocalic position. The evidence for this is (1) that Latin d in this
position has disappeared in Modern French (ˈnuːda > ˈnyːə > ny(ː),
etc.), and that a preliminary weakening of d to ð would have
naturally preceded this disappearance, (2) that the spelling *dh* is
found in Old French texts in positions corresponding to Latin
intervocalic d. The ultimate disappearance of this ð is thus the
disappearance of a subsidiary member of a phoneme. It seems
to have begun in the speech of some people about the tenth century,
and to have become general by the twelfth century.

---

[22] As in *para* (Portuguese ˈpɐrɐ, Brazilian ˈpara). The Portuguese nasalized
ẽ has remained unaltered in Brazilian speech. Incidentally, the phonemic
classification of the nasalized vowels in the Portuguese of Portugal and Brazil
is somewhat obscure. (See JONES and DAHL, *Fundamentos de Escritura
Fonética.* p. 17.)

[23] This latter substitution presumably took place simultaneously with the
change in the principal member of the b-phoneme from b to β (§711).

747.   (17) *Replacement of a sound by a sequence of two sounds.*—
An example of this is the replacement of Latin short ε in stressed
open syllables by jε and iε in French, as in ˈfɛbre(m) > fjɛːvr(ə),
ˈbrɛve(m) > Old French *brief* (at one time no doubt pronounced
briɛf, in one syllable). This development may have started with a
narrow diphthongization of the type eε which was gradually
widened to iε. It is perhaps impossible to discover at what date
the diphthong became a sequence of two sounds. It may be
remarked, however, that there would probably have been a long
period during which it would have been possible to regard the
iε either as a single diphthongal sound constituting a phoneme
or as a sequence of two sounds belonging to two phonemes. It
was no doubt the appearance of disyllabic iε from other sources,
and particularly as the result of the elision of intervocalic d (ð),[24]
which finally caused the diphthongal iε of such a word as *brief* to
become disyllabic. As for the alternative form jε, which is
practically indistinguishable in sound from the rising diphthong
ĭε, it may be presumed to have been thought of as a sequence of
two sounds as soon as sequences like ja and jo appeared in the
language[25]; for the existence of such sequences would mean that j
was definitely a phoneme of the language.

748.   Another replacement of a sound by a sequence of two
sounds occurred during the development of Latin e: into French
wa (me: > mwa, etc.). This development was presumably of the
type e: > eĭ > əĭ > oĕ > ŏε (which practically = wε) > wa. Here
again there must have been a period during which the sound could
be regarded either as a diphthong or as a sequence of two sounds.
The diphthong would doubtless have to be considered definitely
as having become a sequence of two sounds at the time when w
became established as a phoneme by the reduction of disyllabic
oˈi to the monosyllabic wi in the word *oui* (§740).

749.   Yet another example of the replacement of a sound by a
sequence of two sounds is seen in the development which has given
rise to the modern English juː. In Old English the corresponding

---

[24] As in Old French *oblider* (probably pronounced obliˈðɛr) which has
become in Modern French ublie (*oublier*). (The other modern form ublije
is doubtless a quite recent development of ublie, formed on analogy with
brije (*briller*), etc., after ʎ had been replaced by j.)
[25] See §740.

sound is believed to have generally been a diphthong eŭ or in some words a diphthong ɛŭ: eŭ (*eow*, you), neŭ (*neowe*, *niwe*, *newe*, new), kneŭ (*cneow*, knew), dɛŭ (*deaw*, dew), fɛŭ (*feawe*, few). It seems pretty certain that the first of these became iŭ at an early date, and that ɛŭ caught up with it later (perhaps not until the sixteenth or even the seventeenth century).[26] These were no doubt single diphthongal sounds until the modern pronunciation juː, which can hardly be regarded as other than a sequence of two sounds, supervened.[27]

750. (18) *Replacement of a sound-quality by a length.*—Sometimes when a sound has been dropped compensation has been made by lengthening a neighbouring sound in the words affected. The disappearance of r before consonants in South Eastern English provides an example. Words like *heart* and *purse* doubtless had at one time (fifteenth and sixteenth centuries) pronunciations of the type haɹt, pəɹs,[28] etc. The ɹ's in such words were doubtless retroflex continuants with vowel-colouring corresponding to the preceding vowel, these sounds being members of the r-phoneme. Subsequently in the Court language these ɹ's ceased to be sounded, and there was left in their stead a lengthening of the vowel; hence resulted the modern South-Eastern pronunciations haːt, pəːs, etc. A second chroneme thus came into being, affecting the sounds a and ə which previously had been subject only to one chroneme (short).

751. The different development of words like *purse* in South Western English and in American English illustrates the same process. There it was the ə which disappeared, while the ɹ remained

---

[26] JOHN WALLIS in his *Grammatica Linguae Anglicanae* (1653), p. 63, said that *few*, *beauty* were pronounced more correctly with "*è* clarum" and *w*, but that some people pronounced "more sharply" as if the words were written *fiw*, *biwty*.

[27] This may have been in the seventeenth century. The question is discussed in VIËTOR's *Shakespeare's Pronunciation*, Vol. I, Chapter V.

[28] More precisely pɤɹs. The vowel in this word was no doubt derived from a previous short u. Most of the short u's of Middle English are represented in Modern English by ʌ, having presumably undergone a development of the type u > ɤ (a variety of ə) > ʌ; see my article on *Shakespeare in the Original Pronunciation* in *English Pronunciation through the Centuries*, p. 39, §1 (Linguaphone Institute). But when ɹ followed, this development would seem to have been arrested (in South Eastern English) at the time of the disappearance of the ɹ.

and received a compensatory lengthening resulting in pronunciations of the type pɹːs. It will be observed that in neither of these developments of *purse* was there any change of phoneme.[29] It was the manner of using the phonemes in particular words that altered.

752. Another example of the appearance of a new chroneme by compensation for the loss of a sound is seen in French words like mɛːtr (*maître*), ɑːn (*âne*) which replace earlier forms mɛstrə (< Latin ma'gistrum), asnə (< Latin 'asinum).[30]

753. Yet another example is afforded by the treatment of French "feminine *e*" in some parts of France and in Belgium and in French-speaking Switzerland. In these localities various masculine and feminine words are distinguished by vowel-length: *bout* and *boue* are pronounced bu and buː respectively, *œil* has a short vowel (œj) and *feuille* a long one (fœːj), and the masculine and feminine forms of such an adjective as *original* are distinguished as ɔriʒinal (*original*) and ɔriʒinaːl (*originale*).[31] These lengthenings of vowels in feminine words can hardly be other than substitutions for a formerly pronounced ə, buː replacing an earlier buə,[32] ɔriʒinaːl replacing an earlier ɔriʒinalə, and so on. The development is presumably a comparatively recent one.

754. Sometimes a sound has disappeared from a sequence leaving compensation in the shape of syllabic character in another sound of the sequence. This is a special case of a substitution of a length for a sound-quality, since in order to be syllabic a sound

---

[29] Except that subsequently the American ɹ has acquired a quality differing somewhat from the South Western English ɹ. As far as I am able to judge, the syllabic South Western and American ɹ's still belong to the same phoneme as the consonantal r; its use appears to me to be comparable to the use of syllabic and non-syllabic l.

[30] It is believed that this disappearance of s was complete by the fourteenth century (BONNARD and SALMON, *Grammaire Sommaire de l'Ancien Français*, p. 65).

[31] These distinctions are not made in ordinary Parisian speech. In that type of French all final vowels are short, *boue* being pronounced bu, like *bout*; and with most speakers final j is accompanied by lengthening of the vowel, *œil* being pronounced œːj, and the feminine termination *-ale* is pronounced with a short vowel like the masculine *-al* (-al).

[32] Earlier still probably bɔə. (See NYROP, *Grammaire Historique de la Langue Française*, Vol. I, §189, where dʒɔə is given as a probable early form of *joue*.)

must be comparatively long. Examples are seen in such English words as *mutton* and *sudden* which are now 'mʌtn, 'sʌdn with syllabic n, but which must be presumed to have been said with a vowel between t or d and the n when the words were first taken into the language from French.

755. (19) *Appearance of a new phoneme through a change of length.*—As has been pointed out in §§510 ff. and elsewhere, minimal distinctions are often effected by complexes of quality and duration. If in the course of time changes of length occur in such cases, the distinction comes to be by quality only, so that new phonemes appear. One case of this has already been quoted in §734. Another is the shortening of the traditionally long and close i in the Scottish pronunciation of such words as *week*, *keen*, which has caused the presumably older short and open i (ɩ) to become a separate phoneme in that form of English (see §520).[33]

756. (20) *Replacement of a sound-quality by a tone.*—It will no doubt be found on examination that sound-qualities have sometimes been replaced by tones. It seems likely, for instance, that Chinese dialects which at present do not make use of final p, t, k or ʔ, possessed sounds of this kind at an earlier period, and that sometimes when the sounds disappeared special tones took their place. It is probable too that the two tones of modern Panjabi are derived from aspirations in an earlier form of that language. (The low-rising tone, denoted in GRAHAME BAILEY's *Panjabi Phonetic Reader* by ˏ, corresponds to the aspirations of the consonants bh, dh, etc., of Urdu, while the high-falling tone ˆ corresponds to the breathy voice often applied to Urdu vowels.[34] Compare Panjabi kˏər (house), bɜ̂ot (much) with Urdu ghər, bəɑht.)

757. In languages making use of significant length or stress or voice-pitch one may expect these attributes to undergo modifications in course of time. One may expect also that the modes of

---

[33] It will be seen from what has been said in this and previous paragraphs that new phonemes can come into a language in a variety of ways, the chief of which are (*a*) introduction of a sound from a foreign language, (*b*) isolative change resulting in detachment from an old phoneme (§§716, 717), (*c*) elision of a "determining" sound (§§729–733), (*d*) contraction (§740), (*e*) change of length (§§734, 755). There are also cases for which we are unable to account, such as the appearance of ɑ in addition to a in modern Northern French.

[34] Represented in romanic writing by *h* following the vowel.

using them should sometimes change. The significant function of these attributes may be preserved in spite of such alterations, or on the other hand their significant function may disappear. Moreover, one of the attributes may come to have significant function in a language where it was previously not so used. Below are examples of some types of change in these attributes. There are doubtless many more.

758. (21) *Change in length not effecting significance.*—Example: the (apparently recent) lengthening of French **a** before **b**, **d** and **g**, as in **taːbl**, **baːg** for the more usual and presumably older **tabl**, **bag** (*table, bague*).

759. (22) *The appearance of significant length where it did not exist previously.*—Examples: the appearance of significant length affecting certain French vowels and exemplified in **mɛːtr** (*maître*) and **mɛtr** (*mettre*), and affecting the Scottish English close **i** and exemplified in the Scottish pronunciation of **grid** (*greed*) (with short close **i**) and **ʌˈgriːd** (*agreed*).[35] (See also the examples in §§750–753.)

760. (23) *The disappearance of significant length,* as for instance in Vulgar Latin,[36] or in the English of those who pronounce such words as *thick, stop, book* with full length (**θɪːk, stɒːp, bʊːk**).[37]

761. (24) *Change in a type of stress,* as for instance when a falling diphthong is replaced by a rising diphthong (see example in §748).

762. (25) *Shifting of the position of strong stress,* as in many English words of French origin, e.g. *courage,* which no doubt first appeared in English in the form **kuˈraːdʒə** and has since become **ˈkʌridʒ**.[38]

763. (26) *Changes in the values of tone in tone languages,* such as those which must be presumed to have occurred in various Chinese languages, if they have a common origin.

---

[35] See §§377, 520.

[36] Length, which had been significant in Classical Latin, remained a noteworthy feature in Vulgar Latin, but it became linked with stress and was no longer significant.

[37] See §§130, 734, footnote 8 to §513, footnote 1 to §592.

[38] Changes in the position of strong stress in English have generally been accompanied by changes of sound-quality.

764. (27) *Appearance of new tones and disappearance of old ones in tone languages,* as evidenced by the varying numbers of tones in present-day Chinese languages.[39]

765. (28) *Substitution of strong stresses for special tones,* such as that believed to have taken place in Greek.

766. (29) *Complete disappearance of significant tones from a language which was previously a tone language, without replacement by any other attribute,* as is believed to have happened in Swahili.

767. Other possibilities are the replacement of length by stress or by tone, the replacement of stress by length or by tone, the replacement of tone by length or by stress, and many changes affecting complexes of attributes.

768. It should be added that though the attributes length, stress and voice-pitch can be and are employed for the purpose of distinguishing words, their use for this purpose is rather restricted.

---

[39] The number is said to vary from four to nine. (See B. KARLGREN, *La Phonologie Chinoise*, Vol. I, Chapter XVI.) It should be noted, however, that KARLGREN's statement that Cantonese contains nine tones (*Phonologie Chinoise*, p. 591) needs some amplification. If "tone" is used as a translation of the Cantonese terms _sœŋ (tone of the upper series) and _ha (tone of the lower series), it means not only musical pitches but also what the Chinese call "entering tones," i.e. musical pitches combined with a final stop consonant (unexploded p, t or k). In the *classical* style of Cantonese there are nine of these, six being musical pitches without final stop and three being musical pitches with final stop. They are: high fall (with variant high level in the same toneme), high rise, mid level, low fall (with variant very low level in the same toneme), low rise, low level, high with stop, mid with stop, low with stop. In *colloquial* Cantonese there are, in addition, a high rise with stop and a very high level (a separate toneme), making eleven in all.

If one adopts what seems to me to be the better course of using the term "tone" in its common European sense of musical pitch only—the stops being taken for what they really‚are, viz. articulated sounds—the numbers are: for the *classical* style of Cantonese six (high fall, high rise, mid level, low fall, low rise, low level) and for *colloquial* Cantonese seven (the same with the addition of the very high level). The "upper entering tone" (i.e. high pitch with stop) has the same pitch as the level variant of the high falling, the mid level with stop has the same pitch as the mid level, and the "lower entering tone" (i.e. low pitch with stop) has the same pitch as the low level.

According to KARLGREN (*Phonologie Chinoise*, p. 594) there are, in other types of Chinese, cases where one tone has split into two and where two different tones have merged into one.

Very extensive use of them is, however, made for the purpose of superimposing meanings on *sentences*. The ways in which they are employed to fulfil functions of this type are very varied and complicated, and it is only to be expected that the methods of applying them in sentences should undergo considerable variations in course of time.[40] This subject does not, however, come within the scope of this book.

769. I would conclude this chapter by pointing out that the investigation of phonemic changes occurring in the history of languages may prove to be of assistance towards determining the nature of the phoneme itself. It would be useful, for instance, to ascertain whether such developments as a change causing a sound to leave one phoneme and join another, or the substitution of a length for a sound-quality, are compatible with a mentalistic view of the phoneme. It is to be hoped that such questions will in due course receive the attention of specialists in the psychological aspects of phonetics.

---

[40] The following are two examples. French has evolved a special method of denoting intensity-emphasis by strong stress combined with a particular type of intonation (see COUSTENOBLE and ARMSTRONG, *Studies in French Intonation*, Chapters XIX, XX) and contrast-emphasis by another type of intonation (see Chapters XXIII, XXIV of the same book). Cantonese and Pekingese have different ways of giving prominence to a word in the sentence. In Cantonese it is done by giving extra length to the words, while in Pekingese it is done by making the non-prominent words "toneless" or nearly so. If, as is supposed, the two languages are derived from a common original, one or both of these methods of rendering words prominent must have come into existence by some sort of evolution.

APPENDIX

LIST OF PUBLICATIONS REFERRED TO IN THIS BOOK

The black type numerals show the paragraphs in which the references are made. (Most references are in footnotes to the paragraphs.)

Z. M. AREND, *Baudouin de Courtenay and the Phoneme Idea*, in *Le Maître Phonétique*, Jan., 1934. **652.**

L. E. ARMSTRONG, *The Phonetics of French*, Bell, London. **297, 411, 692.**

L. E. ARMSTRONG, *The Phonetic and Tonal Structure of Kikuyu*, Oxford University Press, 1940. **79, 353, 635, 692.**

L. E. ARMSTRONG, *The Phonetic Structure of Somali*, in *Mitteilungen des Seminars für Orientalische Sprachen zu Berlin*, Vol. XXXVII, Part 3, 1934. (Offprints obtainable from the Dept. of Phonetics, University College, London.) **366, 485, 580, 675.**

L. E. ARMSTRONG, summary of the phonetics of Luganda, in WESTERMANN and WARD, *Practical Phonetics for Students of African Languages*, Oxford University Press, 1933. **83.**

L. E. ARMSTRONG and PE MAUNG TIN, *A Burmese Phonetic Reader*, University of London Press, 1925. **586.**

L. E. ARMSTRONG and I. C. WARD, *Handbook of English Intonation*, Teubner, Leipzig, and Heffer, Cambridge, 1926. **348, 446, 574.**

T. GRAHAME BAILEY, *Panjabi Phonetic Reader*, University of London Press, 1914. **277, 366, 756.**

M. L. BARKER, *Handbook of German Intonation*, Heffer, Cambridge. **574.**

W. BARKLEY, *The Two Englishes*, Sir Isaac Pitmen & Sons, London, 1945. **705.**

J. BAUDOUIN DE COURTENAY, *Próba teorji alternacyj fonetycznych* (Essay on a theory of phonetic alternations), Cracow, 1893. **652.**

D. M. BEACH, *Phonetics of the Hottentot Language*, Heffer, Cambridge, 1937. **17.**

B. BLOCH, Note on English transcription in *Le Maître Phonétique*, Jan., 1943, p. 4. **204.**

B. BLOCH, *Phonemic Overlapping*, in *American Speech*, Dec., 1941. **311.**

L. BLOOMFIELD, *Language* (revised edition), Allen & Unwin, London, 1935, and Henry Holt & Company, New York. **657.**

L. BLOOMFIELD, *German* ç *and* x, in *Le Maître Phonétique*, April, 1930. **232.**

J. BONNARD and A. SALMON, *Grammaire Sommaire de l'Ancien Français*, H. Welter, Leipzig and Paris, 1904. **752.**

S. C. BOYANUS, *The* ı̵ *Phoneme*, appendix to the 2nd edition of his *Manual of Russian Pronunciation*; also published separately by the Association Phonétique Internationale, and obtainable from the Dept. of Phonetics, University College, London. **505.**

S. C. BOYANUS, *Russian Pronunciation*, Lund, Humphries, London, 1955. **95, 183, 348.**

S. C. Boyanus and N. B. Jopson, *Spoken Russian*, Sidgwick & Jackson, London, 1939. **348, 574**.

J. P. Bruce, *Linguaphone Chinese Course*, 1st edition, Linguaphone Institute. **257**.

A. Camilli, *Pronuncia e grafia dell' italiano*, 2nd edition, 1946, Sanzoni, Viali Mazzini 46, Florence. **692**.

A. Camilli, *I rafforzamenti inizziali in italiano*, in *Le Maître Phonétique*, July, 1909, and May, 1911. **692**.

J. Cantineau, *Principes de Phonologie* (translation of Trubetzkoy's *Grundzüge du Phonologie*), Klincksieck, Paris, 1949. **288, 505, 655, 656, 663, 733**.

J. C. Catford, *Specimen of Kubardian with Notes on the Pronunciation*, in *Le Maître Phonétique*, July, 1942. **674**.

H. N. Coustenoble, *La Phonétique du Provençal Moderne*, Stephen Austin & Sons, Hertford, 1945. **145, 157, 454**.

H. N. Coustenoble and L. E. Armstrong, *Studies in French Intonation*, Heffer, Cambridge, 1934. **348, 432, 768**.

C. M. Doke, *Phonetics of Zulu*, University of the Witwatersrand Press, 1926. **17**.

A. Egan, *German Phonetic Reader*, University of London Press, 1913. **91**.

E. E. Elder, *Egyptian Arabic Phonetic Reader*, Oxford University Press, 1927. **673**.

A. J. Ellis, *Essentials of Phonetics*, Pitman, London, 1848. **5**.

English Language Teaching, a journal devoted to methods of teaching English to foreign learners, published by the British Council, 65, Davies Street, London, W.1. From 1946 onwards. **348**, footnote 7.

J. R. Firth, *Short Outline of Tamil Pronunciation*, published as an appendix to the current edition of Arden's *Grammar of Common Tamil*, Christian Literature Society for India, Madras, 1934. **85, 272, 373, 438, 531**.

J. R. Firth, *The Word "Phoneme,"* in *Le Maître Phonétique*, April, 1934. **652**.

D. B. Fry and D. Kostic, *A Serbo-Croat Phonetic Reader*, University of London Press, 1939. **466, 547, 556, 558**.

W. H. T. Gairdner, *Egyptian Colloquial Arabic*, Oxford University Press, 1926. **673**.

W. H. T. Gairdner, *The Phonetics of Arabic*, Oxford University Press, 1925. **93, 673**.

Sun-Gi Gim, *The Phonetics of Korean*, thesis for the M.A. degree of the University of London, 1937. May be consulted in the Library of the University of London. **194**.

W. Grant and B. H. A. Robson, *Phonetics for Scottish Students*, Cambridge University Press, 1926. **520**.

A. Gugushvili and D. Jones, *Specimen of Georgian with Notes on the Pronunciation*, in *Le Maître Phonétique*, Jan., 1944. **17**.

E. Henderson, *Specimen of Annamese with notes on the Pronunciation*, in *Le Maître Phonétique*, Jan., 1943. **528, 587**.

J. W. Jeaffreson, *The Mensuration of French Verse*, thesis for the M.A. degree in the University of London, 1924. **205**.

J. W. JEAFFRESON, *Stress and Rhythm in Speech*, in *Transactions of the Philological Society*, 1938. **205**.

O. JESPERSEN, *The Philosophy of Grammar*, George Allen & Unwin, London, 1924. **7**.

D. JONES, *The History and Meaning of the Term "Phoneme,"* Association Phonétique Internationale (I.P.A.), University College, London, W.C.1, 1957. Preface, **652**.

D. JONES, *Outline of English Phonetics*, 8th edition, Heffer, Cambridge, 1956. **14, 90, 130, 142, 160, 178, 199, 201, 205, 237, 249, 348, 403, 427, 446, 461, 462, 513, 517, 574, 602, 616, 692**.

D. JONES, *An English Pronouncing Dictionary*, 11th edition, re-written, Dent, London, 1956. **462**.

D. JONES, *The Pronunciation of English*, 4th (re-written) edition, Cambridge University Press, 1958. **605**.

D. JONES, *Intonation Curves*, Teubner, Leipzig, 1909. **645**.

D. JONES, *Concrete and Abstract Sounds*, in the *Proceedings of the Third International Congress of Phonetic Sciences*, Ghent, 1938. **20, 38, 625, 649, 660**.

D. JONES, *Some Thoughts on the Phoneme*, in *Transactions of the Philological Society*, 1944. **25, 29, 34, 210, 231, 282, 650, 688**.

D. JONES, *Chronemes and Tonemes*, in *Acta Linguistica*, Copenhagen, Vol. 4, No. 1, 1944. **40**.

D. JONES, *The Problem of a National Script for India*, Stephen Austin & Sons, Hertford, and the Pioneer Press, Lucknow, 1942. **163, 277, 700**.

D. JONES, *The Tones of Sechuana Nouns*, International African Institute, 10, Fetter Lane, London, E.C.1, 1927. **386**.

D. JONES, *Experimental Phonetics and its Utility to the Linguist*, in *Proceedings of the Royal Institution*, Vol. XXII, pp. 8–18, published in 1919. (Report of a lecture delivered on 9th Feb., 1917.) **403**.

D. JONES, *Dhe Fonetik Aspekt ov Speling Reform*, published for the Simplified Spelling Society by Sir Isaac Pitman & Sons, London, 1944. **706**.

D. JONES, *Differences between Spoken and Written Language*, Association Phonétique Internationale (I.P.A.), 1948. **706**.

D. JONES, article on Shakespearian pronunciation in *English Pronunciation through the Centuries*, Linguaphone Institute. **707, 718, 750**.

D. JONES and I. DAHL, *Fundamentos de Escritura Fonética*, Association Phonétique Internationale, 1944 obtainable from the Dept. of Phonetics, University College, London. **47, 743**.

D. JONES and S. T. PLAATJE, *A Sechuana Reader*, University of London Press, 1916. **81, 386**.

D. JONES and KWING TONG WOO, *Cantonese Phonetic Reader*, University of London Press, 1912. **354, 475**.

B. KARLGREN, *La Phonologie Chinoise*, Stockholm, 1915. **257, 764**.

J. S. KENYON, *American Pronunciation*, George Wahr, Ann Arbor, 10th edition, 1950. **646**.

R. KINGDON, *Groundwork of English Intonation*, Longmans, 1958. **348**.

R. KINGDON, *Tonetic Stress-marks for English*, in *Le Maître Phonétique*, Oct., 1938. **348**.

H. KLINGHARDT, *Übungen in Deutschem Tonfall*, Quelle & Meyer, Leipzig, 1927. **348, 561, 574**.

H. KLINGHARDT and G. KLEMM, *Übungen im Englischen Tonfall*, Schultze, Cöthen, 1920. **348**.

H. KLINGHARDT and R. OLBRICH, *Französische Intonations-Übungen*, 2nd edition, 1925, Quelle & Meyer, Leipzig. **348**.

L. KRASS, *The Phonetics of Estonian*, thesis for the M.A. degree of the University of London, 1944. May be consulted in the Library of the University of London. **184, 419, 420, 423, 529**.

R. J. LLOYD, *Northern English*, Teubner, Leipzig, 2nd edition, 1908. **277**.

K. LUICK, articles on relations between quality and pitch, in *Germanisch-Romanische Monatsschrift*, Vol. 18, p. 364, and *Englische Studien*, Vol. 65, p. 337. **114**.

C. MEINHOF, *Die Sprachen der Hamiten*, Abhandlungen des Hamburgischen Kolonialinstituts, Vol. IX, Friederichsen, Hamburg, 1912. **580**.

P. MENZERATH, *Beobachtungen zur deutschen Lautquantität*, in *Le Maître Phonétique*, July, 1934. **561**.

E. A. MEYER, *Deutsche Gespräche, mit phonetischer Einleitung und Umschrift*, Reisland, Leipzig, 3rd edition, 1917. **561**.

E. A. MEYER, *Englische Lautdauer*, Akademiska Bokhandeln, Uppsala, and Harrassowitz, Leipzig, 1903. **391**.

T. NAVARRO TOMÁS, *Manual de Pronunciación Española*, Revista de Filología española, Madrid, 4th edition, 1932. **417**.

G. NICHOLSON, *A Practical Introduction to French Phonetics*, Macmillan, London, 1909. **411**.

K. NYROP, *Grammaire Historique de la Langue Française*, Vol. I, 4th edition, 1938, Gyldendal, Copenhagen. **725, 753**.

H. E. PALMER, *English Intonation*, Heffer, Cambridge, 1922. **348, 459**.

H. E. PALMER, *Principles of Romanization*, Maruzen Company, Tokyo, 1930 **325, 327, 330, 628, 738**.

L. R. PALMER, *Introduction to Modern Linguistics*, Macmillan, 1936. **7, 656**.

G. PANCONCELLI-CALZIA, *Italiano*, Teubner, Leipzig, 1911. **366**.

P. PASSY, *Petite Phonétique Comparée*, Teubner, Leipzig, 1912. **197**.

P. PASSY, *Les Sons du Français*, Didier, Paris. **299, 692**.

P. PASSY, *Premier Livre de Lecture*, 1917 edition, Didier, Paris. **277**.

H. S. PERERA and D. JONES, *A Colloquial Sinhalese Reader*, Manchester University Press, 1919. **438**.

H. S. PERERA and D. JONES, *The Application of World Orthography to Sinhalese* in the *Bulletin of the School of Oriental Studies*, London, Vol. IX, Part 3, 1938, p. 705. **260**.

W. PERRETT, *Some Questions of Phonetic Theory*, Heffer, Cambridge, 1916. **245**.

Phonetic Reader (Scottish), Bon Accord Press, Aberdeen, 1918. **520**.

O. PLETNER, article on Japanese pronunciation in the *Japan Weekly Chronicle*, 14th April, 1938. **327**.

The Practical Orthography of African Languages, International African Institute, 10, Fetter Lane, London, E.C.1. **277**.

Principles of the International Phonetic Association, new edition, Association Phonétique Internationale, 1949, obtainable from the Dept. of Phonetics, University College, London. **47**.

W. RIPMAN and W. ARCHER, *New Spelling*, 6th edition, 1948, Sir Isaac Pitman & Sons, London. **616**.

H. A. ROSITZKE, *A Note on Final Stops in General American*, in *Le Maître Phonétique*, Oct., 1938. **380**.

E. SAPIR, *La Réalité Psychologique des Phonemes*, in *Le Journal de Psychologie*, Jan., 1933, published by Librairie Félix Alcan, 108, Boulevard St. Germain, Paris 6e. **653, 687**.

E. SAPIR, *Sound Patterns in Language*, in *Language*, Vol. I, 1925. **653**.

N. C. SCOTT, *An Experiment in Stress Perception*, in *Le Maître Phonétique*, July, 1939. **456, 459**.

E. W. SCRIPTURE, *The Nature of Speech*, in *Proceedings of the Second International Congress of Phonetic Sciences*, Cambridge University Press, 1936. **3**.

TH. SIEBS, *Deutsche Hochsprache*, 16th edition, 1957, Walter de Gryter & Co., Berlin. **561**.

E. SIEVERS, *Grundzüge der Phonetik*, 5th edition, 1901, Breitkopf & Härtel, Leipzig. **561**.

L. SPRAGUE DE CAMP, *American Retroflexed Vowels*, in *Le Maître Phonétique*, July, 1942. **726**.

E. M. STÉPHAN and D. JONES, *Colloquial French for the English*, H.M.V. Gramophone Co., London, 1927. **692**.

H. SWEET, *Handbook of Phonetics*, Clarendon Press, Oxford, 1877. **5, 652**.

H. SWEET, *The Practical Study of Languages*, Dent, London. **661**

H. SWEET, *Elementarbuch des gesprochenen Englisch*, Oxford University Press. **241**.

H. SWEET, *Primer of Spoken English*, Oxford University Press. **199, 241, 713**.

M. VON TILING, *Die Sprache der. Jabárti mit besonderer Berücksichtigung der Verwandtschaft von Jabárti und Somali*, in *Zeitschrift für Eingeborenen Sprachen*, Vol. XII, No. 1, 1922. Also published separately by Dietrich Reimer, Berlin. **580**.

M. VON TILING, *Somali-Texte*, Dietrich Reimer, Berlin, 1925. **580**.

G. L. TRAGER, *Serbo-Croatian Accents and Quantities*, in *Language*, Vol. XVI, No. 1, Jan., 1940. **466**.

G. L. TRAGER, *Serbo-Croatian Dialect*, in *Le Maître Phonétique*, Jan., 1940. **466, 542**.

G. L. TRAGER, transcriptions in *Le Maître Phonétique*, Jan., 1935, and April, 1941. **204**.

G. L. TRAGER and B. BLOCH, *The Syllabic Phonemes of English*, in *Language*, Vol. XVII, No. 3, July, 1941. **152, 204, 462**.

G. L. TRAGER and H. L. SMITH, *An Outline of English Structure*, Norman, Oklahoma, 1951. **462**, footnote 26.

N. TRUBETZKOY, *Grundzüge der Phonologie*, Travaux du Cercle Linguistique de Prague, Vol. 7, Prague, 1939. **288, 505, 655, 656, 663, 733.**

A. N. TUCKER, *Comparative Phonetics of the Suto-Chwana Group of Bantu Languages*, Longmans, 1929. **127, 680.**

A. N. TUCKER, *Eastern Sudanic Languages*, Vol. I, Oxford University Press, 1940. **125.**

A. N. TUCKER, description of Nuer in WESTERMANN and WARD'S *Practical Phonetics for Students of African Languages*, Oxford University Press, 1933. **278.**

A. N. TUCKER, *Sotho-Nguni Orthography* in the *Bulletin of the School of Oriental and African Studies*, Jan., 1949. **482**, footnote 18.

W. F. TWADDELL, *On defining the Phoneme*, Language Monographs, published by the Linguistic Society of America, No. XVI, 1935. **657.**

H. J. ULDALL, *A Note on Vowel Length in American English*, in *Le Maître Phonétiqu.*. Oct., 1934. **380.**

W. VIËTOR, *Die Aussprache des Schriftdeutschen*, Analle & Meyer, Leipzig. **525.**

W. VIËTOR, *Deutsches Ausspracheworterbuch*, 5th edition, revised by E. A. MEYER, Reisland, Leipzig, 1925. **28, 149, 224, 561.**

W. VIËTOR, *Shakespeare's Pronunciation*, Vol. I, Elwert, Marburg i.H., 1906. **749.**

J. WALLIS, *Grammatica Linguæ Anglicanæ*, London, 1653. **732, 749.**

I. C. WARD, *Introduction to the Ibo Language*, Heffer, Cambridge, 1936. **353, 509.**

I. C. WARD, *Phonetic and Tonal Structure of Efik*, Heffer, Cambridge, 1933. **19.**

D. WESTERMANN and I. C. WARD, *Practical Phonetics for Students of African Languages*, Oxford University Press, 1933. **83, 278, 630.**

J. WILKINS, *Essay towards a Real Character and a Philosophical Language*, London, 1668. **742.**

F. S. WINGFIELD, *Bulletin* (of reformed spelling), Feb., 1940, published by the author, 4617, Grace Street, Chicago. **26.**

INDEX OF LANGUAGES REFERRED TO IN THIS BOOK

References are to paragraphs

INDEX OF SUBJECTS

References are to paragraphs

OTHER WORKS BY THE SAME AUTHOR

The History and Meaning of the Term "Phoneme," Association Phonétique Internationale, 1957 (University College, London).

An Outline of English Phonetics (Heffer, Cambridge).

The Pronunciation of English, 4th edition, 1958 (Cambridge University Press).

An English Pronouncing Dictionary, 11th edition (re-written), 1956 (Dent, London).

Phonetic Readings in English, new edition, 1956 (Winter, Heidelberg).

Colloquial French for the English, by E. M. Stéphan and D. Jones. Complete Course (586 pp.) with 15 double-sided gramophone records, together with Key-book and Pupils' Book (H.M.V. Gramophone Co., London).†

100 *Poésies Enfantines,* recueillies et transcrites phonétiquement, avec illustrations par E. M. Pugh (Teubner, Leipzig).*

Intonation Curves (Teubner, Leipzig).†

Shakespeare in the Original Pronunciation. Texts in phonetic transcription with notes, on pp. 36–45 of *English Pronunciation through the Centuries* (Linguaphone Institute, London). Accompanies a double-sided Linguaphone record of passages from Shakespeare in the original pronunciation spoken by D. Jones and E. M. Evans.

Dhe Fonetik Aspekt ov Speling Reform (published by Sir Isaac Pitman & Sons, for the Simplified Spelling Society).

Concrete and Abstract Sounds (off-print from the *Proceedings of the Third International Congress of Phonetic Sciences,* Ghent, 1938).*

The Great English Vowel Shift, by D. Jones and C. L. Wrenn.*

The Problem of a National Script for India (Pioneer Press, Lucknow).*

A Colloquial Sinhalese Reader, by D. Jones and H. S. Perera, 1919 (Manchester University Press).

A Sechuana Reader, by D. Jones and S. T. Plaatje, 1916 (University of London Press).

A Cantonese Phonetic Reader, by D. Jones and Kwing Tong Woo, 1912 (University of London Press).

The Tones of Sechuana Nouns, 1927 (International African Institute, 10, Fetter Lane, London, E.C.1).

The Principles of the International Phonetic Association, 1949, with Specimens of 51 Languages.*

* Obtainable from the Department of Phonetics, University College, London, W.C.1.
† Out of print.